Studies in the
Bábí and Bahá'í Religions
Volume Twelve

Evolution and Bahá'í Belief

D1738767

STUDIES IN THE
BÁBÍ AND BAHÁ'Í RELIGIONS

(Formerly *Studies in Bábí and Bahá'í History*)

Anthony A. Lee, General Editor

Studies in Bábí and Bahá'í History, Volume One, edited by Moojan Momen (1982).

From Iran East and West, Volume Two, edited by Juan R. Cole and Moojan Momen (1984).

In Iran, Volume Three, edited by Peter Smith (1986).

Music, Devotions and Mashriqu'l-Adhkár, Volume Four, by R. Jackson Armstrong-Ingram (1987).

Studies in Honor of the Late H. M. Balyuzi, Volume Five, edited by Moojan Momen (1989).

Community Histories, Volume Six, edited by Richard Hollinger (1992).

Symbol and Secret: Qur'an Commentary in Bahá'u'lláh's Kitáb-i Íqán, Volume Seven, by Christopher Buck (1995).

Revisioning the Sacred: New Perspectives on a Bahá'í Theology, Volume Eight, edited by Jack McLean (1997).

Modernity and the Millennium: The Genesis of the Baha'i Faith in the Nineteenth-Century Middle East, distributed as Volume Nine, by Juan R. I. Cole, *Columbia University Press* (1999).

Paradise and Paradigm: Key Symbols in Persian Christianity and the Bahá'í Faith, distributed as Volume Ten, by Christopher Buck, *State University of New York Press* (1999).

Religion in Iran: From Zoroaster to Bahau'llah, distributed as Volume Eleven, by Alessandro Bausani, *Bibliotheca Persica Press* (2000).

Evolution and Bahá'í Belief: 'Abdu'l-Bahá's Response to Nineteenth-Century Darwinism, Volume Twelve, edited by Keven Brown (2001).

Reason and Revelation, Volume Thirteen, edited by Seena Fazel and John Danesh (2001).

Bahá'ís in the West, Volume Fourteen, edited by Peter Smith (2002).

'ABDU'L-BAHÁ

*"In the world of existence, man has traversed successive
degrees until he has attained the human kingdom."*

STUDIES IN THE BÁBÍ AND BAHÁ'Í RELIGIONS

Volume Twelve

General Editor

Anthony A. Lee

Evolution and Bahá'í Belief: 'Abdu'l-Bahá's Response to Nineteenth-Century Darwinism

by
Keven Brown
and
Eberhard von Kitzing

Edited by Keven Brown

KALIMÁT PRESS
LOS ANGELES

Library of Congress Cataloging-in-Publication Data
Evolution and Bahá'í belief:
'Abdu'l-Bahá's response to nineteenth-century Darwinism /
by Keven Brown and Eberhard von Kitzing; edited by Keven Brown.
p. cm.—(Studies in the Bábí and Bahá'í religions; v. 12)
Includes bibliographical references.
ISBN 1-890688-08-8
1. 'Abdu'l-Bahá, 1844-1921. 2. Bahai Faith—Doctrines.
[1. Evolution—Religious aspects—Bahai Faith.]
I. Von Kitzing, Eberhard, 1954-   II. Title. III. Series.
BP388.E94 B76 2000   297.9'317—dc21
00-044407

Kalimát Press
1600 Sawtelle Blvd., Suite 310
Los Angeles, CA 90025

www.kalimat.com
KalimatP@aol.com

The authors wish to dedicate this volume to
their beloved children
Minea and Anja Brown
and
Arianne, Nora, Mona, Fabian,
Carmel, and Constanze von Kitzing

May each carry forward an ever advancing civilization by cultivating the special gifts and talents with which they have been endowed by their Creator and by sharing these with the world. May they also live to witness a cherished desire of their fathers: science and religion both honored as the two wings of one bird, both working together to obtain a more balanced understanding of reality.

Religion assures us that life's purpose is not arbitrary, that it is designed by a loving Creator in the best way possible. It instills hope and optimism that our efforts will be crowned by success, that our destiny is glorious. Faithful adherence to the scientific method, on the other hand, enables us to separate fancy from fact, to discover new technologies for the betterment of all, and to come ever closer to understanding the workings of our universe.

Contents

PART TWO

**The Origin of Complex Order in Biology: 'Abdu'l-Bahá's
Concept of the "Originality of Species" Compared to
Concepts in Modern Biology** *by Eberhard von Kitzing*

Section 1: Evolution and Bahá'í Belief

CHARLES R. DARWIN (1809-1882)
Immediately after his *Origin of Species* was published
(1859), thoughtful people began to ponder its implications
for the status of human beings and the biblical concept of
creation.

Foreword

It is now over 140 years since Darwin published his famous book *The Origin of Species*, but the intense controversy surrounding his theory of evolution has not died down, especially in America. The classical worldview that predominated up until the middle of the nineteenth century understood all species as having been created by God in essentially their present forms all at one time. Modification of populations was allowed in recognition of the fact that organisms do adapt to changing environmental conditions, but any change beyond the strict bounds of a species' essential characteristics was not considered possible. This is also the view accepted by many contemporary Christian denominations, a view that a 1993 Gallup poll found to be supported by 47% of Americans.[1]

This view, however, stands in stark contrast to the position put forward by Darwin, and now accepted by the scientific community, which holds that no act of supernatural creation is necessary to explain the origin of the diverse biological populations that inhabit our planet. Instead, the mechanical processes of random variation and natural selection of the fittest are sufficient to account for all the divergent organisms that exist on earth today. In contrast to the classical view, which believes that all kinds were specially created for a preexisting purpose, many modern writers propose that no preexisting plan or purpose is necessary for the origin of man or any other species.[2]

Darwin's theory had profound repercussions, not only for every scientific discipline (including history and social science), but also for religion. By denying special creation, Darwin's theory threatened to undermine one of the most cherished doctrines of religion. If the diversity of species didn't need a creator, the role of God was diminished. If speciation is arbitrary and occurs through a blind, natural process, then the laws that govern human beings could also be arbitrary and constructed on a merely pragmatic basis, not in accord with an intelligible order created by God. Social Darwinism, which viewed society and the economy as an arena in which the fittest nation should rise to the top at the expense of other nations, was one consequence of this view. Materialism, which denied the existence of an incorporeal soul and a spiritual world, also gained fresh converts on account of Darwin's theory.

It is not surprising, therefore, that during the twentieth century religion and science have continued to find themselves at odds with each other, not only in people's minds but in the courts. In 1925, a young biology teacher named John Scopes was put on trial and fined $100 for defying a Tennessee state law prohibiting the teaching of "any theory which denies the story of the Divine creation of man as taught in the Bible" in public schools. Although the Tennessee appellate court overturned the verdict two years later, such laws were not declared unconstitutional until 1968.

In the late 1970s, Arkansas and Louisiana passed laws requiring that whenever evolution is taught in public schools "creation science" must also be taught. A number of other states introduced similar "creation science" bills in their state legislatures before the United States Supreme Court rejected such laws in 1987.[3] The latest effort to promote "creation science" in public schools occurred in 1999, when the Kansas Board of Education voted to remove evolution theory from the state's science curriculum, while not formally banning its instruction or insisting on equal time for "creation science."

At the beginning of the twentieth century, the controversy

between the materialistic interpretation of Darwin's theory and biblical special creation was even more intense in the public mind. Fundamentalists saw it as a confrontation between "theism versus atheism, morality versus immorality, angel-man versus monkey-man," while scientists and others saw it as a contest between "reason versus superstition, enlightenment versus obscurantism, scientific skepticism versus blind commitment to religious dogma."[4]

It was in this divisive atmosphere that 'Abdu'l-Bahá, during his visits to Europe and America between 1911 and 1913, presented the Bahá'í principle that true religion and sound science are complementary and can never oppose one another. 'Abdu'l-Bahá repeated this principle again and again in his talks to Western audiences. For example, in Paris on November 12, 1911, he said:

> If a religious statement is found which categorically contradicts reason and science, then that statement is mere fancy. . . . Therefore make all of your beliefs congruent so that science and religion are in harmony, for religion is one wing of man and science is the other. Man can fly with two wings but not with one. All religious beliefs that are contrary to reason and science are not part of the reality of religion. Rather, such blind beliefs and absolute convictions are the cause of hatred and enmity between the children of men. But if religion is made congruent with science, the truth will appear. Therefore, let your aim be this: to make science in accord with religion and religion in accord with science.[5]

In a talk given at a Unitarian Church on June 9, 1912, he affirmed:

> Science must recognize the truth of religion, and religion must recognize the truth of science. A perfect relationship must be obtained between them, for this is the root of truth. . . . Therefore, we must abandon superstitions and investigate reality, and that which we see corresponding to reality, we should accept. That to which science does not assent and reason does not accept is not reality; rather it is blind imitation. We must cast these misguided beliefs far away from us and hold fast to reality. Any religion that is in harmony with science and reason is worthy of acceptance.[6]

It was from this perspective of the complementarity of religion and science, and the need to maintain harmony between them, that

'Abdu'l-Bahá addressed the question of evolution. Although 'Abdu'l-Bahá accepted evolution, as he understood the meaning of this word, as a fact, he did not accept Darwin's theory as it was taught by the scientists of his time. Instead, 'Abdu'l-Bahá presented an understanding of evolution harmonious with the religious idea of creation and the philosophical concept of essences. The details of his manner of reconciling evolution and creation are discussed in the articles that follow.

It is important to determine here what 'Abdu'l-Bahá means by the term "science" (*'ilm*), since it is obvious 'Abdu'l-Bahá is referring to something that does not necessarily accord with any particular scientific theory or even with the scientific consensus of an age. Let us consider the following statement:

> You have asked how we can harmonize scientific theories with the ideas of religion. Know that this material world is the mirror of the Kingdom, and each of these worlds is in complete correspondence with the other. The correct theories of this world which are the result of sound scientific thinking are in agreement with the divine verses without the slightest divergence between them, for the truth of all things is laid away in the treasuries of the Kingdom. When that truth is manifested in the material world, the archetypes and realities of beings attain realization. If a scientific theory does not correspond with the divine verses, it is certain that it is the essence of error.[7]

In other words, the Bahá'í principle of the harmony of science and religion is based on the assumption that the world of the Kingdom (i.e., the atemporal, placeless dimension) contains all the realities and potentialities upon which the material world is founded. Since divine revelation is also based upon the same source, its true meaning cannot be in conflict with any categorical facts of the external world. In the same letter quoted above, 'Abdu'l-Bahá goes on to explain how for over a thousand years learned consensus followed the Ptolemaic system in which the earth was viewed as the fixed center of the universe around which the sun moved, while two verses of the Qur'an, according to 'Abdu'l-Bahá's interpretation, indicated the fixity of the sun relative to the planets and the movement of the earth around it.

This does not mean, however, that particular religious ideas and doctrines are inherently superior to particular scientific theories, and vice versa, because 'Abdu'l-Bahá also explains that the criteria by which humans judge the veracity of a proposition (i.e., sense perception, reason, scriptural authority, and inspiration) are all liable to error due to human subjectivity. Consequently, he concludes that the most reliable standard of judgement is all four in combination:

> But a statement presented to the mind accompanied by proofs which the senses can perceive to be correct, which the faculty of reason can accept, which is in accord with traditional authority and sanctioned by the promptings of the heart, can be adjudged and relied upon as perfectly correct, for it has been proved and tested by all the standards of judgment and found to be complete.[8]

In other place, he adds that the standard of the "inmost heart" (*mízán al-fu'ád*) through the aid of the Holy Spirit is capable of apprehending the truth of things.[9] In summary, the Bahá'í principle of the harmony of science and religion not only implies the essential unity of the material and spiritual dimensions of existence, but means that human beings must rely upon both science (empirical data interpreted through reason and inspiration) and religion (scripture interpreted through reason and inspiration) to obtain a truer picture of reality.

Originally this volume was planned to include three articles, one by a historian, one by a physical scientist, and one by a practicing evolutionary biologist. Unfortunately, the third article being prepared by Dr. Ronald Somerby, the biologist, was not ready in time and he has urged us to publish without him. As such, the views presented here do not represent the full richness of different backgrounds that this subject deserves. Somerby's article proposed to cover such questions as the meaning of complementarity, the principle of "unity in diversity" in modern evolutionary theories, and the need for a new paradigm shift that transcends both classical metaphysics and the modern mechanization of nature. We urge him to complete his article soon.

Eberhard von Kitzing's article, "The Origin of Complex Order in Biology," focuses on 'Abdu'l-Bahá's concept of the *originality of species*, places it within the context of the nineteenth-century conflict between the views of classical biology and Darwin's theory of evolution, and compares 'Abdu'l-Bahá's views with concepts in modern biology and cosmology. Kitzing explains that his essay is based on the assumption that 'Abdu'l-Bahá's statements on the subject of evolution are not intended to be explanations of biological fact. In other words, 'Abdu'l-Bahá was not a biologist; rather he approached the subject from the standpoint of religious knowledge. As such, his arguments reflect his interest in the philosophical and spiritual consequences of Darwinism as it relates to questions of religion, such as the purpose of life. He was especially concerned with the theory's potential, as represented by "certain European philosophers," to undermine the essential principles of religion.

If all of 'Abdu'l-Bahá's statements on evolution are to be understood literally as referring to biological fact, then these statements need to be supported by evidence from applied biology just like any other hypothesis, if they are to be taken seriously. Kitzing proposes that the *parallel evolution model*, which results from interpreting 'Abdu'l-Bahá's statements literally and as doctrine, not argument, "produces more problems than it solves." He presents a series of five questions that he believes need to be successfully answered for parallel evolution to be accepted as a serious theory by scientists. Kitzing also gives a non-literal interpretation of 'Abdu'l-Bahá's statements on evolution that he finds more in harmony with current scientific thought. For should the literal meaning of 'Abdu'l-Bahá's statements become categorically proven to contradict biological facts, Bahá'ís will have to answer this question posed by historian Susan Maneck: "Should Bahá'ís feel compelled to accept that earlier theory [of parallel evolution] because of 'Abdu'l-Bahá's use of it, or is it sufficient to simply accept the point of it all, that our Reality is ultimately related to our intended end, not our origins, and allow science to figure out the rest of it?"[10]

My own article, "'Abdu'l-Bahá's Response to Darwinism," explores in detail the philosophical and historical context within which 'Abdu'l-Bahá spoke and from which he and his audience drew the understanding which informed their discourse. I start with the conflict between the essentialists and Darwinists during the latter half of the nineteenth century in Europe and America, and then move to the parallel controversy that took place over Darwinism in the Near East. Since 'Abdu'l-Bahá indicated in one of his talks that his views on evolution are generally congruent with the system of thought of the "philosophers of the East," by which he means Plato and Aristotle, and the philosophers of Iran, I devote a lengthy chapter to examining the ideas of these philosophers as they relate to the concepts of "species," "essence," and "becoming."

With the views of the "philosophers of the East" presented as necessary background, my last chapter is devoted to a careful analysis of 'Abdu'l-Bahá's teachings on evolution based on the context presented in the first three chapters. The original Arabic or Persian writings and talks of 'Abdu'l-Bahá are relied upon throughout, and revised translations are provided where necessary.

My approach is to assume that 'Abdu'l-Bahá intended his words on this subject to be taken at face value, and that he was responding to Laura Clifford Barney's questions on "the modification of species" and "the theory of the evolution of beings" with unambiguous and non-symbolic language.

Both authors agree, however, that 'Abdu'l-Bahá's response to Darwinism was more philosophical in nature than scientific and that his main objective was to establish by *rational arguments* the existence a divinely ordained purpose for life, the special place of humanity in creation, the need of final causes (i.e., teleology), and the existence of timeless natural laws in the universe.

Numerous religious leaders and scientists during the twentieth century have found science and religion to be not the least bit contradictory. Each, working in the sphere that it knows best, gives us a fuller and truer picture of reality than either could by itself. Neither should dominate the other, but each should recognize the complementary and mutually beneficial role of the other in human society.

As 'Abdu'l-Bahá desired: "Science must recognize the truth of religion, and religion must recognize the truth of science. A perfect relationship must be obtained between them, for this is the root of truth."[11]

The Catholic Church is to be praised for its recent efforts to harmonize the teachings of the Bible with the facts of science and the fruits of reason. As the Vatican II Council expressed it: "Research performed in a truly scientific manner can never be in contrast with faith because both profane and religious realities have their origin in the same God."[12] The Catholic Church therefore deems evolution and Christianity to be compatible. It holds that "God created the matter and laws of the universe" and that "evolution is the manner in which these laws have unfolded."[13] In another move on the side of science and reason, Pope John Paul II recently declared that "rather than a place, hell indicates the state of those who freely and definitively separate themselves from God." He added that hell is "not a punishment imposed externally by God" but the natural consequence of the unrepentant sinner's choice to live apart from God.[14]

The Bahá'í principle of the harmony between science and religion is connected to another Bahá'í principle which holds that "religious truth is not absolute but relative."[15] This means that religious statements should be understood from the perspective of the historical and cultural context within which they were revealed and in the light of the purpose for which they were revealed. It is with respect to the purpose of religious statements that universality applies, whereas the literal words and images of sacred writings are very time and culture bounded. The changing understanding of the concept of hell is illustrative of this point. According to a Catholic scholar: "to people living in early Christian centuries, infernal images of hell no doubt conveyed quite effectively the horrific consequences of rejecting God. One thing people feared most then was the burning and pillaging of their towns. If you had described hell to them in terms of relationships and psychological experiences like loneliness, they wouldn't have known what you were talking about."[16]

Such time- and culture-bound concepts and statements are also found in the writings of Bahá'u'lláh and 'Abdu'l-Bahá. For example, when Bahá'u'lláh refers to "the fourth heaven" of classical astronomy in the Kitáb-i Íqán, Shoghi Effendi explains that this book "was revealed for the guidance of that sect [the Shí'ah]," where "this term was used in conformity with the concepts of its followers."[17] In the same manner, such terms as "essence," "species," "evolution," and "creation" have specific meanings to 'Abdu'l-Bahá relative to the cultural and philosophical background with which his audience was familiar. One should not automatically assume that such terms, or 'Abdu'l-Bahá's usage of them, are limted by that background. But their meaning should be properly understood through a careful study of their original context, and then they should be interpreted and applied in terms that make sense today. This is in keeping with the dynamic character of the Bahá'í Faith, which Shoghi Effendi says, has the capacity "even as a living organism, to expand and adapt itself to the needs and requirements of an ever-changing society" and "has been so fashioned" as "to keep it in the forefront of all progressive movements."[18]

How should the Bahá'í community interact with scientists and discuss scientific theories? With a combination of frankness and humility, in the spirit of a fellow-seeker searching for the truth about reality, questioning assumptions that preclude the existence of metaphysical causes, but willing to discard preconceptions and always being open to new perspectives. Why is this important? Because, as 'Abdu'l-Bahá states: "religion is one wing of man and science is the other. Man can fly with two wings but not with one."[19] Furthermore, 'Abdu'l-Bahá explains that "if religion is contrary to science and reason, it is not possible for it to instill confidence in the heart. . . . Therefore, religious teachings must be congruent with reason and science so that the heart may be assured and mankind find true happiness."[20]

The articles presented in this volume have as one of their aims, in addition to exploring the philosophical and historical background of the evolution question in Europe and the Near East at the end of the nineteenth century, presenting interpretations of 'Abdu'l-Bahá's statements on evolution (from the side of religion) that may be more congruent with reason and with scientific facts. The full answer of how evolution and creation have worked together to bring the universe into existence is very complex, and many more questions need to be explored and answered. It is our hope that this volume will help stir our fellow Bahá'ís and interested scientists to work harder to raise the science and religion dialogue to new heights of agreement and understanding.

KEVEN BROWN
March 2001

NOTES

1. Cited by Chet Raymo, *Skeptics and True Believers* (New York: Warner, 1998) p. 122.
2. Richard Dawkins, "God's Utility Function," *Scientific American*, vol. 273, no. 5, (1995) pp. 80-85.
3. Ashley Montagu, *Science and Creationism* (New York: Oxford University Press, 1984) pp. 4-5; Stephen Jay Gould, "Dorothy, It's Really Oz," *U.S. News and World Report* (August 23, 1999) p. 59.
4. Raymo, *Skeptics and True Believers*, p. 121.
5. 'Abdu'l-Bahá, *Khiṭábát,* vol. 1 (Talks of 'Abdu'l-Bahá) (Hofheim-Langenhain: Bahá'í-Verlag, 1984) pp. 155, 157-158; corresponds to *Paris Talks*, 11th Edition, pp. 141-146. The original, free English translation contains much material that is not in the Persian.
6. Ibid., vol. 2, pp. 136-137; *Promulgation of Universal Peace*, (Wilmette: Bahá'í Publishing Trust, 1982) pp. 175-176, revised translation.
7. 'Abdu'l-Bahá, *Makátíb-i 'Abdu'l-Bahá*, vol. 3 (Collected Letters) (Cairo 1921) pp. 172-173.
8. 'Abdu'l-Bahá, *Promulgation*, p. 255.
9. 'Abdu'l-Bahá, *Min Makátíb-i 'Abdu'l-Bahá*, vol. 1 (From the Collected Letters) (Rio de Janeiro: Editora Baha'i Brasil, 1982) p. 85.
10. Susan Maneck on Baha'i Studies List, August 1, 2000.
11. 'Abdu'l-Bahá, *Khiṭábát*, vol. 2, p. 136.
12. Quoted in Robert Root-Bernstein, "On Defining a Scientific Theory," in *Science and Creationism*, p. 82.
13. Ibid., p. 83.
14. Quoted in "Hell Hath No Fury," *U.S. News and World Report* (January 31, 2000) pp. 45, 48.

15. Shoghi Effendi, *World Order of Bahá'u'lláh* (Wilmette: Bahá'í Publishing Trust, 1974) p. 58.
16. Rev. Thomas Reese, quoted in "Hell Hath No Fury," *U.S. News and World Report* (January 31, 2000) p. 49.
17. Quoted in a letter written on behalf of the Universal House of Justice, 3 November 1987.
18. Shoghi Effendi, *The World Order of Bahá'u'lláh*, pp. 22-23.
19. 'Abdu'l-Bahá, *Khiṭábát*, vol. 1, p. 158.
20. Ibid., vol. 2, p. 227; *Promulgation of Universal Peace*, pp. 298-299, revised translation.

Studies in the
Bábí and Bahá'í Religions
Volume Twelve

Evolution and Bahá'í Belief

PART ONE

'Abdu'l-Bahá's Response to Darwinism: Its Historical and Philosophical Context

by
Keven Brown

The translations and revised translations of 'Abdu'l-Bahá's writings and talks contained in this essay are provisional and have not been authorized by the Universal House of Justice.

Acknowledgments

I would especially like to thank Eberhard von Kitzing for encouraging me to write this article. It was he who, in the beginning, asked me if I would assist him by checking the original Persian and Arabic writings of 'Abdu'l-Bahá on the subject of evolution and by examining the philosophical background with which 'Abdu'l-Bahá was familiar. He has remained throughout this project a source of support and of constructive criticism. I would also like to give a special thanks to David Garcia who took the time to read this essay carefully and respond with many specific criticisms that helped me to see new perspectives on 'Abdu'l-Bahá's words. Without his input the subject of this essay would have received a less balanced treatment. Equally critical was the feedback of Ronald Somerby, who pointed out to me the importance of reading Arthur Lovejoy's book *The Great Chain of Being* and Ernst Mayr's *The Growth of Biological Thought*. Both books proved to be indispensable sources for the subject of this article. Lastly, thanks to Stephen Friberg for reading the manuscript and helping me to avoid the dangers of excessive "historical contextualism."

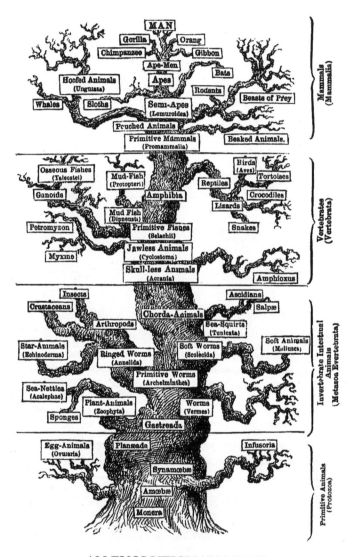

AN EVOLUTIONARY TREE

An illustration from Ernst Haeckel's Evolution of Man (1879) showing the evolution of life from "Amoebae" and "Monera" to "MAN." The drawing conceals the highly imprecise and speculative nature of the relationships shown.

Preface

Many Westerners first became acquainted with 'Abdu'l-Bahá (1844-1921) during his missionary journeys to Europe and America between 1911 and 1913, undertaken for the purpose of spreading the teachings of his father, Bahá'u'lláh, founder of the Bahá'í Faith. During his busy schedule of meeting his American followers, visiting dignitaries, speaking at churches, social organizations, and universities, and associating with people from all walks of life, 'Abdu'l-Bahá emphasized his father's progressive social principles, which included such teachings as the equality of men and women, the oneness of the human race, the establishment of a world federal government, the adoption of a universal auxiliary language, and the harmony of science and religion.

'Abdu'l-Bahá's views on the theory of evolution, as it was understood at the beginning of the twentieth century, fall within the context of the last principle. In one talk of 'Abdu'l-Bahá at the Open Forum in San Francisco, dated 10 October 1912, he speaks particularly about the theory of evolution and contrasts the modern Western idea of the transmutation of species with the idea of evolution within a species of the "philosophers of the East" (*falásifiyyih sharq*), with whom he associates his own views (see Section 3). Among these philosophers, he includes "Aristotle and Plato, and the philosophers of Iran."[1] 'Abdu'l-Bahá had previously discoursed on this subject to Laura Clifford Barney, an American who visited him in 'Akká between 1904 and 1906. She records at least five talks of 'Abdu'l-Bahá specifically addressing the questions of evolution and the diversification of species. In several of his letters, 'Abdu'l-Bahá also writes on this subject.

In order to accurately analyze 'Abdu'l-Bahá's ideas and compare them to the understanding educated Westerners had of Darwin's theory at the time, it will be necessary to use the original texts of 'Abdu'l-Bahá and ensure their accurate translation into English. It will also be necessary to study in depth the views of the "philosophers of the East" and the responses of Darwin's contemporaries to his theory. The tasks to be accomplished in this article, therefore, are four-fold: (1) to present revised translations of 'Abdu'l-Bahá's writings and talks on the subject of evolution where necessary;[2] (2) to explain the relevant theories of certain Greek and Islamic philosophers on the ideas of "species," "essence," and "becoming"; (3) to describe the contemporary response to Darwinism during the last half of the nineteenth century and the beginning of the twentieth century in Europe and, more especially, in the Arab world; and (4) to analyze 'Abdu'l-Bahá's doctrine in the light of this historical context and philosophical background.

After having accomplished these tasks, I believe it will be demonstrated that 'Abdu'l-Bahá is a teleologist (or essentialist), who maintains the original creation of "species" by God outside of time, and that he was a proponent of evolution in a sense that is harmonious with the doctrine of creation. As the essay will attempt to make clear (especially in Sections 2 and 3), 'Abdu'l-Bahá is not an Aristotelian essentialist but a Platonic one. In other words, 'Abdu'l-Bahá's essences (*máhiyát*) and species (*naw'iyát*) are equivalent to Platonic Forms, not to Aristotelian substances and the logical essences derived from them.

Section 1

The Historical Context

EUROPE[3]

Darwin's *The Origin of Species by Means of Natural Selection* (published in 1859) disturbed the scientific community, for it struck at the foundations of a long-established worldview in which religion and science worked side by side without interfering in any fundamental way in the domain of the other. That God had created all species according to a divine plan and linked them together in the great Chain of Being was taught by religion and almost universally accepted; it was the role of scientists to discover the material details of that plan and reveal the wisdom of the Creator. English naturalist John Ray's work *The Wisdom of God Manifested in the Works of the Creation* (1691) is typical of the thinking of the time. The pre-Darwinian worldview was well summed up by Newton, who said: "A God without dominion, providence, and final causes, is nothing else but Fate and Nature. . . . All the diversity of natural things which we find, suited to different times and places, could arise from nothing but the ideas and will of a Being necessarily existing."[4]

1.1. Teleological Thinking vs. Population Thinking

The assumption of the design and creation of the natural world by a supreme being are fundamental to teleological thinking, which had been dominant since the days of Plato and Aristotle, and which is still favored by the general American population.[5] In this view, each species was created by design and for a purpose in the great plan of life. In other words, it is not by chance that humanity is at the apex of the animal kingdom. According to the Judeo-Christian tradition, every species of plant and animal was independently created prior to the creation of Adam. Called "special creation," this view holds that an essential discontinuity separates species from each other. As the French biologist, Georges Cuvier (1769-1832), wrote to a friend: "We imagine that a species is the total descendence of the first couple created by God."[6] The British physiologist, William Carpenter (1813-1885), summed up the prevailing belief at the time Darwin published *The Origin of Species*:

> Now it seems to be a received article of faith, both amongst scientific naturalists and with the general public, that all these reputed species have a real existence in nature; that each originated in a distinct act of creation; and that, once established, each type has continued to transmit its distinctive characters, without any essential change, from one generation to another, so long as the race has been permitted to exist. This idea of the permanence of species . . . is commonly regarded at the present time [1860] as one of those doctrines which no man altogether in his right senses will set himself up seriously to oppose.[7]

At the present time, this view of the special creation of species is still widely believed, especially among fundamentalist Christians for whom it is an essential doctrine. One of the leading contemporary proponents of special creation is Dr. Duane Gish of the Institute for Creation Research. He explains:

> By creation we mean the bringing into being of the basic kinds of plants and animals by the process of sudden, or fiat, creation described in the first two chapters of Genesis. . . . We do not know how God cre-

ated, what processes He used, for God used processes which are not now operating anywhere in the natural universe. This is why we refer to divine creation as special creation. . . .

During the creation week God created all of the basic animal and plant kinds, and since then no new kinds have come into being, for the Bible speaks of a finished creation (Gen. 2:2). . . .

The concept of special creation does not exclude the origin of varieties and species from an original created kind. It is believed that each kind was created with sufficient genetic potential, or gene pool, to give rise to all of the varieties within that kind that have existed in the past and those that are yet in existence today.[8]

The problem with explaining the origin of species by special creation, argued the early critics, is that it does not explain how species have actually appeared, survived, and vanished in the real world. No one had witnessed an act of special creation taking place, and it was evident by this time from the fossil record that innumerable different species had appeared and then become extinct in the long course of geologic time. Did this mean that the Creator continued to create new species independently as older species vanished? Charles Lyell, author of *Principles of Geology*, thought so; he proposed that God uniformly replaced extinct species by new special creations after each extinction.[9] But if this was true, then an act of special creation should at some time be observable.

Darwin's theory excited the scientific community because his proposed natural mechanism for the origin of species was feasible and explained many observable facts of nature that had not been satisfactorily explained by earlier theories. In short, it brought the explanation of species forms into the realm of science and out of the realm of theology. Darwin was saying that most ancient extinct species did not really vanish but were earlier evolutionary stages of the species on earth today.[10] His field observations of structurally similar but reproductively isolated populations in close geographic proximity suggested to him that biological species are not specially created by divine intervention, nor are they fixed realities of nature. Instead, he proposed that the diversity of species is due solely to the natural selection of the random individual variations of organisms which best suit them to adapt to a changing environment. All the species existing today have resulted, he said, from the gradual transformation of one or several first primitive forms into which God breathed the spirit of life. Although Darwin allowed creation for the first primitive form, the new theory contradicted the fundamental premise of special creation: the real existence of distinct species in nature and their essential discontinuity from each other.

Darwin's view is called *population thinking* by modern biologists because it considers only the individual members of populations as real, not the "species," which is a mental construct used for classification. Darwin explained: "I look at the term species as one arbitrarily given, for the sake of convenience, to a set of individuals closely resembling each other."[11] Since every individual has variations or unique characteristics, Darwin proposed that if some members of a homogeneous population become geographically separated from the parent population, they can become—through the gradual evolution of those unique variations—a new reproductively isolated population, or a new "species." Darwin felt he had found sure evidence of this with many similar but reproductively isolated species on the Galapagos Islands.

Mayr explains: "The concept of a static type is replaced by that of a highly variable population. New variations are produced continuously, some of them superior and some of them inferior to the existing average."[12] Superior variations that help the population adapt to changes in the environment or compete better with similar populations tend to be preserved in the gene pool—this is natural selection.[13] The random variations, according to Darwin, occur accidentally, but their "selection" is neither accidental nor predetermined. Beneficial variations are simply preserved because they better meet the survival needs of an organism. Given time and geographic isolation, this is how Darwin conceived of new species gradually deriving from parent species. By implication, Darwin postulated that all organisms, including man, have descended from common ancestors by a continuous process of branching. Each animal, plant, or micro-organism is but a link in a chain of ever-changing, never-repeated forms, and these forms are determined solely by the environment.

The significance of this change of view to Western thought has been eloquently expressed by Thomas Kuhn:

> All the well-known pre-Darwinian evolutionary theories—those of Lamarck, Chambers, Spencer, and the German Naturphilosophen— had taken evolution to be a goal-directed process. The "idea" of man and of the contemporary flora and fauna was thought to have been present from the first creation of life, perhaps in the mind of God. That idea or plan had provided the direction and the guiding force to the entire evolutionary process. Each new stage of evolutionary development was a more perfect realization of a plan that had been present from the start. For many men the abolition of that teleological kind of evolution was the most significant and least palatable of Darwin's suggestions. *The Origin of Species* recognized no goal set either by God or nature. Instead, natural selection, operating in the given environment and with the actual organisms presently at hand, was responsible for the gradual but steady emergence of more elaborate, further articulated, and vastly more specialized organisms. Even such marvelously adapted organs as the eye and hand of man—organs whose design had previously provided powerful arguments for the existence of a supreme artificer and an advance plan—were products of a process that moved steadily from primitive beginnings but toward no goal. The belief that natural selection, resulting from mere competition between organisms for survival, could have produced man together with the higher animals and plants was the most difficult and disturbing aspect of Darwin's theory.[14]

Darwin never pretended to explain how life arose to begin with. He proposed that God had breathed life into one or several first primitive forms. Then he thought God had stepped back from His work and allowed the mechanism of natural selection, which Darwin had just discovered, to take over and "select" the random variations best suited for survival in an ever-changing environment. The forms of the species resulting over the vast course of time were determined strictly by natural forces, not by conscious design. "There is a grandeur in this view of life," explained Darwin, "with its several powers, having been originally breathed by the Creator into a few forms or into one; and . . . from so simple a beginning

endless forms most beautiful and most wonderful have been, and
are, being evolved."[15] Although his theory dealt a blow to teleology, as traditionally understood, he allowed that God had established
the general laws of nature but not the details. In his words:

> There seems to me too much misery in the world. I cannot persuade
> myself that a beneficent and omnipotent God would have designedly
> created the Ichneumonidae with the express intention of their feeding
> within the living bodies of Caterpillars, or that a cat should play with
> a mouse. Not believing this, I see no necessity in the belief that the eye
> was expressly designed. . . . On the other hand, I cannot anyhow be
> contented to view this wonderful universe, and especially the nature of
> man, and to conclude that everything is the result of brute force. I am
> inclined to look at everything as resulting from designed laws, with the
> details, whether good or bad, left to the working out of what we may
> call chance.[16]

1.2 Evidences Favoring Darwinism

Just as Newton had deduced an invisible force called gravity to
explain the movements of the heavenly bodies (now more accurately
explained by Einstein's general theory of relativity), Darwin deduced
his theory from a wide range of observable evidence, which gave his
theory scientific credibility. That scientists were not able to find a particular set of "essential characteristics" universally distinguishing one
biological species from another was an apparent victory for the
Darwinists. Geometrical figures and atomic elements are universally
and clearly defined, but the situation with organic species, when these
are defined by reproductive isolation, is more problematic. For example, except for inability to interbreed, two or more species of finches
may look and act nearly identical to each other. By what then are their
essences (i.e., their essential characteristics) distinguished?[17]

Still, Darwin's critics saw no reason for one species to evolve into
another; this would be, they thought, like lead evolving into gold.[18]
To them, the kinds of biological organisms required by nature
should be just as fixed as the kinds of elements in physics.

Other evidences used by Darwin and his followers to support evolution include the following: (1) The existence of vestiges or rudimentary organs no longer used suggests that the species has evolved from a form in which those organs were necessary. (2) The similarity of reproductively isolated species in geographic proximity suggests that they have branched from each other recently. This is especially evident in the case of the animals in Australia, which bear a family resemblance. (3) The taxonomic hierarchy and morphological similarity of organisms is evidence of descent from a common ancestry (the tree model of evolution).[19] (4) The stages of embryological development (ontogeny) appear to recapitulate the stages of evolution (phylogeny). For example, if biological species had been specially created, asked Darwin, why shouldn't their ontogeny take them by the most direct path to the adult stage, so that the wing of a bat or the fin of a porpoise would be "sketched out with all their parts in proper proportion, as soon as any part became visible [in the embryo]"?[20] But instead we find detours, such as the embryos of land-living vertebrates going through a gill-arch stage. (5) Darwin's strongest evidence, he felt, was in the ability of breeders and domesticators to alter the shape and constitution of wild species. Given time and a larger gene pool, nature should be able to alter a species into a completely different species. Based on such evidences, Darwin asserted against the essentialists: "On the ordinary view of each species having been independently created. . . . I do not see that any explanation can be given."[21]

1.3 Essentialist Objections to Darwinism

1.3.1 *The Role of Natural Selection and Chance.* What biologists who favored the special creation of species by a transcendent, ruling mind (such as Lyell, Herschel, Cuvier, Owen, Agassiz, and von Baer) found most objectionable in Darwin's theory was, as Frederick Hutton put it, "its reliance on *natural* causes and *chance* in affecting the changes." We should be more inclined," he continued, "to refer the modifications which species of animals or plants have undergone to the direct will of God."[22] Most essentialists accepted that random variations did occur in nature, but these variations, they claimed, could never stray from the limits set by the "species essence."

Darwin's critics held that every species has an immutable essence, or law, or idea present in the mind of God which determines the essential attributes of its biological counterpart, such as the important organs, basic body structure, and behaviors necessary to fulfill a niche in an environmental system. These remain constant through time and make each species what it is. Accidental properties, like color, amount of body hair, and size, in contrast, may vary from individual to individual depending on the environment. Natural selection, from this perspective, merely serves to ensure that accidental characteristics that stray too far from the norm are eliminated, while the essential form is preserved through time. This was the general position of classical biology, which is designated today as *typological thinking*, because of the assumed close correlation between fixed essences (types) and static biological populations.

Classical biology also held that these essences and their biological counterparts formed an unchanging, continuous Chain of Being. The Creator "did not make kinds separate without making something intermediate between them," so that a "wonderful linkage of beings" exists, wherein "the highest species of one genus coincides with the lowest of the next higher genus, in order that the universe may be one, perfect, and continuous."[23] The static understanding of the Chain of Being, however, began to change after Leibniz (1644-1716) added the concept of dynamic becoming to it (see Section 1.4).

One of Darwin's arguments was that natural selection could, over time, transmute the so-called essential form, just as domesticators modified animals and plants by artificial selection. But Agassiz countered:

> It is not true that a slight variation, among successive offspring of the same stock, goes on increasing until the difference amounts to a specific distinction. On the contrary, it is a matter of fact that extreme variations finally degenerate or become sterile. . . .[24] Our domesticated animals, with all their breeds and varieties, have never been traced

back to anything but their own species, nor have artificial varieties, so far as we know, failed to revert to the wild stock when left to themselves.[25]

Darwin remained adamant, however, that it is precisely the accidental properties, the chance individual variations, that, if beneficial, in time could become typical of a group, and hence the basis of a new species. He stressed: "Unless such [profitable variations] occur, natural selection can do nothing."[26]

Herschel in his *Physical Geography of the Globe* objected strongly to this line of thinking:

> We can no more accept the principle of arbitrary and casual variation of natural selection as a sufficient condition, per se, of the past and present organic world than we can receive the Laputan method of composing books [by randomly striking the keys of a typewriter] as a sufficient account of Shakespeare and the Principia. . . . Equally in either case, an intelligence, guided by a purpose, must be continually in action to bias the directions of the steps of change—to regulate their amount—to limit their divergence—and to continue them in a definite course. We do not believe that Mr. Darwin means to deny the necessity of such intelligent direction. But it does not, so far as we can see, enter into the formula of this law; and without it we are unable to conceive how far the law can have led to the results.[27]

1.3.2. *The Lack of Intermediate Forms.* The slow and gradual change of an older species into a new species was another component of Darwinism that nineteenth-century essentialists found difficult to accept. On the whole, the essentialists agreed that Darwin's theory was based on assumptions. If what Darwin proposed was true, then there should be a wealth of transitional fossil forms in the geological strata, which would prove that one class of animals had gradually evolved from another. For example, there should be many intermediates between fishes and amphibians, between reptiles and mammals, and so forth. Many of the essentialists were paleontologists, and what they found in the fossil record was exactly the opposite of what Darwin required. Instead, they said, species appear suddenly in the fossil record, persist relatively unchanged for most of their existence, and then abruptly disappear from the fossil record. As the British paleontologist, Richard Owen (1804-1892), observed:

> When we see the intervals that divide most species from their nearest congeners, in the recent and especially the fossil series, we either doubt the fact of progressive conversion, or, as Mr. Darwin remarks . . . one's "imagination must fill up very wide blanks." . . . The last ichthyosaurus, by which the genus disappears in the chalk, is hardly distinguishable from the first ichthyosaurus. . . . The oldest pterodactyle is as thorough and complete a one as the latest.[28]

The same objection was put forth by the American paleontologist, Louis Agassiz (1807-1873):

> [Darwin's] doctrines, in fact, contradict what the animal forms buried in the rocky strata of our earth tell us of their own introduction and succession upon the surface of the globe. . . . Let us look now at the earliest vertebrates, as known and recorded in geological surveys. They should, of course, if there is any truth in the transmutation theory, correspond with the lowest in rank or standing. What then are the earliest known vertebrates? They are the selachians (sharks and their allies) and ganoids (garpikes and the like), the highest of all living fishes, structurally speaking. . . . The Silurian deposits follow immediately upon those in which life first appeared, and should therefore contain not the highest fishes, but the fishes next in order to the myzonts ["fishes structurally inferior to all others"]. . . . The presence of the selachians at the dawn of life upon earth is in direct contradiction to the idea of a gradual progressive development.[29]

Cuvier had similarly objected against Lamarck's evolutionary theory: "If the species have changed by degrees, we should find some traces of these gradual modifications; between paleotherium and today's species we should find some intermediary forms: This has not yet happened."[30] He also called attention "to the fact that the mummified animals from the Egyptian tombs which were many thousands of years old were quite indistinguishable from the living representatives of these species."[31]

Though Darwin recognized the lack of evidence in the geological strata for intermediate forms, he attributed such lack of evidence to "the extreme imperfection of the geological record."[32] Today evolution biologists claim to have discovered a number of preserved transitional species in the fossil record. One of the most famous is *Archaeopteryx*, considered to be an intermediate between reptiles and birds. Contemporary evolutionists Stephen Jay Gould and Niles Eldredge do not argue against transitional lineages between kinds, but they do contest Darwinian gradualism between them. Their theory of punctuated equilibrium, says Gould, accounts for "two outstanding facts of the fossil record—geologically 'sudden' origin of new species and failure to change thereafter (stasis)."[33]

Another paleontologist, Francois Jules Pictet (1809-1872), pointed out another problem with the gradual development of intermediate forms:

> Admit, for instance, that they [birds] sprang from a common progenitor with mammals and reptiles. The wing then must have been formed by successive alterations in the anterior limb of the prototype. But I do not see how natural selection could act for the conservation of future birds, since this modified member, this future wing, being neither a real arm nor a real wing, could not possibly be of any physiological value.[34]

He also noticed that the explosion of diverse, complex life forms appearing in the earliest part of the fossil record, with nothing more complicated than bacteria beforehand, contradicted Darwin's idea of life starting from only one or a few primitive types.[35]

1.4 Essentialist Alternatives

For some essentialists, such as T. H. Huxley and William Bateson, the only way evolution was viable was by the sudden origin of new species by saltation, i.e. evolutionary jumps in which earlier species are used as building blocks for new species via an extensive mutation.[36] In this way, distinct species essences are preserved and act as the laws defining the field of favorable mutations. This idea was also noticed by the physical scientist, Fleeming Jenkin. In 1867, he wrote in *The North British Review*:

> If . . . the advantage given by the sport [a radical mutation] is retained by all descendants . . . then these descendants will shortly supplant the old species entirely, after the manner required by Darwin. But this theory of the origin of species is surely not the Darwinian theory [of gradual change]; it simply amounts to the hypothesis that, from time to time, an animal is born differing appreciably from its progenitors, and possessing the power of transmitting the difference to its descendants. What is this but stating that, from time to time, a new species is created? It does not, indeed, imply that the new specimen suddenly appears in full vigour, made out of nothing.[37]

Jenkin also argued that just as there is a set number of chemical elements and possible combinations of these, the forms of species and possible variations are also limited, though seemingly infinite. He explained that

> organized beings may be regarded as combinations, either of the elementary substances used to compose them, or of the parts recurring in many beings, . . . [so it is not] surprising that newly discovered species and varieties should almost invariably occupy an intermediate position between some already known, since the number of varieties of one species, or the number of possible species, can only be indefinitely increased by admitting varieties or species possessing indefinitely small differences one from another.[38]

Another possibility, which was foreshadowed by Leibniz, is that evolution is really change within the same species, in other words, the temporal unfoldment of the preexisting potentialities of the original kinds created by God. Leibniz stated:

> Although many substances [species] have already attained a great perfection, yet on account of the infinite divisibility of the continuous, there always remain in the abyss of things slumbering parts which have yet to be awakened, to grow in size and worth, and in a word, to advance to a more perfect state. . . . There is a perpetual and a most

free progress of the whole universe in fulfillment of the universal beauty and perfection of the works of God, so that it is always advancing towards a greater development.[39]

According to Mayr, although Leibniz's idea "helped to prepare the ground for evolutionary thinking," it was not a genuine theory of evolution, in a strict Darwinian sense, since it did not allow for the transmutation of one species into another. Transformation *within* a species and the development of varieties out of original kinds does not count as "evolution" to Mayr. He argues that Leibniz's view, which maintains fixed underlying essences but allows for the gradual transformation of physical forms toward greater perfection, should be called, as Lovejoy coined it, "the temporalizing of the Chain of Being."[40] In other words, the Chain of Being became construed by Leibniz and his followers "as a process in which all forms are gradually realized in the order of time."[41]

Although the British naturalist, Thomas Wollaston (1821-1878), chose special creation over evolution, he allowed a greater range of plasticity within the species limit to help account for Darwin's observations: "Whilst 'individual variation' in each species is literally endless, it is at the same time strictly prescribed within its proper morphotic limits (as regulated by its specific range), even though *we may be totally unable to define their bounds*."[42] Because of this, "if a formerly acknowledged species can be shown to be descended from another formerly acknowledged species, then these two forms were not actually species but varieties [even if they can no longer interbreed]."[43]

This again is a form of "evolution" *within* an original species or kind, and can be termed "parallel evolution" since the original kinds develop in parallel or independently from each other. (The modern concept of "microevolution," which recognizes the undisputable fact that living things change as they adapt to their environment, is amenable to both the supporters of special creation and of parallel evolution.) These two essentialist alternatives will be examined again when we come to the writings of 'Abdu'l-Bahá on this subject.

As early as 1690, the English philosopher John Locke had given an answer as to why a particular set of "essential characteristics" universally distinguishing one biological species from another would never be found. This, as mentioned in Section 1.2, was one of the main objections Darwinists held against the essentialist claim that each natural species has an essence which determines it. Locke granted the existence of "real essences" that are known by God, but he distinguished these from the purely "nominal essences" conceived by human beings. Because of the essential limitation of human knowledge and its inability to encompass every detail of an entity, he proposed that the precise boundaries of real essences cannot be known. Thus, he says, "our distinguishing substances into species by names is not at all founded on their real essences; nor can we pretend to range and determine them exactly into species, according to essential internal differences."[44] In other words, real essences, just like real laws of nature, can never be completely defined and will always be the subject of further inquiry. What humans deal with are nominal and provisional representations of these real things.

Morphologists also answered this same objection by proposing that there is no one-to-one correspondence between the species essence and what Darwinists define as a biological species. In other words, mutual interbreeding does not define a single species in the metaphysical sense. Instead, an ideal type determining a common form and common function in a certain environmental niche underlie the evident variability of things.[45]

Under the naturalists' definition of "real species" as "all forms related by blood descent to a common ancestor," Darwin would have to say, had he believed in species as other than nominal constructs, that there is only one or several species and countless varieties. This is because Darwin allowed special creation to one or several first primitive organisms, from which everything else has subsequently derived by slow and gradual variation. But, as already mentioned, Darwin's theory represents a radical change in thinking, because he proposed that God had no preconceived plan for how the first organism(s) should evolve. This was left to the mechanism of chance variations followed by their necessary selection by the environment.

Since Mayr says most biologists did not agree on the significance of natural selection as the main agent of evolution until the "evolutionary synthesis" of the 1930s and 40s, we can assume that during 'Abdu'l-Bahá's visits to Europe and American between 1911 and 1913, the debates between the essentialists and the Darwinists were far from settled.[46] The implications of the two alternatives (species as fixed realities of nature determining biological populations versus biological populations as productions of natural selection and species as mere theoretical constructs) would not have been lost to his educated audience. We may now turn to the reception of Darwinism in the Arab world.

THE ARAB WORLD[47]

Under the impact of Western ideas, the late nineteenth-century in the Arab world was a period of intellectual ferment and increasing interest in secular learning and social change. One of the most important vehicles for the dissemination of Western scientific ideas into the Arab world was the magazine *al-Muqtataf*, founded by Yaqub Sarruf and Faris Nimr in Beirut in 1876. It moved to Egypt in 1885. The editors of *al-Muqtataf* were open-minded Christian Arabs who were generally favorable to Darwin's theory. The discussion on Darwinism in *al-Muqtataf* was frequently countered by the journal *al-Mashriq*, founded in 1898 by an Arab Catholic, Father Louis Cheikho.[48] Darwin's theory was introduced and discussed in *al-Muqtataf* in its first volume in an article by Rizqullah al-Barbárí.[49]

1.5 Rizqullah al-Barbárí's Description of Darwinism

Barbárí commences with the biblical view that the first man was created at once by God's power, not by evolution. Contrary to the biblical view, he says that certain ancient philosophers believed in the spontaneous generation of all organisms. "They assumed that the earth was full of the 'seeds' or 'germs' of all organic species, which then evolved of their own accord with the appearance of suitable conditions."[50] Some modern scientists have returned to this view, Barbárí continues, which teaches that creatures arise "from inert matter by their own power when conditions are right . . . emerging by natural causes without needing an intelligent creator. To be sure, many natural scientists oppose this . . . and say that every living thing is due to fixed natural laws."[51]

Darwin, he says, is not to be counted among the materialists, because he accepts a Creator as the cause of existence. Both groups agree, though, that "all the differences among animals and plants occur solely from natural causes without the interference of a conscious power in their production."[52] At the end of his article, Barbárí refutes this theory for four reasons: (1) Matter or the original germ cannot by itself differentiate into all that exists today; an intellectual power is needed. (2) Although Darwin did not deny the existence of God, his theory leads to the refutation of all the proofs for God's existence. (3) This theory requires that everything now existing was generated from a single germ in the space of 500 million years by a natural action; but no proof for this exists. (4) This theory is against sound intelligence.[53]

As Ziadat notes, "Arab interest in Darwinism centered on its philosophical, social, and political implications, rather than on its status as a biological theory."[54] In other words, the educated public was more interested in knowing how this theory affected their religious and political views than in understanding how well it stood up to empirical evidence. This explains Barbárí's cursory review of Darwinism and his focus on its philosophical and theological meaning. In the Arab world, Darwin's *The Origin of Species* was not known firsthand until 1918 with the translation of the first five chapters by Ismail Mazhar. Before that, Darwin's theory was known through translations of works by some of his commentators, like Herbert Spencer, Ernst Haeckel, and Ludwig Büchner, and through articles in journals like *al-Muqtataf.*

The real debate over Darwinism began in 1882 when an American professor, Edwin Lewis, gave a speech appearing to favor Darwinism to the graduating class at the Syrian Protestant College in Beirut. As a result, several professors who sided with Lewis were forced to resign. The debate continued in the pages of *al-Muqtaṭaf* between Louis, supported by *al-Muqtaṭaf's* editor, Yaqub Sarruf, and an Egyptian, Yusuf al-Ḥá'ik, on one side, and James Denis, an American theologian, and other dissenters, on the other side.[55]

1.6 Yaqub Sarruf's Article Supporting Darwin

Darwin's position, explains Sarruf, is that everything on earth, whether extinct or living, has derived gradually from something else, so biological species, in this case, could not be independently created. This chain of descent goes back to one or several roots for all plants and animals. Sarruf reminds us that Aristotle also spoke of the "great Chain of Being" and saw nature as one interconnected whole linked together from the lowest plant to the highest animal with very little difference between neighboring links, but it was a fixed and eternal whole that did not evolve.[56] Arabic speaking philosophers, states Sarruf, adopted Aristotle's concept of a fixed Chain of Being, but they added to it the ideas of creation and "progress toward perfection" (*taraqqí ila'l-kamál*), "not in the sense that man was an ox and became a donkey, then a horse, an ape, and finally man," but in the sense that independently created species progress within themselves. For example, according to medieval natural science, gold is a metal that gradually reaches perfection by first passing through less perfect stages. So first it is lead, tin, copper, and silver, before becoming gold, but all the while it has remained within the same species.[57] In other words, these metals were not recognized as separate elements in essence. Sarruf says this view is called "independent creation" (*al-khalq al-mustaqill*), wherein species have remained independent from each other since the beginning of their creation.[58] The position of Sarruf's "Arabic speaking philosophers," by which he probably means those after Mullá Ṣadrá (see Section 3.9), is obviously very similar to that of Leibniz (see Section 1.4).

In the remainder of the article, Sarruf discusses some of the problems with the independent creation of biological populations. First, he says, as more and more species became classified scientists began to recognize that they could no longer find unique attributes distinguishing one species from another. For example, butterflies were found to consist of many different species with no apparent fixed distinction between them.[59] "Furthermore," continues Sarruf, "when scientists examined the composition of plants and animals, they found that all plants and animals belonging to one taxon or one class are formed according to a common pattern, so that vertebrates, for example, all have bones according to one pattern, no matter how different the species. . . . Thus the bones in the hand of a man, the foot of a horse, the wings of a bird, and the fins of a fish are all homologous."[60] This similarity of structure indicates common descent.

Another evidence against independent creation, explains Sarruf, was the discovery of trace organs, or vestiges, no longer being used by a species. For example, the whale has teeth which never break through its gums and the boa constrictor has vestiges of legs hidden under its skin, each of which indicate its descent from other vertebrates which had use for these organs.[61]

Scientists also used to believe, he says, that just as mature animals differ in their forms, their embryos similarly differ. But then it was proven by close examination that the embryos of different species are virtually indistinguishable, a sign of their common origin. If the species were independently created, why don't their embryos differ?[62]

With the discovery of fossils buried in the strata of rock, scientists found that the living animals of one region resembled the extinct animals of the same region, although their species were apparently different; thus the marsupials of Australia resemble the extinct marsupials of the same continent, and these species are not found elsewhere. The same geographical isolation and species resemblance was found with the armadillo and its extinct predecessors, which are found only in South America. "Therefore," asks Sarruf, "if the species of animals had been created independently, why do the animals living now in one country resemble those that lived there formerly and are now extinct?"[63] He proposes that Darwin's answer is more satisfying: "some species descended from others, so those living today are naturally similar to their now extinct ancestors."[64]

The fossil remains in the great depths of sedimentary rock also provided evidence favoring Darwin's theory, claims Sarruf. "It was found that the animals of the earth since the beginning of its existence until today had succeeded one another gradually. . . . The most ancient layers of rock contained nothing but sea shells and the bones of fishes very different from those living today. . . . The next layer contained traces of animals having legs."[65] Sarruf concludes that the more recent geological strata contain the fossils of mammals and primates, and that those animals more recent in time resemble each other more closely than those more distantly separated. "The links connecting these species to each other," he explains, "are not seen because it is said that one species has changed into another species gradually by the change of its individual members."[66] Although he adds that the discovery in America of the fossilized remains of an animal with the body of a bird and the jawbone and teeth of a reptile provides a link between the reptile and the bird.

As for the reason organs change and variations appear, Sarruf holds that this is due to an organism's need to adapt to the environment to survive. For example, the giraffe's long neck developed from its need to feed on the leaves of high branches. "God did not create its front legs longer than its hind legs or its neck very long, as is widely believed, but it was compelled to eat the leaves of trees; its preference for this over moving to a more verdant region changed its body from its original form."[67] The snake, he says, also lost its legs because of its need to adapt to a changing environment.

Darwin's great law of natural selection, by which beneficial variations are preserved, depends on two things, says Sarruf. The first is that all creatures multiply in large numbers in a short time, but only the fittest survive to reproduce and carry on subsistence. Were it not for this the earth would soon become overpopulated and resources would become depleted. The second is that offspring inherit the characteristics of their parents, so if a parent has a characteristic that increases its life span or ability to reproduce, it is sure that some of its offspring will inherit this quality. They, in turn, will pass it on to their descendants. In this way, over a long period of time, the species changes.[68] Darwin's most famous evidence for this, continues Sarruf, is in how far human breeding of domesticated plants and animals has altered them from their wild relatives. Nature does the same thing, only much more slowly.[69]

As for species that do not change over time, Sarruf says this is because they are well-suited to their environments, and this situation may continue indefinitely.[70] As for how today's species reached their present state from one origin, "it is not," clarifies Sarruf, "that the flea became a frog, the frog became an eagle, the eagle became an ox, and the ox became an elephant, but their first ancestor was the same. The flea was produced from one branch [of the evolutionary tree] and the elephant from another over a long period of time."[71] So it is not correct to say that man has descended from the ape, because these are contemporary species, but both descended from a common primate ancestor.[72]

Sarruf ends his defense of Darwinism by acknowledging that certain of its proofs are weak, as Darwin also admitted. But he says, despite this, "it contains established truths, has greatly benefited scientists, and opened a number of doors to hidden mysteries."[73] His depiction of Darwinism is surprisingly accurate and very similar to Mayr's construction, which I have summarized in Sections 1.1-2.

1.7 James Denis' Refutation of Darwinism

Referring to Sarruf's article and Edwin Lewis's address, the theologian James Denis complains that Darwin completely separated religious truth from the conclusions of science and denied God's role in creating plants and animals as they appear today. He accuses Darwin of being an unbeliever and rejecting the truth of the Bible. The whole of Denis's refutation consists in summoning authorities to back him up. The Apostle Paul, for example, refuted Darwin, when he wrote: "For by Him were all things created that are in heaven and that are in earth, visible and invisible" (Colossians 1:16). Denis next turns to certain scientists of his time: A German naturalist states that "none of the human fossils found so far prove that man was at one time inferior to his present state."[74] The French philosopher Pouchet asserts: "Species are not theoretical concepts created by human intellects, but they are created by the all-powerful Hand of God in numerous stages. They cannot change into other species, but they change independently . . . and are limited by certain timeless laws."[75] The American geologist Professor Dana claims: "The distance between man and the ape is enormous. The area of the brain in the lowest humans is 68 square inches and in the highest apes only 34. . . . No links between man and the apes have been found in the geological strata."[76] In short, many brilliant scientists, including Agassiz, Dawson, Beal, Pasteur, and Owen, have objected to Darwin's theory. Denis ends by arguing that Darwin's theory should not be confused with a religious theory of "evolution by a divine power" (*al-irtiqá' bi-quwat ilahiyah*), because evolution may be a law by which the Creator operates, so long as self-creation and the transmutation of species are not included.[77]

1.8 Edwin Lewis Responds to James Denis

In his response to Denis, Lewis focuses on his belief that science and religion are in essential harmony. Denis had accused Darwin of being an unbeliever. Lewis explains that Darwin only meant that one's relationship with God is a personal matter, which does not conflict with a scientist's duty to investigate reality impartially. Whatever we think of Darwin's theory, he was a model example of using the scientific method to further our knowledge of reality. "We should not make a rigid judgment against the value of this theory, since it hasn't been sufficiently test yet."[78] Lewis continues: "It is clear that the scientific method correctly applied does not make men turn away from their religion," and Darwin had testified to God's greatness and acknowledged Him as the Creator of the laws of nature. "By studying nature, we learn about the way God established it, but through revelation we learn who and what God is."[79] Lewis concludes that whoever follows a revealed religion should rejoice in God and in the progress of science, for whatever appears in one contrary to the other will vanish in the course of time and the reality will be made manifest.[80]

1.9 Yusuf al-Ḥá'ik Responds to One of Lewis' Critics

A scholar had written a letter to *al-Muqtataf* objecting to Lewis's speech to the graduating class at the Protestant College. The scholar wrote: "He [Lewis] referred to Darwin as a model scientist, showed esteem for his ideas, and did not attempt to refute them, nor did he mention that many of the greatest scientists of our time consider them to be absurd and devoid of proof."[81] Ḥá'ik counters this criticism in a reasonable manner:

> We know that many of the scientists are unbelievers, but this does not mean their works, discoveries, and inventions should not be accorded great respect. . . . True religion does not contradict science . . . for what is science except an explanation of the laws by which God caused the universe to operate. Scientists who believe in God and those who don't both agree in investigating realities, but they differ in that the former recognize God as the originator of the laws and the latter do not. There is no objection, therefore, if a believer refers to the theory of a learned nonbeliever in a scientific meeting. . . . If it is not correct, science itself will disprove it; if it is correct, man will not be lowered from his high station.[82]

1.10 Shiblí Shumayyil and Ludwig Büchner

In 1884, Shiblí Shumayyil, a Lebanese Catholic, published his translation of Ludwig Büchner's commentary *Sechs Vorlesungen über die Darwinsche Theorie*[83] in his book *Falsafat al-Nushú' wa'l-Irtiqá'* (The Theory of Evolution), raising a vehement intellectual response among Muslims and Christians alike. The reason for this response was that Shumayyil, via Büchner, understood Darwin's theory as a call to materialism. Büchner wrote, in defense of materialism: "Perhaps the greatest philosophical achievement of Darwin's theory is its removal, by categorical proofs, of the belief in final causes from the sphere of the natural sciences and from science in general. . . . His theory has explained to us the correct causes [of speciation], and its proofs are derived not only from philosophy but from nature and living specimens as well."[84]

The materialist does not accept as explanations for natural phenomena what the senses or scientific instruments cannot detect. Thus Shumayyil states: "Man . . . and whatever is in him derives from nature. This is the truth, and there is no reason for doubting it today. . . . Nothing in his composition indicates a connection to the world of spirit or to a hidden reality. . . . He is like the animal physiologically and like the mineral chemically. He is distinguished from them only in quantity, not quality, and in form not essence."[85]

Büchner held that matter never disappears but is simply transformed from one form or state into another according to the law of change, which applies not only to living organisms, as Darwin demonstrated, but to energy and the atomic elements as well. All result from the continuous transformations of matter.[86] Matter and its motion, therefore, are the ultimate, self-evident basis of all that exists.[87] Shumayyil says that Darwin proved the transmutations of biological populations with scientific certainty and disproved the fixity of species through special creation, showing instead that they are produced necessarily by the laws of nature and never cease to be generated and destroyed as one succeeds another.[88]

One of Shumayyil's followers, Salama Musa, wrote *Muqdimat al-Superman* (The Advent of Superman) and *Nazariyat al-Tatawwur wa Asl al-Insán* (The Theory of Evolution and the Origin of Man). He was very interested in eugenics and wished his countrymen to discontinue allowing physically or mentally handicapped persons to marry. Instead of natural selection, which he felt was no longer feasible in the case of human beings, he wanted to use artificial selection to produce children with optimum physical and mental characteristics.[89]

1.11 Refutations of Materialism

The editors of *al-Muqtataf*, unlike Shumayyil, denounced materialism. Faris Nimr in an address titled *Fasád Falsafat al-Máddiyín* (The Falsity of Materialistic Philosophy), published in *al-Muqtataf* in 1883,[90] rejected the opinion of the materialists that the actions of the soul are no more than the effects of matter, and likewise that feelings, intelligence, and human will are merely the actions of the brain.[91] He upheld instead that the mind is independent of the brain, which is only the instrument of the former.[92] Sarruf, in his own commentary against materialism at a latter date, called World War I the end result of materialistic philosophy unguided by morality or belief in the divine force that created, organizes, and controls the world.[93]

Another critic of the materialists' use of "struggle for survival" to justify the war was Jurji Zaydan, the editor of *al-Hilal.* Influenced by Henry Drummond's philosophy in *The Ascent of Man,* that "love, cooperation, and friendship are also laws of nature and are necessary for evolution in all living organisms," he emphasized that the more a society exhibits cooperation and self-sacrifice, the more evolved it is.[94]

A letter of 'Abdu'l-Bahá (which will be discussed in Section 4) makes the very same pionts. Although not favoring religion, Ismail Mazhar also opposed materialism because it did not answer the question of the origin of life. He admitted that the forces acting to produce speciation were still unknown and he interpreted the law of struggle for survival to mean "struggle against an adverse environment," whereas "mutual aid governed living organisms."[95]

1.12 Arabic Speaking Essentialists

Among the Arab Christians, Father Louis Cheikho took a strong stand against Darwinism and opposed the moderates at *al-Muqtataf.* In regard to species, he held that each was a special creation, similar to a "small seed which contains in it the roots, branches, and flowers of a tree," such that "wheat seeds do not produce beans and the seeds of beans do not yield wheat. Therefore, animals could not produce humans or man evolve from animals."[96] Another Christian, Rufail Hawawini, writing in 1906 in the Arabic paper *al-Kalimah* published in New York, said that "all species were created separately and that man, no matter how diverse, came from one root, Adam."[97]

1.12.1 *Jamál al-Dín al-Afghání.* Among Muslims, Jamál al-Dín al-

Afghání was a firm opponent of Darwin's theory. He wrote *al-Radd 'ala'l-Dahriyín* (The Refutation of the Materialists) in 1881 in Persian; it was later translated into Arabic by his follower, Muhammad Abduh, and published in Egypt. Although he was not well-informed about Darwin, whom he classified among the materialists, his views were typical of many of his fellow Muslims. He commences by reminding his readers that one of the first materialists was Democritus, who believed that the "whole universe is composed of small hard particles that are naturally mobile, and that they appear in their present form by chance."[98]

Referring to Darwin and his supporters, he explains that they "decided that the germs of all species, especially animals, are identical, that there is no difference between them, and that the species also have no essential distinctions. Therefore, they said, those germs transferred from one species to another and changed from one form to another through the demands of time and place, according to necessity and moved by external forces."[99] Mistakenly, he relates that Darwin has man descending from the ape and the orangutan. In short, he is especially critical that the diversity of species and the perfection of organs could occur by chance without the benefit of intelligent direction. He says:

> If one asked him [Darwin]: What guided those defective, unintelligent germs to the production of perfect and sound external and internal members and limbs, whose perfection and soundness the wisest men are unable to fathom, and whose benefits the masters of physiology are unable to enumerate; and how could blind necessity be the wise guide of the germs toward all these perfections of form and reason—naturally he could never raise his head from the sea of perplexity.[100]

Against the idea of some materialists that the simple elements form themselves into complex and stable forms, he asks:

> How did these separate, scattered particles become aware of each other's aims and by what instrument of explanation did they explain their affairs? In what parliament and senate did they confer in order to form these elegant and wonderful beings? And how did these separate

particles know that if they were in a sparrow's egg they must there take on the form of a grain-eating bird, and that its beak and maw should be so formed as to make its life possible?[101]

1.12.2 *Hussein al-Jisr.* Hussein al-Jisr, a Shi'ite jurist from Lebanon, won a prize from his patron, Sultan 'Abdu'l-Hamíd, for his book *Al-Risála al-Hamídíya fí Haqíqa al-Diyána al-Islámiya wa Haqqíya al-Sharí'a al-Muhammadíya* (The Praiseworthy Epistle on the Truth of Islam and Islamic Canon Law) published in Beirut in 1887. In one part of the book, he argues against Darwin's theory and supports "the theory of creation and the independence of species" (*madhhab al-khalq wa istiqlál al-anwá*). He is reasonable enough, however, to state that should the evolution "hypotheses become established by categorical proofs which haven't a chance of contradiction or refutation, Muslims should accept them" and interpret the Holy Book so that the two views are compatible.[102] But he is clear that Muslims would continue to hold God as the real First Cause of the universe, who had chosen to create the world via natural laws and secondary causes. Whether God created the species independently and all at once in the beginning or gradually by means of evolution, deriving some from others, Jisr maintains that "either of these two beliefs . . . would suffice Muslims to prove the existence of God and to ascribe to Him the attributes which these signs indicate."[103]

Jisr argues, however, that the proofs for the theory of evolution are weak and against the obvious meaning of the Qur'án and the Bible, which indicate that God created species independently, not derivatively (cf. Genesis 1:10-31). He adds that although the Holy Texts are clear on independent creation, they are not clear on whether species were created all at once or gradually.[104]

As for the proofs used to support Darwin's theory, Jisr relates and then refutes three of them, saying that none are categorical evidence for evolution. The first proof is that the existence of trace members or vestiges, which now have no use, indicate that the species has changed. If each species was independently created, why are these useless vestiges present? They must have been of use to an earlier species which has since evolved so that they are no longer necessary, and only their traces remain; or they indicate that the species is currently changing into something else where they will be of use.[105] In response, Jisr asks: "What prevents these vestiges from having a use? They may have a wisdom which is hidden to you, just as the uses of many things existing in plants and animals are hidden from you."[106]

The second proof is that the oldest layers of sedimentary rock contain fossils of the most primitive plants and animals, and the layers higher up contain more evolved species. If the theory of independent creation is true, both the most primitive and the most advanced species should be found in each of the geological strata, but this is not the case. Consequently, the origin of the higher species must be the ancient primitive species, which changed in form and evolved until they appeared as they do today.[107] Jisr counters that God may have created the most primitive plants and animals first in accordance with the earth's primitive state. Then when the earth's environment began to change, He created independently a new group of more advanced species suitable to the new conditions, not deriving them from the more primitive species. The old species became extinct due to natural disasters or from competition with the new species. This process of new independent creation and extinction continued, proposes Jisr, until the present species appeared and accounts for the fossils of ancient extinct species found in the strata of rocks.[108] This was also the position of the British geologist Charles Lyle mentioned above.

The third proof constitutes the four laws by which the transmutation of species and the extinction of the primitive by evolution take place. The first is the law of inheritance, which states that the offspring will inherit the characteristics of the parents. The second is the law of variation, which means, inheritance notwithstanding, the offspring will differ in some characteristics from the parents. The third is the law of struggle to survive, in other words, species compete with each other to acquire the means of subsistence, and some are destroyed by others or by natural disasters. The fourth is the law of natural selection, which means the strongest and most fit will endure, while the weakest and least fit will perish.[109] Jisr accepts two of the laws without hesitation, because they do not contradict creation. He says: "As for the law of inheritance, this is an evident thing which Muslims do not deny. . . . Similarly, we do not object to the struggle to survive. As a result of this law, some species survive while others perish and return to God."[110] But he interprets the law of variation in a different way. Similar to other essentialists, he says the variations that occur in individuals are accidental and not essential, so that they cannot become the means of transforming one species into another.[111] Even if the variations of individuals within a species continue for millions of years, this could not change the species, which is fixed. The law of natural selection, explains Jisr, is a natural consequence of the other three, so it is also compatible with the existence of species by creation.[112] With his refutation finished, Jisr concludes that the theory of creation is superior to that of evolution.

1.12.3 *Abu al-Majd al-Isfahání.* The last Muslim thinker to be considered here, also a contemporary of 'Abdu'l-Bahá, is Abu al-Majd Muhammad Ridá al-Isfahání, a Shi'ite theologian from Iraq. He was acquainted with the views of Darwin's critics and supporters and wrote a two volume work called *Naqd Falsafah Darwin* (Critique of Darwin's Philosophy), which appeared in 1914. Of all the critiques of Darwinism yet presented, his is the most knowledgeable and penetrating. He accepted evolution in a special sense, as long as God remained the Creator of all things by design (*qasd*) and choice (*ikhtiyár*). In his introduction he warns his fellow believers to not thoughtlessly reject Darwinism, and he castigates the materialists for denying God:

> As for how things were created, although all these species were created independently and came into existence from the seal of nonexistence without changing from what they were at the beginning of their creation, there is no clear text in the Book or the Sunna which is in opposition to this theory. Whether the primordial ancestor of the camel was a camel or not, or the most distant ancestor of the elephant was an elephant or not, the evidence of their creation in each case is manifest and testifies to the existence of a wise Creator. Therefore the rejoicing

of the materialists over this theory and making it the basis of their heresy is most strange.[113]

By the materialists, Iṣfahání means specifically Ludwig Büchner and his Lebanese follower, Shiblí Shumayyil, who were promoting a concept that Iṣfahání considered extremely dangerous to the positive teachings of religion. He is eager to disassociate Darwin's name from the materialists, and he affirms that Darwin was a believer in God by quoting his words in *The Origin of Species*: " 'The origin of all these genera is five or six [ancestors] into which the Creator breathed the spirit of life.' But," laments Iṣfahání, "the ignorant among his supporters eclipsed this star and brought the utmost dishonor upon him and his theory."[114] Another reason Iṣfahání admired Darwin was because he admitted the hypothetical nature of his ideas, and Iṣfahání quotes him again, this time from *The Descent of Man*: "Many of the ideas I have proposed are very hypothetical and I do not doubt that some will be disproved by categorical proofs."[115]

Iṣfahání believed that scientific theories can only be established by categorical proofs, and that no categorical proofs can contradict the essential truth of religion. The believers, he is quick to point out, do not deny the natural laws by which the Creator causes things to occur.[116]

Despite his praise for Darwin, Iṣfahání has some serious criticisms of Darwin's theory. He starts with Darwin's affirmation that man is able to change just like other animals and is subject to the law of inheritance, which allows the transmission of new characteristics to the offspring.[117] He observes: "The utmost that is proved by the capacity to change is the possibility of transformation, but the acquisition of the human form by this means does not refute its occurrence by another cause, like creation."[118]

A second proof of Darwin for the descent of man from the animal is based on the similar construction of their bodies, so that the pattern of human bones, muscles, nerves, blood vessels, cells, and brain are like that of an ape, bat, seal, and so on, indicating that man is physiologically closely related to the animal and that they share common descent. Iṣfahání states that Muslim thinkers have long noted the physiological similarity between men and certain animals, especially the ape, but they have not deduced from this their descent from a common ancestor. That the organs are analogous does not mean they are also homologous, i.e., they may be similar by design but not necessarily because of a common physical ancestor. He includes an especially interesting statement attributed to the Imam Ja'far al-Ṣádiq, according to al-Mufaḍḍil, from the *Kitáb al-Tawḥíd*:

> Ponder upon the creation of the ape and its resemblance to man in most of its members, i.e. its head, face, and shoulders. Its intestines are also like the intestines of man. It is endowed with a mind and nature by which it understands its master and imitates many of the things it sees man doing, so much so that it is the nearest among created things to man. Its characteristics . . . serve as an example to man with respect to himself that he should know he is from the clay of beasts and their origin. . . . Were it not for the excellence which makes man superior to the beasts in thought, intellect, and speech, he would be like some of the beasts. Although the ape has different features in the nose-mouth structure, hanging tail, and hair enveloping its body, this would not prevent the ape from catching up to man, were it given thought, intellect, and speech like those of man.[119]

Notwithstanding physiological similarity, Iṣfahání argues that "mere resemblance between two things does not require their transmutation from a third thing, or the change of one into another" because these species are different in essence.[120]

Darwin's third proof is that the embryo of man in the beginning is almost no different from the embryos of other vertebrates. Then gradually, differences appear, indicating that the legs of lizards, the limbs of mammals, the wings of birds, and the arms and legs of man have all evolved from one original form. Iṣfahání rejects this idea that ontogeny recapitulates phylogeny, firstly, because of the revelation of Haeckel's forgeries of the stages of embryonic forms; but also for the following reasons: (1) the comparison is limited to species that reproduce sexually; (2) some animals jump from one stage to another but omit the stages in between; (3) some animals may advance, then decline, then advance again. As an example of the second, Iṣfaháni says: "You find two animals of one species . . . whose embryos grow in different ways. Frogs usually pass through the stage of having gills, but in America there is a species of frog that doesn't pass through this stage."[121]

Darwin's fourth proof is that the existence of vestiges, or trace organs, in man and the higher animals, such as breasts in the human male, the wisdom teeth, etc. indicate common descent. They have become vestiges due to lack of use.[122] Iṣfaháni counters that the science of physiology, which studies the functions of organs, did not at first know the functions of many of the organs. For example, heart valves used to be considered trace organs until their use in the circulation of the blood was discovered. The small number of remaining vestiges may also have functions of which we are still unaware.[123] Iṣfaháni also undermines the proof in another respect:

> If we agree there is no actual use for these organs now, how do we know they were functional to man in the past. Perhaps they will be functional in the future. According to evolution, the organs do not come into existence all at once, but they are completed gradually. . . . They began to appear in one of the ancient epochs and did not cease to become more perfected over millions of years until they reached maturity and were ready to perform their functions. It is evident that in those past eras, these presently active members would have been considered an excess.[124]

As an example, Iṣfaháni says the breasts of a girl at first are not functional, but they grow gradually until maturity, when their function is realized for nursing children. He holds that such changes to species through evolution do not negate the immutability of the species forms of things. He concludes: "The utmost they have proven is that these organs were in man formerly, and he had need of them, but is now independent of them. This does not prove that he was an animal, even according to their principles. . . . Rather, the hand of divine wisdom produced them [changes in organs] as they were needed."[125]

Iṣfaháni also discusses the discovery of fossil remains like

Neanderthal and Java man, which were being put forward as intermediate links to prove the descent of man from the animal. He says
of Java man: "Its skull being intermediate in size between apes and
man does not prove that its owner was intermediate between them.
Some men have brains smaller than some animals, and some animals have larger brains."[126] In regard to the discovery of
Neanderthal man, he similarly concludes: "All that these discoveries succeed in proving is the existence of a kind of primate . . . nearer
to man than the presently evolved apes. The descent of man from it
is not proved."[127]

The depth of Iṣfahání's understanding of Darwinism is evident in
his criticism of some contemporary scientists who were trying to
find a link between man and present-day apes. Iṣfahání asserts they
have misunderstood an important aspect of Darwin's theory, which
is that no present forms derive from other present forms; rather
Darwin holds that each species is the end of a long series of transformations from a common unknown ancestor.[128]

Similar to Jisr's response to the four laws of evolution above,
Iṣfahání has no trouble accepting them from the standpoint of religion, except for the law of variation. Darwin based this law on the
premise that no two individuals are alike. Everything has some new
variations, and these variations are the cause of new species by continuous deviation from the parent population.[129] Iṣfahání responds:
"These philosophers insist that this [i.e. random variation] is the
cause of all beings . . . but it is necessary for them to prove that these
variations are not limited by a law or that there is not a law behind
the species which derives some of them from others."[130] Later in his
book, he perceptively notes that the main problem with Darwin's
"theory are the laws of differentiation, which still aren't known, and
are preserved for the twentieth century to discover."[131]

At this point, Iṣfahání has arrived at the heart of the controversy
between the essentialists and the Darwinists, and he is commend-
ably candid about the problems both sides face on the issue of speciation: "What they say [i.e., in favor of Darwinism] could be true if
there is no distinction between accidental and essential attributes, or
if they are able to prove that variations apply to essential things."[132]

He next quotes Büchner's response to the essentialists:

> The opponents of Darwin . . . claim changes apply to accidents only, like color, skin, and stature, and say such changes do not apply to the essence (*jawhar*), but Darwin explained the error of their claim and established that the tendency to change does extend to the essence. He said that the distinction between the species and the variants is difficult to ascertain and scientists maintain many differences over this issue; they do not have an accepted definition for it [species].[133]

Isfahání answers Büchner in a manner reminiscent of John Locke and Thomas Wollaston (see 1.4 above): "We say that establishing [the limits of] the species is a question belonging to the Exalted Wisdom, and it cannot be attained by way of the natural sciences."[134] In other words, Isfahání believes that the laws determining independent species are known only to God and cannot be ascertained by physical classification.

The next part of Isfahání's criticism turns upon the supposition of the Darwinists that random variation and natural selection are sufficient to explain the countless variety of living beings. These laws do not explain, he argues, "the causes by which things exist" nor the causes of their order and perfection. "They only explain the causes of their survival and the reason they are not destroyed after their existence."[135] Like Pictet (see Section 1.3), he objects to the idea that natural selection by itself should select organs that as yet have no benefit, and which may even be detrimental to the organism's immediate survival, because "nature according to them [Darwin and his supporters] is blind; if this is so how can it single out the augmentations which have no benefit except after a long period of time?"[136]

Isfahání, having undermined Büchner's interpretation of Darwinism, explains that "what is meant by the philosophy of creation is the theory of the independence of species (*istiqlál al-anwá'*) and their non-evolution from each other. If we have defended this philosophy, it is a purely scientific defense, not religious."[137] Although upholding independent creation, Isfahání combines it with a special understanding of evolution. A definition of evolution (*al-irtiqá*') which he finds acceptable is the following: "It is the movement of living bodies toward perfection."[138] "The universe," he says, "has a wise director who brings all things into existence as they are needed and annihilates them when they serve no purpose. He does so gradually, both bringing into existence and destroying, according to the requirements of the divine system."[139]

In other words, he believes that species are more or less evolved in relation to themselves but not in relation to each other, because each creature is perfect in its place and its organs suit its environmental niche. So he argues against Spencer, who defined evolution as a decrease in homologous organs and increase of diverse organs:

> In short, if one organ fulfills a number of functions without deficiency and fulfills all the animal's needs, then there is no need for other organs to divide up its functions; nay, those organs would be an excess and could be harmful. . . . The existence and state of these things is not evolution and their lack is not considered a decline. For example, you may consider the mole primitive because its eyes are undeveloped, but it does not need its sight.[140]

As for how evolution and creation work together, Iṣfahání concludes with the following conception:

> What can we say against the Divine Power if He created the horse after numerous transformations due to His knowledge that it cannot at once become the form of a horse, but according to the most perfect system, must first wear other more primitive forms? Or what can we object if different exigencies due to different times, new changes in the environment, and changes in the means of subsistence, required the forms of the ancestors of the horse to change, so that their shape in each stage was conformable with what suited the circumstances and conditions of the environment. How absurd to consider the destruction of the pillars of teleology the fruit of this philosophy![141]

*　　　　　*　　　　　*

In summation, Muslim thinkers, in general, rejected Darwin's theory insofar as it called for speciation by random variation and natural selection alone and failed to allow for the role of God's wisdom in the creation of species. This is because they belonged to the same teleological worldview supported by a large number of Darwin's contemporaries in Europe (see Section 1.1). Very few Arab thinkers, whether Christian or Muslim, accepted materialism. Most rejected it as a dangerous and unworkable doctrine. The editors of *al-Muqtaṭaf*, Sarruf and Nimr, can be considered deists like Darwin who believed that God had set the laws of nature into motion but did not preplan the boundaries of species.

From the writings and talks of 'Abdu'l-Bahá on the subject of evolution, which will be examined in Sections 2 and 4, it is evident that 'Abdu'l-Bahá was familiar with the contemporary debate on this theory in the Arab world and knew, generally, the views of Darwin's supporters and detractors. It is also possible that 'Abdu'l-Bahá subscribed to the journal *al-Muqtaṭaf*, and that he had an opportunity to familiarize himself with the issues.[142] In his table talks, published as *Some Answered Questions*, given to Laura Clifford Barney in 'Akká', Palestine, between the years 1904-1906, 'Abdu'l-Bahá does not mention by name any of Darwin's supporters. He calls those who uphold speciation by transmutation "certain European philosophers," and designates those who believe in the divine creation of species "theologians" (*ilāhíyún*). He reserves the term "materialists" (*máddíyún*) for those who allow for no ultimate reality beyond matter.

'ABDU'L-BAHÁ

"Man was always a distinct species, a man, not an animal."

Section 2

The Originality of Species

Among the key concepts that 'Abdu'l-Bahá proposes in his talks on evolution is the concept of the "originality of species" (*aṣálat-i naw'*), which is pivotal to understanding his response to Darwinism. By "originality" here is probably meant the state of being "the source or cause from which something arises" or "not secondary or derivative." The expression *aṣálat-i naw'* (originality of species) is used by 'Abdu'l-Bahá in *Some Answered Questions*,[143] twice in Chapter 47, twice in Chapter 49, and once in Chapter 50 in the variant form *aṣlíyah*. In each case, it is used as an alternative to the Western theory of the "transmutability of species" (*taghyír-i naw'*) proposed by "certain European philosophers" (i.e., Darwin, Spencer, Büchner, etc.). The position of the latter theory is that all species, including man, are successive modifications of earlier species through the natural selection of random variations in the struggle to survive. 'Abdu'l-Bahá, standing within the teleological tradition, counters this theory by asserting that species are not derived from each other; rather each has its own originality, or primary reality (*aṣálat*), and independence (*istiqlál*).

While affirming that evolution (*taraqqí*) of the biological form has occurred, he qualifies this by saying that "progress and development take place within the species itself," not "from the genus to the species."[144] Various Arabic words have been used by Arabic speakers to translate "evolution," such as *taraqqí*, above, and its variant *irtiqá'*, both of which mean to ascend, progress, and advance. The word *nushú'*, meaning to grow and develop, is also used, and the theory of evolution has been specifically termed *madhhab al-nushú' wa'l-taraqqí*. These words, however, do not capture the significance of Darwin's particular use of the term "evolution," which implies the transmutation of one species into another without any underlying goal. It is clear that when 'Abdu'l-Bahá uses "evolution" favorably, it is not in the particular Darwinian sense of the word, but in the general sense of progress leading to greater complexity and perfection over time. Confusion may arise for the reader of 'Abdu'l-Bahá's writings because he uses the same term to refer both to Darwin's theory, and to his own idea of evolution within the boundaries of species. Because of this, it is important to remember that when 'Abdu'l-Bahá uses the term "evolution" (*taraqqí*) favorably, he means it in the general sense of the term.

Some may maintain that what 'Abdu'l-Bahá is supporting is not evolution at all but rather the temporalization and continuous becoming of the great Chain of Being, a concept posited by some of the philosophers already discussed. This is true if one defines "evolution" in the Darwinian sense, but it is clear that "evolution" has many other connotations, all of which are widely accepted in the English language and all of which would be acceptable to 'Abdu'l-Bahá. For example, *Merriam Webster's Collegiate Dictionary* (10th edition) defines "evolution" as (1) "a process of change in a certain direction: unfolding"; (2) a process of continuous change from a lower, simpler, or worse to a higher, more complex, or better state"; (3) "a process of gradual and relatively peaceful social, political, and economic advance"; (4) "the historical development of a biological group (as a race or species): phylogeny"; (5) "a theory that the various types of animals and plants have their origin in other preexisting types and that the distinguishing differences are due to modifications in successive generations"; (6) "a process in which the whole universe is a progression of interrelated phenomena." Since

only definition number five is the Darwinian definition, it is fully
justified to say that 'Abdu'l-Bahá supported evolution in the general meaning of this word.

The doctrine of the originality of species and the idea that species
only progress within themselves but do not transform gradually into
other species are consistently maintained by 'Abdu'l-Bahá in both
his talks and his letters. For example:

> Question.—What do you say with regard to the theory held by some
> European philosophers on the evolution of beings? Answer. . . .
> Briefly, this question will be decided by determining whether species
> (naw') are original or not. For instance, has the species (naw'íyah) of
> man been established from the beginning, or was it afterward derived
> from the animal?[145]

> Now assuming that the traces of organs which have disappeared actu-
> ally existed, this is not a proof of the lack of independence and non-
> originality of the species (naw'). At most it proves that the form,
> appearance, and organs of man have progressed. But man has always
> been a distinct species (naw'), man, not animal. So, if the embryo of
> man in the womb of the mother passes from one form to another so
> that the second form in no way resembles the first, is this a proof that
> the species (naw'íyah) has changed? that it was at first an animal, and
> that its organs evolved until it became a man? No, indeed! How puerile
> and unfounded is this idea and this thought! For the originality of the
> human species (naw'), and the independence of the essence (máhiyah)
> of man, is clear and evident.[146]

> In regard to "creation," say to the historian that in the same way that
> "divinity" and "lordship" have no beginning, "creativity" and "provision,"
> and the other original divine perfections, also have no beginning and no
> end. In other words, creation has existed from the beginning that has no
> beginning and will last until the end that has no end. The species
> (naw'íyah) and essences of all things are permanent (báqí) and established
> (bar qarár). Only within the limits of each species (naw'íyah) do progress
> and decline occur.[147]

In these quotations, as well as in other passages on this subject,
'Abdu'l-Bahá frequently uses the term naw'íyat (specificity or

species-ness), which is the abstract noun form of *naw'* (species). Since translating *naw'íyat* as "specificity" or "species-ness" is awkward in English, and also confusing, both *naw'* and *naw'íyat* have been translated in this article by the single English term "species." What is critical now is to determine what 'Abdu'l-Bahá intended by the term "species" (*naw'* and *naw'íyah*).

It is the opinion of the author that 'Abdu'l-Bahá had a particular meaning in mind for "species" different from what most modern readers understand by this term. Today, "species" primarily indicates the theoretical classification of a biological form as determined by its ability to reproduce sexually with similar organisms. This view was probably also held by many of 'Abdu'l-Bahá's European and American listeners in 1912, under the influence of Darwinism. Although 'Abdu'l-Bahá often does use the term species in a biological sense,[148] it is evident that he understood "species" primarily in a Platonic sense. This is supported by the fact that he uses "essence" (*máhíyah*) correlatively with "species" above. Among the philosophers of Iran the term *máhíyah* has two precise philosophical meanings. Professor Izutsu explains:

> *Máhíyah* in Islamic philosophy is used in two different senses: (1) *máhíyah* "in the particular sense" (*bi-al-ma'ná al-khass*), which refers to what is given in answer to the question about anything "what is it?", the expression, *má huwa* or *má hiya* "what is it?" being the source of the word *máhíyah* in this sense; and (2) *máhíyah* "in the general sense" (*bi-al-ma'ná al-'ámm*) referring to that by which a thing is what it is, i.e. the very "reality" (*haqíqah*) of the thing.[149]

The word *máhíyah* in the particular sense is best translated by the term "quiddity," which refers to "what something is" without requiring its actual existence. In other words, it is strictly a concept in the mind, such as when we think of "man" in general apart from any concrete instances of man. *Man*, in this sense, is called a "universal," which in philosophy means the logical classification of individual beings under a certain general type. Thus, individual human beings are classified under the "species" humanity, which has been conceptually abstracted from those same individuals, and so forth for other species. "Species," "quiddities," and "universals" in this sense refer to mental constructs derived from actual biological particulars. This is exactly the way modern science uses the concept of "species" and it was also Aristotle's understanding. But 'Abdu'l-Bahá is not using the terms *máhíyah* and *naw'íyah* in this sense.

It is the second meaning of *máhíyah*, "that by which a thing is what it is," which corresponds to 'Abdu'l-Bahá's meaning. This is the Platonic understanding, in which the terms *máhíyah* (essence) and *naw'íyah* (species) refer to a divine reality existing in a realm outside of space and time, not to a human concept (see Sections 3.1 and 3.2 for more on the differences between Plato's and Aristotle's views). The Greek *eidé*, translated into English as Platonic "Form" or "Idea," was the same word used for "species" among the Greek philosophers. In Sufi terminology such reality is also called a "fixed archetype" (*al-'ayn al-thábitah*), in other words, the universal idea of something posited in God's knowledge prior to its actual manifestation as concrete existents in time. This usage of the term *'ayn* was commonly accepted among Islamic philosophers and mystics by the time of Mullá Ṣadrá, who identified *'ayn* (pl. *a'yán*) with the Platonic Ideas.[150] William Chittick points out, however, that in Ibn 'Arabí's writings *'ayn* should not be translated as "archetype," but rather as "entity," because Ibn 'Arabí did not regard it as a model for many individual things in the Platonic sense.[151] Though the archetypes of things are commonly said to be *fixed* (*thábitah*), this term would probably be better translated in the technical sense of the *posited*. In other words, they are *posited* in God's knowledge, not necessarily *fixed* in God's knowledge. Among Islamic philosophers, *máhíyah* is also closely related in meaning to *dhát* (quintessence) and *haqíqah* (reality).

Given this context, where "species" is the correlative of "essence" in a Platonic sense (Izutzu's second definition above), it is seen that 'Abdu'l-Bahá's concept of "species" (*naw'* or *naw'íyah*) is not equivalent to the modern scientific definition. Therefore, in order to avoid the ambiguity that the term "species" standing alone conveys, the expression "species essence" will often be used in this essay to signal the Platonic meaning (as opposed to the modern or

Aristotelian meaning) of 'Abdu'l-Bahá's concept of species. Although some readers trained in modern sciences will find this expression awkward, it is not altogether contrived, since Shaykh Aḥmad also uses it (see Section 3.10).

Such species essences are necessary, according to Mullá Ṣadrá, for two reasons: First, there must be one director for each biological species which regulates, determines, and preserves its members; otherwise those species will not be continuous but discontinuous, so that a non-horse could eventually evolve from a horse, and a non-human from a human, etc.[152] Second, God must know things as universals before He knows them as particulars in order to have a plan (*'ináyah*) for the cosmos; otherwise the universe would not be a system but a haphazard flow of events.[153]

As an archetype, the species essence is in a special sense a universal, but in an entirely different way than the logical universal. In God's knowledge, archetypes are causative of actual existents, not derivative from them (as are logical universals). Because it is one in relation to the many that it causes, it is in this sense only a universal. Temporal or biological existents are accidents dependent on their species essences. 'Abdu'l-Bahá also follows this way of thinking. For example:

> This general [external] existence is one of the accidents inhering in the realities of beings, while the essences (*máhíyát*) of beings are the substance (*jawhar*). . . . Certainly, that which is the substance is superior to that which is the accident, for the substance is the origin, and the accident is the consequence; the substance is dependent on itself, while the accident is dependent on something else; that is to say, it needs a substance in which it subsists.[154]

The word *jawhar*, usually used to translate Aristotelian "substance," is another Arabic philosophical term which is sometimes used in a sense nearly equivalent to *máhíyah*.

Inasmuch as the essences or potentialities of all possible creatures exist timelessly "with" God, 'Abdu'l-Bahá proposes that "the species and essences of all things are permanent and established."[155] In short, when 'Abdu'l-Bahá refers to a "species" he means the species reality, not its accident or reflection in matter at some particular time point in its changing reflection. Although the biological definition of a species as "able to have fertile offspring" is a good working definition, at root it is the characteristics of the definer of the species, the actual species essence, that determine the species (cf. John Locke's idea of a "real essence" in Section 1.4).

The debate, then, between 'Abdu'l-Bahá and "certain European philosophers" who have proposed the theory of the transmutation of species is more philosophical than scientific in nature. The question is: Does the present form of a biological population depend solely on material factors (such as natural selection and random mutations), or does it depend also on timeless laws designed by a transcendent Creator? This is not a scientific question, according to scientists, because its answer, one way or the other, cannot be falsified by observation and experimentation.[156] To be scientific, a hypothesis must be subject to a process of empirical verification which may falsify it. A philosophical argument, on the other hand, may have as its object things which cannot be proven or disproven by science (such as the existence of God, purpose, and timeless laws of nature) but which can be established by reason and rational proofs.

The difference between how 'Abdu'l-Bahá and his Western audience understood the implications of the term "species" would account for the ambiguity that is apparent in discussions of the writings and talks of 'Abdu'l-Bahá on this subject. 'Abdu'l-Bahá concurred with the views of "the philosophers of the East," in other words, the philosophers of Islam and the Greek philosophical tradition from which they borrowed. In one of his talks, as already mentioned, he associates his views on the originality of species with these Eastern philosophers. It is this tradition which will now be examined in hopes of coming to a clearer understanding of 'Abdu'l-Bahá's position.

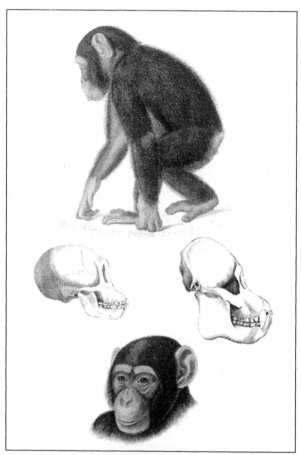

CHIMPANZEE ILLUSTRATED

in a drawing from *The Animal Kingdom* (1817). By this time, both chimps and orangutans were well known in Europe. The gorilla had not yet been described. Still, the discovery of apes so similar to human beings gave rise to questions about the relationship of humanity to other members of the animal kingdom.

Section 3

Species, Essence, and Becoming: The Views of the "Philosophers of the East"

3.1 Aristotle

The two variant understandings of what a species is go back to the dispute between Plato and Aristotle on the nature of form. Is a species: (a) determined solely by the biological form and, therefore, a mental construct? or (b) determined by an immaterial, archetypal form which is beyond the direct grasp of the human mind and is, therefore, a reality of nature? For Aristotle (384-322 B.C.E.), the only form of things is the form immanent in the matter of actual existents, the form of particular individuals: this tree, this man, this horse, etc. He called these "primary substances." Mayr says that historians of science have recently recognized in Aristotle's immanent form the equivalent of the genetic program of modern biology by which the next generation assumes the form of its parents.[157]

According to Aristotle, primary substances are the fundamental realities of the world to which accidents, such as quantity, quality, relation, place, position, time, state, activity, and passivity can be predicated. "All the other things," he explained, "are either said of the primary substances as subjects or in them as subjects. . . . If the primary substances did not exist it would be impossible for any of the other things to exist."[158] Although individual entities undergo change in respect to coming-into-being and going-out-of-existence, alteration of quality, growth or diminution, and change of place (motion), the essences of these primary substances are fixed and unchanging. In other words, it is not the substance itself, as subject, that is changing but only its accidental qualities. Change is the exchange of one accidental quality for another, and is therefore an accidental feature of reality. This type of philosophy, based on unchanging primary substances, is therefore called *substance metaphysics*—as opposed to *process metaphysics*, which places change itself into the category of substances.

The very first things predicated of primary substances, before any other qualification, are *species* and *genera*, which Aristotle termed "secondary substances." Secondary substances do not subsist independently, but because of things predicated they most reveal the primary substance, they have been honored by the designation "secondary substance." They are not, however, true substances, because they have only a mental reality. Aristotle says:

> Of the secondary substances the species is more a substance than the genus, since it is nearer to the primary substance. For if one is to say of the primary substance what it is, it will be more informative and apt to give the species than the genus. For example, it would be more informative to say of the individual man that he is a man than that he is an animal.[159]

> As regards the primary substances, it is indisputably true that each of them signifies a certain "this"; for the thing revealed is individually and numerically one. But as regards the secondary substances, although it appears from the form of the name (when one speaks of man or animal) that a secondary substance likewise signifies a certain "this," this is not really true; rather, it signifies a certain qualification, for the subject is not, as the primary substance is, one, but man and animal are said of many things.[160]

The species form, Aristotle stated, is coincidentally identical in all members of a species but not numerically one. Only primary substances, i.e. actual individuals, are one. The logical universal abstracted by the mind from concrete individuals (which are the primary realities), such as "man" abstracted by observing human individuals, corresponds to the real specific form immanent in them. But it does not exist apart from individual concrete beings in any manner whatsoever, except as a derivative mental construct.[161]

In such a cosmos, where the individual entities themselves are the ultimate realities, Aristotle did not see the need for Forms, or Ideas, separated from the physical world, as taught by Plato, to act as causes to the biological forms of species taken as a whole. For Aristotle another member of the same species is sufficient to provide the form (concealed in the seed or sperm) unchanged to the next generation of the species. "So it is evident that there is no need at all of setting up a Form as a pattern . . . but that which begets [i.e., a man, a horse, etc.] is sufficient to produce and to be the cause of the form in matter."[162] In other words, the species form is passed on by the biological begetter, which is Aristotle's "efficient cause," and this efficient cause must precede that which it generates and be fully developed itself.[163]

A beginning for this process, or a source of its existence, is not envisioned by Aristotle. In Aristotle's system, God (or the First Mover) is the "final cause" of things, not actively, but passively as an object of desire, for God's only act is to eternally contemplate himself. In other words, as the supreme and most perfect being in the universe, He indirectly moves other beings to emulate Him and thus obtain their own inherent perfection.[164] God does not bestow existence on anything, nor is He concerned with the other beings in the universe, since He confines His activity to contemplating himself as the only object worthy of His thought. Unlike Plato, for whom species are planned by a ruling, ordering Mind (*Phaedo* 97c) and are materially created in time, for Aristotle biological species are causes-to-themselves, always have been as they are, and repeat themselves endlessly in a universe co-eternal with God. There is no possibility of an act of divine creation in the biblical or quránic sense in Aristotle's system, nor for any form of evolution. However, his conception of species as mental constructs and not realities of nature, and his emphasis on the individual, is almost identical to the position held by modern population biologists.

3.2 Plato

Plato (428-348 B.C.E.), on the other hand, taught the existence of a Creator existing independently of the physical universe, who fashioned the cosmos out of pre-existing materials, which were in a state of chaos, by means of eternal, primary patterns, which Plato called Forms, or Ideas.[165] These are not the conceptual universals originated and comprehended by the human mind taught by Aristotle, but eternal, objective, incorporeal realities, such as "Beauty itself," "Justice itself," "Man himself," etc. Plato arranged these realities (not beings) into a hierarchy of more universal and less universal Ideas, and said it is only possible to know them in this world by the process of dialectic.

The Ideas, which in modern terms are equivalent to laws of nature, correspond to reality itself. To know them is to know the truth about the best order of things, the pursuit of which Plato called the purpose of human existence. For example, Socrates, Plato's principal speaker in the dialogues, would ask: "What is it that makes a beautiful thing beautiful or a just act just?" If what makes something beautiful or just is only relative to the thing itself, as the Sophists claimed, then how is an objective criterion for these attributes in the real world possible? Socrates' answer was that beauty and justice are not relative; rather they subsist in themselves, apart from their particular, temporal expressions, as part of an intelligible natural order of things. It is by the degree of their reflection of "Justice itself" that the acts of particular human beings can be called just.

The best society, therefore, will be that in which the acts of its citizens mirror the principle of justice laid down in the natural order. But none of these acts are Justice itself, only imperfect approximations of it. Similarly, what makes a flower or a work of art both beautiful is their common participation in an ideal standard of beauty in the world of

Forms. What determines the forms of natural species is also not relative or haphazard to Plato, since objective criteria for all species and all natural functions required for the harmonious functioning of the whole cosmos exist in the domain of separate Ideas.

Since the Forms cannot be known directly, one can only approach them through their particular likenesses in sensory experience. This requires one to use inductive reasoning and to engage in dialectic, an objective process of questioning and answering, until one finds an answer coherent with observable facts. Plato explained that insofar as such an answer is based on fluctuating particulars, it is called opinion; but insofar as it accurately reflects the Idea-Forms, it is true knowledge.[166]

Some Forms are inclusive of others, and the supreme, all-encompassing Form Plato called the Form of the Good, which provides both existence and reality to all the other Forms.[167] This is a crucial point, because it implies that the system of Forms is determined by the Good. In other words, the Forms are related to each other in the way they are because this relation is good and results in the best possible universe. The Creator, who is a being with a "mind," is not the same as the Form of the Good, which is a reality. Plato says: "Mind in producing order sets everything in order and arranges each individual thing in the way that is best for it."[168] So the Idea of the Good contains in itself all the kinds of goodness necessary to make a cosmos out of the inherent disorderliness of the preexisting matter.[169]

Proclus, one of Plato's commentators, explains that the hierarchy of causative Ideas ranges from the most general to the most specific. He says:

> By the most general I mean those that are participated in by all beings, so that nothing at all exists without a share in them—for example, Being, Identity, and Otherness, for these extend to all things. . . . By the most specific I mean those Ideas that are participated in by individuals, such as Man, Dog, and others of the sort. Their "makings" have as their immediate result the generation of individual unities— Man [the making] of individual men, Dog of particular dogs, and Horse and each of the rest in like manner. I call intermediate those ideas that have wider application than these, but are not active in

things. Justice, for example, belongs to souls; but how could it be an attribute of bodies. . . . Justice in itself, apart from all other ideas, illuminates only the beings that are capable of receiving it, and that is not all things in general.[170]

Two of Aristotle's criticisms of Plato's Forms, which include the species essences of biological beings, were that Plato did not explicitly locate them anywhere, nor, according to Aristotle, adequately explain how they could be a cause of material forms while they are separate.[171] To Aristotle, a form must be in a material thing to cause something, so how then can the same form be both in one particular thing and in many other things at the same time? Plato's answer, of course, was that the Form *is* separate and acts as the model for the many material forms which bear its likeness. In other words, the material (or biological) form and the archetypal form are two different things. Aristotle, it appears, did not accept Plato's explanation that the connection between the separate Form and the material form is the creative *action* of the Creator, who is the ultimate mover of the forms in matter (cf. *Timaeus* 28a, 53b, etc.). In other words, the Creator fashions the material forms as a whole by taking the eternal Ideas as His patterns, and in this sense the many "participate" in the one of which they are a likeness.[172] (The theory of Natural Law is founded upon this system of Plato.)

According to Plato, the separate Forms "always are and never become," whereas the material forms are "always becoming but never are."[173] The first are "intelligible and unchanging models" (the causes of that-which-changes), the others "visible and changing copies of them."[174] Here we have the beginning of the idea that physical beings progress toward a goal, which was such an important concept to the essentialists who opposed Darwin (see Sections 1.4 and 1.6). In other words, physical beings are always in a state of motion and naturally inclined to fulfill the potentiality determined by their immaterial causes. Plato also proposed a third reality, akin to Aristotle's matter, as necessary for changing things to come into actual existence. He called this "the receptacle" and "the nurse of all becoming and change." It is a formless, receptive medium in which images of the models are enabled to appear and disappear as continually recurrent, similar qualities (cf. *Timaeus* 49a - 51b).[175]

In sum, both Plato and Aristotle made valuable contributions to the question of the nature of form, but from radically different perspectives. Aristotle, recognizing no transcendent cause for the *existence* of things, saw the universe as self-existent and self-ordering, and from the perspective of biology, he determined that an earlier member of one species is sufficient to pass on the specific form, forever unchanged, from one generation to the next. Plato proposed, on the other hand, that a temporal individual is insufficient to account for the existence of the specific form of the whole species, and he recognized the need of a separate organizing and existentializing cause to act as its ultimate origin. Although the terminology is different, it is amazing that here at the very beginning of Western philosophy the basic outlines of the debate between the essentialists and Darwinists of the nineteenth century are already evident.

3.3 The Middle Platonists and the Church Fathers

As time and distance separated Aristotle and Plato from latter thinkers, a movement grew, especially among Neoplatonists, to harmonize the ideas of the two greatest philosophers of the ancient world. Many forgot or overlooked that there were critical differences between the two.

As for where the Forms are located and what their relationship is to the Creator, Plato was ambiguous on this point. In one passage, he does admit that they are created by God (*Republic* x, 597b-e), though elsewhere he says they are uncreated (*Timaeus* 52a). It was left up to latter thinkers to make the connection between God and the Ideas clear. The Middle Platonist, Albinus (c. 2nd century C.E.), said: "The Idea, in relation to God, is his act of thinking," and Wolfson explains, that "by saying that there are Ideas he means that God acts by certain rules and plans and that the order observed in nature is not the result of mere chance."[176] Philo of Alexandria (born c. 15 B.C.E.) and the Fathers of the Church placed Plato's Ideas in God's Word, or Logos, by which He created the world at the beginning of creation. Thus, the Word of God functioned as a kind of intelligible blueprint, synonymous with Plato's domain of transcendent Forms, by which God voluntarily fashioned the form of the world.

Plotinus (205-270 C.E.) posited a trinity of three universal causes each separate in substance: The One, who is beyond being; the Intellect, which is both mind and being; and the Soul, which is the intermediary between the Intellect and changing beings. Plotinus placed Plato's Ideas in the subordinate Intellect, not the One. The doctrine of the Church, on the other hand, held that the three persons of the trinity are one in essence and being, implying that since the Platonic Ideas are the living and eternal thought of the Creator, they are uncreated.

Augustine (354-430 C.E.) developed an idea, which he borrowed from the Stoics, which places him close to the thinking of Darwin's essentialist opponents on how the Chain of Being might unfold in the procession of time.[177] The early Stoics viewed God as the Active Principle containing "the active forms of all the things that are to be," which are like seeds, "through the activity of which individual things come into being as the world develops."[178] Augustine termed these seeds "seminal reasons" (*rationes seminales*). He has God create these seminal reasons at the beginning of the world in the humid element, and they unfold in time and manifest themselves as environmental conditions become suitable for their development. They are not purely passive, but tend to self-development. As Copleston explains Augustine:

> All plants, fishes, birds, animals, and man himself, He created invisibly, latently, potentially in the germ, in their *rationes seminales*. In this way God created in the beginning all the vegetation of the earth before it was actually growing on the earth, and even man himself. . . . For example, God created in the beginning the *rationes seminales* of wheat, which, according to God's plan and activity, unfolded itself at the appointed time as actual wheat, which then contained seed in an ordinary sense. . . . Each species, then, with all its future developments and particular members, was created at the beginning in the appropriate seminal reason.[179]

Similar to but not the same as the seminal reasons are the divine ideas or Platonic Forms, which for Augustine play an essential role in God's creative act. By them God knows things as universals prior to their creation in time. In the *De Ideis*, he explains that the divine ideas are "certain archetypal forms or stable and unchangeable reasons of things, which were not themselves formed but are contained in the divine mind eternally and are always the same. They neither arise nor pass away, but whatever arises and passes away is formed according to them."[180]

3.4 William of Ockham

The view of the Church Fathers was upheld by almost all Christian philosophers in one form or another until the time of Latin Scholasticism, when the nature of universals became an issue. Against the doctrine of Realism, which taught the independent existence of universals as unitary realities outside the human mind, the opposing doctrine of nominalism, primarily associated with William of Ockham (1299-1350 C.E.), was a return to Aristotle's emphasis on the individual form immanent in material things and the mere conceptual existence of species. The term "nominalism" implies that what we call a universal is a name only with no reality outside the human mind, so that what exists in actuality are only singular, separated individuals. It is significant that Mayr singles out scholastic nominalism as the precursor of modern population thinking.[181] Ockham's way marks the beginning of modern empiricism.

3.5 Alfarabi

Alfarabi (c. 870-950 C.E.) was the first of the well-known Islamic philosophers who attempted to harmonize the views of Plato and Aristotle. Most Islamic philosophers considered themselves loyal to Aristotle in one sense or another, but they were really Neoplatonists, influenced by that unique blend of Platonism and Aristotelianism formulated by the successors of Plotinus. Many Islamic philosophers were led astray in regard to Aristotle's genuine position because of the early misidentification of Plotinus's *Enneads* with Aristotle. They did not know Plotinus by name, but knew his work as *The Theology of Aristotle.*[182]

Since Alfarabi's ideas on species are the same as Avicenna's below, I will just mention here his theory of "becoming" as representative of the Arabic-speaking philosophers in general. At the basis of all material things is prime matter, which they share in common. Prime matter receives in succession alternating and contrary forms, which Alfarabi says emanate directly from the Active Intellect, an intellect intermediate between God and creation. The first things to arise from this interaction are the elements, which in turn combine into more complex bodies, such as vapors and solids. In these elements and first simple bodies "arise forces by which they move spontaneously toward the things for which they exist . . . and forces by which they act and are acted upon."[183] Alfarabi continues:

> From these the existence of all the other bodies follows by necessity. First the elements mix with one another, and out of that many contrary bodies arise. Then these contrary bodies mix either exclusively with one another, or with one another and with the elements, so that there will be a second mixture after the first, and out of that, again, many bodies with contrary forms arise. In each of these, again, arise forces by which they act and are acted upon. . . . These mixtures go on being performed, one mixture following the previous one, but so that the following mixture is always more complex than the previous one, until bodies arise which cannot mix with one another. . . . The minerals arise as the result of a mixture which is nearer to the elements and is less complex, and their distance from the elements is less in rank. The plants arise as the result of a more complex mixture than theirs, and they are a further stage removed from the elements. The animals which lack speech and thought arise as a result of a mixture which is more complex than that of the plants. Man alone arises as the result of the last mixture.[184]

Alfarabi's theory of how material things come into being is not a precursor of Darwin's theory of evolution, because the species which appear as a result of the various mixtures of the elements are predetermined by the Active Intellect, and there is no mention of any modification of form after a mixture is completed. There is also no indication here of how long this process of "becoming" takes. Another element that is missing from this description is the idea of "progress toward perfection," which Sarruf noted was a concept that the Arabic speaking philosophers added to Aristotle's great Chain of Being (see Section 1.6).

3.6 Avicenna

In his definitions of *naw'* and *máhíyah*, Avicenna (980-1037 C.E.) uses these terms in the customary manner of the Aristotelian logicians. He says: "As for the species (*naw'*), it is the essential universal which is said of many beings in answer to the question: 'What is it?'" or "The species is described as that which is said of many beings multiple in number in answer to the question: 'What is it?', like 'human' said of Zayd and 'Umar."[185] In regard to *máhíyah*, he defines it in the sense of quiddity: "Whoever asks 'what is it?' only asks what is the quiddity (*máhíyah*) . . . which is realized in the sum of its essential constituents . . . that enter into the quiddity in the intellect."[186] Avicenna reserves the term *'ayn* for concrete, particular existents, equivalent to Aristotle's use of the term "primary substance" (see Section 2.1).[187] As mentioned in Section 2, the Sufis and *Hikmat* philosophers of Iran later adopted this term and used it in the special sense of an immaterial causative essence.[188]

Avicenna maintained unchanged Aristotle's division of being into substance and accident. He also misunderstood the nature of Plato's Forms and made the typical Aristotelian critique: in other words, he understood Plato to say that Forms exist both separately and, at the same time, in the many particulars of which they are the form. He logically rejects this view, saying: "It is impossible for the universal animal to be a particular real animal, for it would then have to be both walker and flyer, as well as not walker or flyer, and be both biped and quadruped. It becomes evident, then, that the idea of universality, for the very reason that it is a universal, is not an actual existent except in thought."[189]

But with his conception of God as not merely the agent of motion

but also the giver of existence, Avicenna did come to a position similar to what Augustine found to be implicit in Plato: God's thoughts
are the causes of the existence of all things.

> The Necessary Existent [God] is . . . a knower of Its own essence. Its
> essence is the existentiator of things according to the order in which
> they exist. . . . All things are known to It, then, due to Its own essence.
> It does not become a knower of things because It is caused by them,
> but on the contrary, Its knowledge is the cause for the existence of all
> things. Similar to such knowledge is the (scientific) knowledge of the
> builder with regard to the form of the house he has conceived. His con-
> ception of the form of the house is the cause of this form in the exter-
> nal reality.[190]

Though Avicenna has God creating things by His knowledge,
God does not create anything directly in Avicenna's system, except
one thing, which is the first and only thing to emanate from God.
This is based on a philosophical principle accepted by most Islamic
philosophers that only one thing can emanate from what is itself
one. But this first emanation, commonly called the First Intellect,
has multiplicity introduced into it; it is hence a unity-multiplicity, a
one-many. Avicenna says: "This intellect is not . . . the True God, the
First. For although in one respect this first intellect is one, it is multiple inasmuch as it consists of the forms of numerous universals. It
is thus one, not essentially, but accidentally, acquiring its oneness
from Him who is essentially one, the one God."[191]
Avicenna did not stop, however, with the universals in the First
Intellect as the formal causes of things. He went on in good
Neoplatonic fashion to add nine additional separate intellects, each
one emanating from the one above it, and each one also emanating
a soul and a heavenly sphere corresponding to its level in the celestial hierarchy. The lowest of these intellects, called the Active
Intellect, emanated not only the matter of the sublunar world but all
of its forms.[192]

3.7 Averroes

Among the Islamic philosophers, Averroes (1126-1198 C.E.) was the most faithful student of Aristotle. He made it his life's work to attempt to return to the true teachings of Aristotle, from which earlier philosophers had strayed. He was surprisingly successful. In the words of Gilson: "Aristotle had taught (*De Anima* i.1) that the notion of animal is . . . posterior to the individuals from which it is formed by the intellect. Averroes had concluded that the definitions of "genera" and "species" are not definitions of real things outside the soul, but of individuals, and that it is the intellect that produces universality in them."[193]

Although Averroes accepted the hierarchy of eternal incorporeal intelligences corresponding to the celestial spheres, he rejected the emanation scheme of Alfarabi and Avicenna and returned to Aristotle's position that the intelligences owe the existence of their matters to themselves, while God is their formal cause only indirectly as the supreme object of desire in the universe.[194] He also held the Aristotelian position that physical forms are due only to physical factors, not to the influence of incorporeal realities as held by Plato. His final view is summed up by Davidson: "At all events, Averroes' *Long Commentary on the Metaphysics* [of Aristotle] unambiguously excludes the Active Intellect or any other incorporeal agent from the process whereby natural forms emerge; no incorporeal being serves as . . . the emanating source of animate forms. . . . In inanimate nature—according to Averroes' final view of things— mechanical physical forces bring forms already existing potentially in matter to a state of actuality."[195]

Averroes' ideas had little influence on other Islamic philosophers, many of whom did not know of his work, but they did have a lasting influence in Europe in the movement known as Latin Averroism, which in turn influenced the thinking of William of Ockham and other Latin scholastics (see Section 3.4).

3.8 Suhrawardí

With the post-Avicennan philosopher, Suhrawardí (1154-1191 C.E.), a more genuinely Platonic view of Plato's theory of Forms is seen by Islamic philosophers for the first time. Avicenna, as mentioned above, did not have a place for Platonic Forms (as he conceived

them) in his system, though he did have God's knowledge, generally speaking, as the cause of the existence of things. Suhrawardí,
however, revived a fully Platonic position. He criticized Avicenna
for holding that only ten intellects can account for the multiplicity of
species in the world while also holding to the principle that a simple
cause can only emanate a simple effect.

Suhrawardí's solution, in brief, was to allow each lower intellect
in the main vertical order to receive effects both directly and medi-
ately from the intellects above it, so that a horizontal order of intellects could also come into being by these accidental relationships.
The number of intellects in the horizontal order is finite, though as
numerous as the number of species in the world and the number of
stars in the heavens.[196] In Suhrawardí's system, all intellects are
self-conscious, self-subsistent, abstract lights, and the horizontal
order corresponds to Plato's realm of transcendent Forms. Each
Platonic Form is the lord of a terrestrial species (*rabb al-naw'*) or
lord of an image (*rabb al-ṣanam*), from which each member of a
biological species ultimately derives the image of its species. The
Platonic Forms, to Suhrawardí, are not realities, but self-conscious
beings; they are celestial angels. He calls them "celestial lords of
species images" that correspond to biological species. He argues:
"The species in our world do not occur simply by chance; otherwise
a non-human could appear from man, and non-wheat from
wheat."[197]

In several places Suhrawardí corrects the common Aristotelian
misunderstanding of Platonic Forms (i.e., understanding them as
"universals" meant in logic) and explains how they can be unitary in
themselves while common to the many and not in the many:

> They [Platonists] did not deny that predicates are mental and that uni-
> versals are in the mind [as in logic]; but when they said, "There is a
> universal man in the world of intellect," they meant there is a domi-
> nating [immaterial] light containing different interacting rays and
> whose shadow among [physical] magnitudes is the form of man. It is
> a universal, not in the sense that it is a predicate, but in the sense that
> it has the same relation of emanation to these individuals.[198]

Do not imagine that these great men [e.g., Plato, Socrates, Hermes], mighty and possessed of insight, held that humanity has an intelligible that is its universal form and that is existent, one and the same, in many. How could they allow something to be unconnected to matter yet in matter? . . . It is not that they considered the human archetype, for example, to be given existence as a copy of that which is below it [referring to the Aristotelian view on logical universals]. No men held more firmly that the higher does not occur because of the lower.[199]

In Suhrawardí's view, then, Platonic Forms are the immaterial roots of the biological members of species. Unlike the Church Fathers, though, Suhrawardí has the Forms function independently of their ultimate Source; in other words, they are not the contents of God's mind. God, therefore, does not create the world through His providence, but instead it necessarily overflows from God and cannot be other than it is.[200] It will be recalled that in Plato's system, the Ideas are "realities," not "beings," and that one Form, although it is unitary, can be associated with many subordinate Forms.

3.9 Mullá Ṣadrá

The seventeenth-century Persian philosopher Mullá Ṣadrá (c. 1571-1640) was responsible for making an important innovation in the traditional substance-based philosophy of Aristotle and Plato that had been the mainstay of the philosophers of the East up until this time. Both Plato and Aristotle had taught that the world subsists by means of fixed and unchanging realities to which ever-changing, impermanent qualities, called accidents, become predicated. While for Plato the fixed realities are Forms or laws beyond this physical reality, for Aristotle they are the immanent forms (or substances) of individual material entities (see sections 3.1 and 3.2). This view of a harmonious cosmos kept in order by static essences dominated Western philosophy until the time of Darwin and underlay the thinking of Darwin's essentialist opponents. Ṣadrá maintained the idea of a harmonious cosmos based on static essences in God's mind, but he made the novel move of adding motion, or becoming, to the category of substance.

Traditional philosophy had categorized motion as an accident occurring in accidents, i.e., in place, quantity, quality, etc., while the substance or substratum of the moving body (its locus of being) remained unchanged. This view implies that motion as a process is subjective, not real. Ṣadrá argued, as Rahman explains, that "movement cannot be established on the basis of a stable entity. Such an entity can have a stable *essence*, but not a stable *being* which must consist simply of change and mutation. *There is, therefore, beneath the change of accidents, a more fundamental change, a change-in-substance.*"[201] This underlying, dynamic substance, according to Mullá Ṣadrá, is existence itself and identical to God's self-manifestation, and it "has a natural impulsion toward taking ever new forms."[202] A "thing" for Ṣadrá is a particular "structure of events" or an "event system" arising from the continuous movement of existence and given temporal coherence and unity by the Platonic Forms, or stable essences, in God's mind. The substance of existence is called "ambiguous" (*tashkík*) by Ṣadrá because it remains the same while unfolding itself in ever different forms, like clay that can be molded into infinite forms yet retains its identity. The movement of existence in Ṣadrá's system is both evolutionary and teleological, because, driven by God's love for the beauty of His own Essence, existence moves unidirectionally and irreversibly toward states of greater perfection as it strives to realize the divine intelligible order and reveal the mysteries of the divine being.

Like Augustine and unlike Suhrawardí, Ṣadrá identified the contents of God's mind with the transcendent Ideas of Plato, and so with the species essences of things. He removed entirely the hierarchy of separate intellects of Alfarabi, Avicenna, and Suhrawardí, and, unlike Suhrawardí, he recognized the Platonic Forms as realities, not separate self-conscious beings. God's providence, or purposive plan (*'ináyah*), is responsible for the order of the universe.[203] Rahman explains, though, that according to Ṣadrá: "God and His knowledge . . . are not two things in any sense except in our conception of Him. Rather, God, by merely being what He is, gives rise to an ideal system of existence—which we may call His mind or the contents of

His mind—and the contents of His mind, merely by being what they are, generate the universe."204

Despite his differences with Suhrawardí, Mullá Ṣadrá agrees with the former in regard to the causative function of the Platonic Forms. He says:

> If you would ponder upon the appearance of species in this world of ours, you will find that they do not occur by mere chance; otherwise those species would not remain preserved and it would be possible for a non-human to be derived from a human, a non-horse from a horse, a non-date palm from a date palm, and a non-wheat grain from a wheat grain. This is not the case; rather, these species are continuous and permanent without alteration or change. . . . The truth is as the ancients have stated: It is necessary for each species among the physical species to have a luminous, incorporeal substance subsisting in itself, which regulates, determines, and preserves it. It is a universal to that species, but they did not intend by this that universal whose conception requires participation [in particulars, i.e., a logical universal].205

Mullá Ṣadrá argues here precisely as Darwin's essentialist opponents argued two centuries later. Biological species do not occur by pure chance; otherwise the kind of non-teleological transmutation of species that Darwin proposed would occur. Ṣadrá and his predecessors held that species are fixed realities of nature on account of the divinely ordained laws which determine and preserve them. Ṣadrá also understood that the Aristotelians, like latter population thinkers, gave the Platonic Forms, or laws of nature, a mere nominal existence. He states:

> As for the error of the Aristotelians, it is in making the divine Forms mere accidents, deficient in existence, and making what is connected to them and subordinate to them in existence [i.e. physical forms] more subsistent, substantial, and real than them. . . . But if this error is laid to rest by making them real entities (mawjúdát 'ayníyah), not conceptual entities, then in this sense, they become like the Forms of Plato. As for the error of the Platonists [i.e., Suhrawardí and his followers], it is in making God's knowledge of things [which consists of these divine Forms] separate from His Essence.206

According to Ṣadrá, if existence itself is in constant flux, then the only thing that can give order to the universe are the permanent essences in God's mind. Although these essences are conceptual in relation to God, they are real in relation to things. Ṣadrá followed the Sufis, and Plato in the *Timaeus*, in saying that what we call a stable material form is really a constantly recurring and moving image of a fixed archetype from which we, in turn, abstract a stable concept, such as man, tree, dog, and the like.[207] Physical species and environments emerge (*takawwun*) in the world process, which is the systematic, unidirectional flow of existence, as soon as matter attains the capacity to receive them. This is progress, movement, and development, but not "evolution" in the Darwinian sense.

3.10 Shaykh Aḥmad Aḥsá'í

Shaykh Aḥmad Aḥsá'í (1753-1825 C.E.) is considered by Bahá'ís to be one of the forerunners of the Báb, whom Bahá'ís believe to be the forerunner of their own prophet, Bahá'u'lláh. Shaykh Aḥmad wrote two voluminous commentaries on two important works of Mullá Ṣadrá called the *Sharḥ al-Mashá'ir* and the *Sharḥ al-Ḥikmat al-'Arshiyyah*. Due to these, and other works like the *al-Fawá'id al-Ḥikmiyyah*, he is a very important transitional thinker between the earlier "philosophers of the East" and 'Abdu'l-Bahá. For the purposes of this article, a fully systematic study of Shaykh Aḥmad's thought was not possible, and reference is only made to his commentary on the *Mashá'ir*.

Shaykh Aḥmad's works contain many original philosophical ideas which distinguish him from his predecessors.[208] Among the most important is his development of a true process metaphysics whereby he makes process or action (*fi'l*), not substance, the ultimate foundation of contingent existence. He also rejects the emphasis of earlier philosophers on the primacy of either existence or essence, and asserts instead the unbreakable polarity of essence and existence.

God creates all things by His action, which is identical to His Will and other attributes connected to creation. He does not create by His

SPECIES, ESSENCE, AND BECOMING   ۽   69

Essence. In other words, the acting of God is a separate reality originated through itself but depending on God as its agent. As Shaykh Aḥmad explains: "The actor (*fāʿil*) originates the acting through itself, that is, through that very acting. As the Imám Jaʿfar al-Ṣādiq has said: *Allah created the Willing through itself. Then He created creation through the Willing.*"[209] Shaykh Aḥmad argues that an infinite regress of causes is avoided in this way because an act does not require another act by which to subsist, just as primary matter does not require another matter to act as its substratum.

The first expression of God's action is matter, or created existence, which necessarily gives rise to form, or essence. Essence and existence denote form and matter to Shaykh Aḥmad, and these two together are the inseparable common ground of all creatures, whether they be eternal and intelligible or perishable and material. Matter (*māddah*), being coextensive with God's action, is itself active (*fāʿil*), but it requires its complement, form (*ṣūrah*), which is receptive (*infiʿāl*), to be realized. (Note that Shaykh Aḥmad is reversing traditional hylomorphism in which matter is receptive and form is active.) Matter has no actual existence apart from form, just as form has no realization apart from matter.[210] Idris Hamid terms this the "ontological polarity principle" by which "every created, contingent thing is a complex of acting (*fiʿl*) and becoming-in-yielding-to-acting (*infiʿāl*)."[211]

Shaykh Aḥmad conceptually divides the actional Will, by which God creates, into two stages depending on the relation this single reality has to things. It is within the actional Will that we find the first hint of Platonic Forms or species essences of things:

> He created the Will from itself, not from another Will besides it, and this is . . . the domain of "tipping the scales" toward existence. By it He made possible the Possible (*al-imkán*), which is the substratum of all possible things and the Most Great Chasm. This is called the possible Will [or Will for the possible], which is connected to all possible things. It is the knowledge which nothing encompasses. . . . When the Eternal Providence ordained that something be brought into being, He created it by His generative Will (*takwíniyah*), and it is connected to all generated things. . . . These are one thing and only differ with

respect to the difference of its relation. . . . So the realities of possible things in the first stage are generated in the second stage. The fixed archetypes exist only in the first stage [that of the possible], not in the Essence of God. . . . So when He desired to manifest something from what is in the treasuries of the first stage and cause it to descend to the treasuries of the second stage, He created matter and form for it by His generative Will. He created it in these two things.[212]

All things, in short, exist first in the possible Will as possible (not actual) realities, and this is why Shaykh Aḥmad says the first stage of every creature is the Will (al-mashiyah). He says elsewhere that the durational mode of the Possible is eternal (sarmad), meaning it is timeless, having neither a beginning nor an end.[213]

As we saw earlier, Ṣadrá identified the archetypes or species essences of things with Plato's transcendent Forms, and Shaykh Aḥmad does the same. He calls them the "first creation" because they are the foundation through which individual entities, termed the "second creation," are called into being. In one reference he says:

Some have charged that Plato established the Forms of things, which are their realities, in . . . the Essence of the True One [which is Mullá Ṣadrá's position]. . . . But as for those who know the intent of Plato, they recognize that he means by the plane of the Platonic Forms (al-muthul) the original foundation from which all things were created, for he follows the meaning of his predecessors, who derived wisdom from the prophets.[214]

It is important to point out here that Shaykh Aḥmad's conception of Platonic Forms differs from that of his predecessors in one critical way: Platonic Forms, to him, are not immutable or fixed in themselves, because they are (to use Hamid's translation of infi‘ál) "becoming-in-yielding-to-acting." Although they are active and constant in relation to what is created through them, they are receptive of God's action, and hence their very essences are also acts of becoming. Whatever is created through the Platonic Forms can only become because they also change in themselves. It is not enough, as Ṣadrá proposed, just for the being of entities to be changeable; the essence also must be changeable in itself. Idris Hamid terms this

Shaykh Aḥmad's "causal principle" whereby "every impression (*athar*) resembles the actional quality of its proximate agent (*mu'aththar*)." The result of this is that, unlike for earlier philosophers who denied the external reality of action and passion, (1) motions or actions are recognized as real, and (2) "whatever characteristics . . . manifest in a given outcome-of-acting (*maf'úl*) are latent in the acting (*fi'l*) from which the outcome-of-acting originated."[215]

Without this even Mullá Ṣadrá's universe, which posited motion in substance, is doomed to a set of fixed, unchanging forms because Ṣadrá located the archetypes of things in God's changeless Essence. But static essences are incapable of capturing the constantly changing modes of delimited existence. Consequently, Shaykh Aḥmad's causal principle allows for a real process of continuous evolution or becoming within individuals and species. All whole systems in the universe are subject to this kind of evolution. It does not, however, allow for some members of one species or system to randomly cross over into another, as in Darwinian evolution.

Furthermore, the Platonic Forms, in Shaykh Aḥmad's conception of them, are not sheer essences devoid of matter. Rather, they are composites of form and matter, or essence and existence, which he terms *al-dhawát* (pl. of *dhát*), which we can translate as "quintessence" or "actual essence" to distinguish it from the purely conceptual essence (*máhíyah*). Using the customary symbolism of his religious milieu, Shaykh Aḥmad says: "In short, what is meant by the foundation [containing the Platonic Forms] is the Inkwell, and it is both the received thing [*maqbúl*, i.e., matter] and the receptacle [*qábil*, i.e., form]. The Pen, which is the First Intellect, is, more properly speaking, derived from the Inkwell and produces the Tablet [upon which the Pen writes]."[216]

Shaykh Aḥmad shares the doctrine of Suhrawardí that God knows things by His created knowledge when He creates them. Before He creates a thing He does not know it, because it does not yet exist and the created knowledge is also identical to His act of creating.

> We say that He knows Zayd in His Essence in the stage of Zayd, not Zayd in the stage of His Essence; otherwise Zayd would be eternally

existent. . . . You are hearing, although there may be no one speaking so that you can hear his words. So when an individual speaks, you hear him; and this occurrence is generated by the generation of what is heard. This is what they mean by "presential illuminational knowledge.". . . So when He created things, then they became known. . . . This knowledge which is connected to and corresponds to things is created with their creation.[217]

From this it should not be inferred that God does not know the Platonic models or universal forms of things (i.e., their species essences) before their particular manifestations in concrete individuals in time, since this atemporal foreknowledge is itself part of God's created knowledge. As stated above, God's "first creation" is the timeless creation of the Platonic Forms. In regard to God's knowledge in the stage of His Essence, Shaykh Aḥmad affirms that we can know nothing about this state:

> As for Allah . . . His existentiation of a thing is not preceded by that thing's having a state in Himself as those ignorant ones, who make comparisons between Him and His creation, profess. . . . From every consideration, drawing parallels with creation constitutes assimilation [of Allah with His creation]. . . . We only ascribe knowledge to Him because He created knowledge within us; with life due to His creating life within us; with existence due to our existentiation; none of this is similar to the state wherein He is.[218]

Shaykh Aḥmad describes the priority of the universal species form to the individual or particular form as follows: "For every possible particular there is a related unlimited universal, which is God's knowledge of things preceding His generative Will. . . . Then He desired by His generative Will the creation of what He had first desired its possibility."[219] This act of creation through the generative Will takes place in four stages, all of which constitute God's existentiational motion (ḥarakat ijádiyyah):

> The creative action that is connected to existence is the Will, and by the archetype (al-'ayn), i.e., the species form (al-ṣúrat al-naw'iyah), it

becomes Purpose (*irádah*), and by the [intelligible] limitation of the created, i.e., design, like length and breadth, stability and change, fixed time, and the like, it becomes Predestination (*qadar*), and by the realization of the act of creation and the thing itself, it becomes Fate (*qadá'*). . . . The fashioning of each existent is completed by these four actions [i.e., Will, Purpose, Predestination, and Fate]."[220]

However, in explaining the sustaining causes by which things subsist, Shaykh Aḥmad relies upon the Aristotelian four causes. He says: "Each thing needs four causes to be brought into being: two causes by which it subsists foundationally, which are matter and form; a cause by which it subsists through emanation (*sudúr*), which is the active cause; . . . and a final cause, which is its reason [for being]."[221] To show that the composite things created in the real world are not composed from (*minhu*) God's action but rather by it (*bihi*), Shaykh Aḥmad often repeats the analogy of a writer composing writing: "For the motion of the hand of the writer is not the source of the writing itself, but only the cause of its coming-into-being. But the writing is composed from the ink and the form of the ink. . . . The recipient of the action (*al-mafʿúl*) is not composed from the action but existentiated by the action and composed from matter and form."[222]

In agreement with earlier philosophers, Shaykh Aḥmad has more simple and indeterminate realities act as the building blocks of more complex and determinate realities in the divine intelligible order, so that each is matter in one respect and form in another depending on its relation. For example, wood is the form of the elements of wood, but wood is the matter of chair, bed, and the like. At the highest level, the totality of universals in the possible Will comprise a hierarchy in which some are matter in relation to what is below them and form in relation to what is above them. For example, Shaykh Aḥmad writes: "What belongs to Zayd of existence and essence is the same as what is in 'Umar, because their matters are portions of 'animal' and their essences are portions of 'rational.'"[223]

Shaykh Aḥmad appears to be saying that the individual members of species, which correspond to the quintessences in the intelligible order, become realized by these quintessences. Shaykh Aḥmad states:

> So the species essence (*al-máhíyat al-naw'íyah*), which is the [active] matter of the real individual at the time of its actualization in the external world, is a general universal belonging to the category of quintessences (*al-dhawát*), as we stated before. A portion of this is "taken" for Zayd and for 'Umar, from which each derives his quintessence. . . . But the characteristics belonging to a particular individual in the external world are delimitations of that existential portion . . . [for] individuals differ with respect to their particular qualities by intensity and deficiency, paucity and abundance, and with respect to degree, aspect, place, time, and situation. For this reason, the individuals of a species differ in most of their states, attributes, stations, and appointed times,[224] despite their equality in respect to species.[225]

The quintessence (*dhát*) thus has "manifestations (*mazáhir*) and effects in the domain of bodies," which Shaykh Aḥmad calls "its accidents."[226] But the quintessence (*dhát*) is not absolute, inasmuch as it is itself an accident in relation to the agent from which it emanates. The quintessence, which is the first composite effect of God's creative action, then becomes by further emanation the cause of another quintessence, which is accidental in relation to it. Shaykh Aḥmad explains: "The truth is that . . . all created things are quintessences in one respect and accidents in another. So the cause is a quintessence to its effect, and the effect in relation to it is an accident, but in relation to its own effect and attribute, it is a quintessence. This is the requisite of all things."[227] All things other than God are called, in this sense, correlational accidents (*a'rád idáfiyyah*) by Shaykh Aḥmad.[228]

What Shaykh Aḥmad delineates here is a typically Neoplatonic process of emanation, but it is combined with a simultaneous process of manifestation at each level of the entity being created. In other words, to Shaykh Aḥmad, every created thing is a multidimensional being with its highest aspect in the possible Will and its lowest aspect in corporeal matter. But each level of the multi-dimensional creature is distinct and has no connection to other levels except through emanation, since each level is an active cause by which subsequent lower levels subsist through emanation. Only mutually necessary form and matter exist at every level of a creature's existence as that by which it subsists foundationally, but form and matter in each level stay within their own level.[229] Each level also shares the characteristics of the level below it, but "in a more sublime way" (*'alay naḥw ashraf*).

As Shaykh Aḥmad puts it in several places:

> The lower was only created from the radiation of the more exalted. . . . Every stage of a reality with respect to its substratum . . . is an effect of what is above it....In this way, until the earth, He created every lower from the attribute of a higher. . . . Every individual in each of these stages [of its being] has a portion which is its configuration, or its form. Whatever of the two kinds of portions [form and matter] exists in each stage, it subsists by what is above it through emanation. Thus, each individual subsists foundationally by its matter and form, but subsists through emanation with respect to the stage above it. . . . Understand what I mean; subsistence by emanation is like the subsistence of speech by a speaker, notwithstanding that the foundational subsistence of the speech is in the air. . . . The stages of every lower thing are the rays from higher things; it is not that the higher things descend to its level . . . nor does anything belonging to the lower stage ascend to the higher stage.[230]

Idris Hamid calls the idea that each level shares characteristics that belong to the realm below it, but "in a more sublime way," Shaykh Aḥmad's "topological principle." He notes that this eliminates the traditional dualism between intelligible and corporeal: "Whatever is corporeal has an intelligible aspect; whatever is intelligible has a corporeal aspect. As one climbs the ladder of existence qua conditioned-by-something, in ascent towards the Divine Will, the corporeal aspect becomes more and more subtle, while the intelligible aspect becomes more intense. . . . Nothing is absolutely incorporeal except God."[231] Another principle coined by Hamid, which is evident in the passage above, is the "codependent origination principle" whereby "whatever is higher in the hierarchy of conditioned existence depends on that which is lower for manifest-ation (*zuhúr*)," while "that which is lower depends on that which is higher for realization (*tahaqquq*). . . . Neither can exist without the other."[232]

Lastly, Shaykh Aḥmad's "creation principle," also coined by Hamid, should be explained. This means that God has created every-thing in the universe in the best possible way in accordance with the dictates of His eternal wisdom. Nothing can be better than it already is. As he so aptly expresses it in the Eighteenth Observation of *al-Fawá'id al-Ḥikmiyyah*: "Allah . . . created what He created in accor-dance with the most perfect of what ought to be, in the way of that which is necessitated by Wisdom deriving from Possibility."[233] God stands outside of and separate from the world-process, and the beings He creates are not fixed substances but units of becoming or "actings."

Furthermore, Shaykh Aḥmad holds that "the act of becoming gen-erated constitutes an act of choice on the part of the created entity in the second creation," which implies that the individual essences of things are, in a certain sense, acts of self-creation.[234] Shaykh Aḥmad derives this idea from a principle of Ibn Síná, overlooked by Mullá Ṣadrá, which recognizes that everything except God is a real composite of essence and existence. Existence, or active matter, is the part bestowed by God; essence, or receptive form, is the part chosen by the creature, according to its disposition, from the set of what is possible. The reason Shaykh Aḥmad includes choice in receiving the act of creation and denies pure determinism is based on his causal principle, explained above, that "every impression [or effect] resembles the actional quality of its proximate agent." Therefore, he explains: "The choice of the Acting is an impression of the Choice of His Quintessence. In the entirety of existence, there is no sheer coercion and no pure compulsion. Rather, everything is a chooser. Every mote of existence is a chooser because the impres-sion of a chooser is a chooser."[235]

3.11 Summary of the Views of the "Philosophers of the East"

Except for Averroes, who had very little influence on other Islamic philosophers, the philosophers of the East were united in the view that a divine intelligible order—either the contents of God's mind or will, or belonging to the subordinate Active Intellect—is the formative cause of the compositions of biological species when they first appear on earth. These compositions appear as soon as the physical environment is suitable to receive them, with simpler compositions, like minerals and plants, appearing first, and more complex structures, like animals and human beings, appearing last. The essential attributes of each of these beings is created in accordance with the predetermined intelligible order, not because of chance.

Although Avicenna mistakenly identified Plato's Idea-Forms with logical universals, he was still a Platonist in the sense that he had the material forms of things result from an incorporeal intellect and in making God's knowledge the cause of the existence of things. The main difference between a logical universal and a Platonic Form is that while the former is abstracted from individuals, the latter is causative of individuals.

Mullá Ṣadrá's novel move of incorporating motion and transformation into the category of substance, and Shaykh Aḥmad's extension of this principle to the essences of things themselves allowed for the real, continuous, and dynamic transformation and evolution of things in the temporal dimension. This was a dramatic departure from the eternal static cosmos of classical biology, a departure which was paralleled by the ideas of Leibniz among the European philosophers.

The views presented represent mainly a "vertical order of becoming" from God to physical things and from physical things back to God, not a "horizontal order of becoming" restricted to the material world, as is the concept of Darwinian evolution. Things "become" as a result of their realities, whether this be gradually or at once. According to Shaykh Aḥmad, a thing's "coming-into-existence" is not completely up to God's will, but is also a voluntary act on the part of the created to receive existence. The important notion here is that everything that exists in the universe exists by design and has a purpose. Movement toward that goal implies the unfoldment of previously existing potentials, whereas "evolution," in the meaning of Darwin, implies the transmutation of species without any underlying goal.

'ABDU'L-BAHÁ IN OAKLAND, CALIFORNIA
at the home of Helen Goodall, October 23, 1912.

*"All the divine teachings can be summarized as
this: that these thoughts singling out advantages to
one group . . . be banished from our midst . . ."*

Section 4

'Abdu'l-Bahá's Response to Darwinism

4.1 The Principle of Cause and Effect

The arguments of 'Abdu'l-Bahá against a materialistic interpretation of the universe, which many thinkers believed to be implicit in Darwinism, depend in one way or another on the principle of cause and effect. 'Abdu'l-Bahá states: "Every cause is followed by an effect and vice versa; there could be no effect without a cause preceding it."[236] According to this statement even random processes, which 'Abdu'l-Bahá refers to by the expression "conditional fate" (*qaḍá'yi mashrúṭ*),[237] have a clear cause and effect relation. For example, throwing dice is a typical random process. When you throw a die (the cause), you know that at the end it will show a number between 1 and 6 (the effect). You only do not know which of the numbers will appear.

This principle of cause and effect is frequently applied by 'Abdu'l-Bahá to prove the existence of a Creator transcending the material world, on the basis that it is inconceivable that this universe should exist without a First Cause.

As we, however, reflect with broad minds upon this infinite universe, we observe that motion without a motive force, and an effect without a cause are both impossible; that every being has come to exist under numerous influences and continually undergoes reaction. These influences, too, are formed under the action of still other influences. . . . Such process of causation goes on, and to maintain that this process goes on indefinitely is manifestly absurd. Thus such a chain of causation must of necessity lead eventually to Him who is the Ever-Living, the All-Powerful, who is Self-Dependent and the Ultimate Cause.[238]

In place of a Creator, materialistic Darwinists, such as Shumayyil and Ludwig Büchner, posited matter and force at the beginning of the chain of causation and attributed matter's orderly transformations to blind necessity (see Section 1.10).

'Abdu'l-Bahá's proof for the existence of God is based on Aristotle's dictum that causes are finite both in series and kind, and that in a series there must be a first cause (*Metaphysics* ii.2). The impossibility of an infinite regress of causes has long been used by both philosophers and theologians as a proof for the existence of God, though not necessarily as a proof of God's nature. Aristotle used this proof to show that there must be a first cause of motion for the universe, which he called the Unmoved Mover, but he did not also assert that this mover was the cause of the existence of the universe.[239]

In another proof, based on the same principle of cause and effect, 'Abdu'l-Bahá states that the very formation of things into orderly structures is proof of the existence of a Creator: "The change of the configuration of particular beings proves the existence of a Creator, for can this great universe, which is endless, be self-created and come into existence from the interaction of matter and the elements alone? How self-evidently wrong is such a supposition!"[240] It will be recalled that Jamál al-Dín al-Afghání made the same argument against certain materialists who believed the simple elements combined themselves into complex and stable forms (see Section 1.12).

4.2 Formation by God's Voluntary Will

'Abdu'l-Bahá rejects both necessary and accidental causation as sufficient to explain the formation of beings:

> Now, formation is of three kinds and of three kinds only: accidental, necessary and voluntary.[241] The coming together of the various constituent elements of beings cannot be accidental, for unto every effect there must be a cause. It cannot be necessary, for then the formation must be an inherent property of the constituent parts and the inherent property of a thing can in no wise be dissociated from it. . . . The third formation remains and that is the voluntary one, that is, an unseen force described as the Ancient Power, causes these elements to come together, every formation giving rise to a distinct being.[242]

In one of his talks in America, 'Abdu'l-Bahá elaborates the same argument, concluding similarly that "composition is effected through a superior will."[243] 'Abdu'l-Bahá is saying that if a thing composed of parts has these parts combined as an inherent property, then there is no possibility of active composition or decomposition. Since the living and non-living objects we are talking about can be taken apart and put together, then our logical choices are now narrowed down to being composed either voluntarily (on purpose) or accidentally (not on purpose). 'Abdu'l-Bahá dismisses the latter option by saying that every effect must have a cause, and, as 'Abdu'l-Bahá argues above, the chain of natural causes must eventually end in God (see Section 4:1). This means that nothing in reality happens accidentally.

This does not imply a dismissal of random occurrences, which obey the cause and effect principle, and which contain a complex order that is hard to see. Also, his rejection of "necessary formation" does not imply a dismissal of natural causality, for 'Abdu'l-Bahá often mentions the "nature" of things: "The nature of fire is to burn; it burns without will or intelligence. The nature of water is fluidity; it flows without will or intelligence."[244] Elsewhere he refers to such necessary cause and effect relationships between things as "decreed fate" (*qadá'yi mahtúm*).[245] The point is that what appears to be necessary causality (i.e., by the nature of something) is really *voluntary* causality, in the sense that God's eternal Will, through the species essences, guides different and contrary elements to form into structures that act and react in certain ways.

'Abdu'l-Bahá states that, in the Bahá'í view, "all of the realities and conditions which the philosophers attribute to nature are the same as have been attributed to the Primal Will in the Holy Scriptures."[246] God's Will, therefore, is recognized by 'Abdu'l-Bahá as the first cause of the formation of beings and the beginning of natural causation. 'Abdu'l-Bahá shares this doctrine with Shaykh Aḥmad Aḥsá'í, who also locates the beginning of natural causation in God's actional Will and not in His Essence (see Section 3.10).

Like Shaykh Aḥmad, 'Abdu'l-Bahá also affirms that the attribute of volition in God's act of creation extends to all created things, and that this is necessary to uphold the justice and mercy of God. He says: "Created things and the recipients of God's action have each accepted a degree of existence according to their own pleasure and desire."[247] Creation thus entails both a voluntary act on the part of the Creator and a voluntary act to receive existence on the part of the created, each according to its own disposition.[248]

Two other important points about the Primal Will need mentioning: First, it is an atemporal, placeless reality which exists "with" God as His action but not as part of God's essence. Because it precedes time and space, time and space are its effects. 'Abdu'l-Bahá explains:

> The first thing to emanate from God is that universal reality which the philosophers of the past termed the First Intellect, and which the people of Bahá call the Primal Will. This emanation, with respect to its action in the world of God, is not limited by time or place; it is without beginning or end. . . . His creation of the possible (*mumkin*) is an essential creation, and not a temporal creation.[249]

In other words, *God's creation of the realities of things takes place outside of time.* As will be recalled from Shaykh Aḥmad, all possible things (*mumkinát*) exist potentially in God's actional Will as part of His "first creation." Second, the Primal Will is identical to the inner reality (*bátin*) of all created things. This is also clearly stated by 'Abdu'l-Bahá: "The Primal Will, which is the world of Command, is the inner reality of all things, and all existing things are the manifestations of the Divine Will."[250] This Will, which corresponds to the possible, manifests the realities of things as a sea manifests itself in the forms of the waves. The actual creatures that have ever lived on earth represent only a fraction of those hidden realities that are potential or possible in God's Will.

'Abdu'l-Bahá explains that the composition, or formation, of things when they first appear on this planet is a result of these realities:

> Each time that the isolated elements become combined in accordance with the divine universal system,[251] one being among beings comes into the world. That is to say, that when certain elements are combined, a vegetable existence is produced; when others are combined, it is an animal; again others become combined, and different creatures attain existence. In each case, the existence of things is the consequence of their realities.[252]

Realities (*haqá'iq*), here, as will be recalled from Section 2, are a close synonym for essences (*máhíyát*), which are equivalent to Platonic Forms and laws of nature.

Another principle that 'Abdu'l-Bahá holds to is that when things come into existence by formation, in the manner described above, they are "created perfect and complete from the first, but their perfections appear in them by degrees (*bitadríj*)."[253] He gives the example of a seed in which all of the vegetable perfections exist in a latent state; it is only later, after the seed is planted, that the vegetable perfections appear, little by little. Here we have the answer to the question which was unanswered by Alfarabi as to how "becoming" takes place in beings. 'Abdu'l-Bahá says it takes place "by degrees" (*bitadríj*), which means "by steps." Sometimes the term *bitadríj* has been translated in the selected passages by the adverb "gradually," but this does not imply a continuum of gradual change, but only a ladder of distinct manageable steps in the development of creatures.

4.3 The Question of Evolution

'Abdu'l-Bahá' does not deny the reality of evolution as a process by which the universe and its creatures change and develop over time, as some essentialists of classical biology did under the influence of typological thinking. He certainly does not believe in a static cosmos of fixed populations corresponding to fixed essences. He appears to confirm the process metaphysics of Shaykh Aḥmad, which requires a real and continuous process of becoming in all created things, whether corporeal or intelligible.

The only entity 'Abdu'l-Bahá excepts from change is God's existentiating Command by which all things are called into being. He states in a letter: "All things are subject to transformation and change, save only the existentiating Command (*al-amr al-wujúdí*), since it is constant and immutable, and upon it is founded the life of every species and kind, of every contingent reality throughout the whole of creation."[254] "Creation," he says in another place, "is the expression of motion, and motion is life. . . . All created forms are progressive in their planes, or kingdoms of existence, under the stimulus of the power or spirit of life. The universal energy is dynamic. Nothing is stationary in the material world of outer phenomena or in the inner world of intellect and consciousness."[255] But this state of motion, which implies transformation, is not a purely random and chaotic motion. It does not imply the transmutation of one species into another or a purely arbitrary unfolding of events, as would be the case in a non-goal-directed universe. 'Abdu'l-Bahá is adamant that physical species evolve purposively within the boundaries of their own essences. As he explains in a letter: "Some of the philosophers of Europe think that evolution takes place from the genus to the species. But the prophets teach that this theory is in error, as we have explained already in the book *Some Answered Questions* (*Mufávadát*). Nay, rather progress and development take place within the species itself."[256]

'Abdu'l-Bahá supports the gradual change of biological species over time, but for him "evolution" means progress toward a preexisting goal, not the mere natural selection of favorable random variations. In commenting on the words of Bahá'u'lláh in the Lawḥ-i Ḥikmat: "That which hath been in existence had existed before, but not in the form thou seest today," he says: "From this blessed verse it is clear and evident that the universe (*kawn*) is evolving (*tarraqí*). In the opinion of the philosophers and the wise this fact of the development and evolution of the world of existence is also established. That is to say, it is progressively transferred from one state to another."[257] He says the same thing about the planet earth, and explains that this law of gradual progress toward greater perfection applies equally to all creatures:

> It is clear that this terrestrial globe in its present form did not come into existence all at once, but that this universal existent gradually[258] passed through different stages until it became adorned with its present perfection. Universal existents resemble and can be compared to particular existents, for both are subject to one natural system, one universal law, and one divine organization. So you will find that the smallest atoms in the universal system are similar to the greatest existents of the universe.[259]

"All beings, whether universal or particular," continues 'Abdu'l-Bahá, "were created perfect and complete from the first, but their perfections appear in them by degrees. . . . So also the formation of man in the matrix of the world was in the beginning like the embryo;[260] then gradually he progressed through various stages, and grew and developed until he reached the stage of maturity, when the mind and spirit became manifest in the greatest power."[261] It will be recalled that "the movement of living bodies toward perfection," which 'Abdu'l-Bahá teaches here, was the only definition of evolution that Iṣfahání found acceptable (see Section 1.12).

From these passages we can see that 'Abdu'l-Bahá teaches that physical beings, whether the universe itself or the creatures within it, evolve step by step, from one distinct stage to another, toward

greater perfection. The fact that creatures may also decline or ret-
rogress, is also recognized by 'Abdu'l-Bahá. But 'Abdu'l-Bahá's
doctrine of the "originality of species" (see Section 2) implies that
this whole process is goal-directed (i.e., guided by laws and
arranged according to divine wisdom), not arbitrary or the result of
blind environmental necessity. Should the transmutation of a population occur, so that it becomes classed as a new species, this is only
possible because of God's prior creation of the possible. "Creation"
and "evolution," to 'Abdu'l-Bahá, are not contrary, but complementary and mutually necessary processes. For God's timeless creation
to become manifested, the evolution of the external universe is necessary; otherwise the potentialities of creation could not unfold as a
temporal process. And for evolution to be realized, the creation of
primordial laws is necessary; otherwise a harmonious cosmos could
not arise out of chaos.

4.4 Some Non-References to Evolution

There are some passages in 'Abdu'l-Bahá's writings and talks that
might be construed as a reference to biological evolution, but which
most likely refer only to the descent and ascent of the soul of man
within human individuals. These passages are those in which
'Abdu'l-Bahá mentions the passage of man through the lower kingdoms of nature. For example, in one of his talks in the United States,
'Abdu'l-Bahá says:

> In the world of existence man has passed through various stages until
> he has attained the human kingdom. In each stage the capacity for
> ascent to the next stage has appeared. While in the kingdom of the
> mineral the capacity to progress to the stage of the plant appeared, and,
> therefore, he came into the vegetable kingdom. In the vegetable king-
> dom the capacity to progress into the world of the animal was
> obtained, and thus he came into the animal kingdom. Similarly, from
> the world of the animal he came into the world of man. . . . In this
> world, also, it is necessary to prepare and make ready for the world to
> come. Whatever is needed in the world of the Kingdom of God, man
> must prepare and make ready for it here.[262]

This idea of the gradual ascent of the soul of man through the three kingdoms of nature has its origin in the Islamic concept of arcs of descent and ascent. According to the Qur'an, as God created things, in a similar manner they will return to Him: "As He created you, so you will return" (7:29). The Sufis and Ḥikmat philosophers of Islam[263] have elaborated this theory and explained it as follows: Individuals commence their lives at conception as an emanation from their Creator, descend through degrees in the incorporeal dimension (the arc of descent) until they reach the level of the corporeal elements, traditionally earth, air, fire, and water, from which are produced the three kingdoms of the material world: mineral, vegetable, and animal. The I-spirit of the individual does not really "descend" but remains in its exalted state. It has, though, successive manifestations which, in Neoplatonic cosmology, are like increasingly darker shadows until the stage of the body composed of the physical elements is reached. This is the lowest point of descent.

The arc of ascent commences with the manifestation of the human spirit in the kingdom of the mineral, from whence it progresses to the plant kingdom, to the animal kingdom, and finally to the human kingdom. In the human kingdom, the soul is ready at last to disengage itself from its attachment to the material world and return toward its point of origin in the world of spirit. To do this it must also traverse many degrees in the spiritual world. The spiritual teachings of religion are directed toward releasing the soul from its bondage to the attributes of the world of matter so that it can attain to the knowledge of its Creator and the perfection of its own reality.

William Chittick explains that in Islam this theory is about the origin and return of individual souls to God and does not prefigure biological evolution. It concerns individuals, not the origin of species.[264] Man only analogously ascends through the kingdoms of nature, not literally. The human body was believed to recapitulate the levels of complexity of the lower kingdoms of nature in its own development. So the human embryo first possesses the faculty of cohesion of the mineral kingdom, then the faculties of growth and metabolism of the plant kingdom, and then in the stage of the infant it possesses the animal faculties of desire, volitional movement, anger, and sense perception. As the child grows, it learns to use these faculties properly, and gradually it acquires and develops the faculties of intellect and the spiritual virtues that belong to the human kingdom. The intellectual faculties and spiritual virtues, in turn, open the door to higher levels of spiritual perfection.

4.5 'Abdu'l-Bahá's Arguments Against Darwinian Transmutation

'Abdu'l-Bahá's arguments against the transmutation of species (*taghyír-i naw'*) from a Darwinian perspective, which occur in *Some Answered Questions*, chapters 46 to 51, and elsewhere, should be understood in the context of his doctrine of the originality of species. In other words, he is not opposed to the modification and change of biological forms but to their haphazard transformation without any underlying goal. According to 'Abdu'l-Bahá, each biological form depends upon a corresponding species essence in the inner world of spirit. This is due to the "perfect harmony and correspondence" of the worlds of God, whereby whatever exists in the material world is the outer expression of the realities of the inner intelligible realm.[265] 'Abdu'l-Bahá states:

> "Know that this material world is the mirror of the Kingdom, and each of these worlds is in complete correspondence with the other . . . for the truth of all things is laid away in the treasuries of the Kingdom. When that truth is manifested in the material world, the archetypes (*a'yán*) and realities (*haqá'iq*) of beings attain realization."[266]

The essential attributes of a biological organism cannot become modified or changed in time into the attributes of an entirely different species, unless the essence itself is replaced. Species, in other words, are original, not derivative, while the material form (the clay of creation) is dependent upon and derived from what precedes it. What is material is only so much clay that can be molded into any form as dictated by the complex system of forces or causes originating in the world of spirit. DNA and genes, from this perspective, are simply tools created in the clay to accomplish purposes on a higher level.

The first argument of 'Abdu'l-Bahá against the transmutation of species (*taghyír-i naw '*), which sees the "clay" itself as fundamental to speciation, is based on the idea of a predetermined harmonious cosmos and the eternal perfection of the creation brought into being by an all-wise Creator. For example, if the human species at one time did not exist, then this chief member of the body of the universe would have been missing, and the creation consequently would have been imperfect. 'Abdu'l-Bahá states:

We have now come to the question of the modification of species and the evolution (*taraqqí*) of organs—that is to say, to the point of inquiring whether human beings have descended from the animal or not. This theory has found credence in the minds of some European philosophers, and it is now very difficult to make its falseness understood, but in the future it will become evident and clear, and the European philosophers will themselves realize its untruth. For, verily, it is an evident error. When man looks at the beings with a penetrating regard, and attentively examines the condition of existents, and when he sees the state, organization, and perfection of the world, he will be convinced that in the contingent world there is nothing more wonderful than what already exists. For all existing beings, terrestrial and celestial, as well as this limitless space and all that is in it, have been created and organized, composed, arranged, and perfected as they ought to be. The universe has no imperfection, so that if all beings became pure intelligence and reflected for ever and ever, it is impossible that they could imagine anything better than that which already exists.

If, however, the creation in the past had not been adorned with the utmost perfection, then existence would have been imperfect and meaningless, and in this case creation would have been incomplete. . . . Now, if we imagine a time when man belonged to the animal world, or when he was merely an animal, we shall find that existence would have been imperfect—that is to say, there would have been no man, and this chief member, which in the body of the world is like the brain and mind in man, would have been missing. The world would then have been quite imperfect. This is a categorical proof, because if there had been a time when man was in the animal kingdom, the perfection of existence would have been destroyed.[267]

By "man" here, 'Abdu'l-Bahá does not mean the body of man but the reality or essence of man within the divine intelligible order, because biological man had a temporal origin on the planet earth. 'Abdu'l-Bahá, speaking with the theologians, says: "The human species on this planet had a beginning and is not eternal. And inasmuch as the existence of the human species [on this planet] had a beginning, surely the first man [Adam] had neither father nor mother."[268] The import of 'Abdu'l-Bahá's argument is that "man" has always been part of God's timeless intelligible creation, which manifests in space and time whenever the material conditions are suitable. Since the perfection of the universe requires a being like man, according to 'Abdu'l-Bahá, and since we cannot ascribe imperfection to God's creation, man, therefore, has always existed. Man is not a haphazard descendant of an animal species, even though his body is physically and genetically related to the animal and "grows develops through the animal spirit."[269]

In a variant of this same argument, 'Abdu'l-Bahá focuses on the necessity of the eternal existence of the human species to act as a comprehensive mirror of God's created names and attributes.

> The proofs which we have adduced relative to the originality of the human species are rational proofs. Now we will give theological proofs. . . . We have many times demonstrated and established that man is the noblest of contingent beings, the sum of all perfections, and that all beings and all existents are centers for the appearance of the divine effulgence—that is to say, the signs of the divinity of God are manifest in the realities of all created things. Just as the terrestrial globe is the place where the rays of the sun are reflected—where its light, heat, and influence are apparent and visible in all the atoms of the earth—so, in the same way, the atoms of every universal existent in this infinite space proclaim and prove one of the divine perfections. Nothing is deprived of this benefit: either it is a sign of the mercy of God, or it is a sign of His power, His greatness, His justice, His nurturing providence; or it is a sign of the generosity of God, His vision, His hearing, His knowledge, His grace, and so on. . . .

The world, indeed each existing thing, proclaims to us one of the names of God, but the reality of man is the collective reality, the general reality, and the center for the appearance of the effulgence of all the divine perfections. That is to say, for each name, each attribute, each perfection which we affirm of God there exists a sign in man. If it were otherwise, man could not conceive these perfections and could not understand them. . . . Consequently, the divinity of God, which is the sum of all perfections, appears resplendent in the reality of man. . . . If man did not exist, the universe would be without result, for the object of existence is the appearance of the perfections of God. Therefore, it cannot be said there was a time when man was not. All that we can say is that this terrestrial globe at one time did not exist, and at its beginning man did not appear on it. But from the beginning which has no beginning, to the end which has no end, this perfect manifestation always exists. This man of whom we speak in not every man; we mean the perfect man (insán kámil).[270] For the noblest part of the tree is the fruit, which is the reason of its existence. If the tree had no fruit, it would have no meaning. Therefore, it is inconceivable that the worlds of existence, whether the stars or this earth, were once inhabited by the donkey, cow, mouse and cat, and that they were without man. This supposition is false and meaningless.[271]

'Abdu'l-Bahá is saying that the universe is designed by God to produce perfect human beings who will reflect His attributes (such as love, mercy, justice, wisdom, beneficence, etc.), and who can therefore know His Essence befittingly. This was the reason why He, as the Hidden Treasure, created the creation. All other things in existence ultimately serve this purpose. "This world," states 'Abdu'l-Bahá, "is in the condition of a fruit tree, and man is like the fruit; without the fruit the tree would be useless."[272] The implication may be that biological manifestations of the species essences of all things always exist in some part of the universe, wherever the conditions are suitable. Or, the perpetual existence of species may indicate only the species essences, because there was a long period in the early phases of the formation of our universe when biological species could not exist. Of course, it is not known whether or not the temporal creation is limited to what arose from the singularity of the Big Bang.

The above arguments regarding the necessity of perfect man apply in a similar sense to all species because each has a necessary purpose in the eternal plan of God: "The difference of degrees and distinction of forms, and the variety of genera and species, are necessary—that is to say, the degrees of mineral, vegetable, animal, and man are inevitable; for the world cannot be arranged, organized, and perfected with man alone."[273] The plan of God for a harmonious cosmos requires the simultaneous presence of many species, so it is inconceivable in this context that any species should exist merely by mechanical causes and be the product of arbitrary evolution.

A second argument of 'Abdu'l-Bahá against the transmutation of species is based on the proposition that each biological organism represents a prescribed composition.[274] In other words, for each species to realize the purpose or function intended for it by its Creator, a certain type of structure or pattern of constituent elements must be present in its make-up. Because of this, as long as man has existed on the earth, even though he has evolved (taraqqí) toward greater perfection, he has always had the same type of composition and structural organization, or at least the specific potential for them in the way that an acorn has the specific potential to become an oak:

There is another more subtle proof: all these endless beings which inhabit the world, whether man, animal, vegetable, or mineral—whatever they may be—are surely, each one of them, composed of elements. There is no doubt that this perfection which is in all beings was realized by the creation of God from the composition of the elements, by their appropriate mingling and proportionate quantities, by the manner of their composition, and the influence of other beings. For all beings are connected together like a chain; and reciprocal help, assistance, and interaction belonging to the properties of things are the causes of the existence, development, and growth of created beings. It is confirmed through evidences and proofs that every being in the universe influences other beings, either independently or through a series of other beings. In brief, the perfection of each individual being—that is to say, the perfection you now see in man and apart from him with regard to parts, organs, or faculties—is due to the composition of the elements, to their measure, to their balance, to the manner of their combination, and to the interaction and influence of other beings. In the case of man, when all these factors are gathered together, then man exists. As the perfection of man is entirely due to the composition of the elements, to their measure, to the manner of their combination, and to the interaction and influence of different beings—then, since man was produced ten or a hundred thousand years ago from these earthly elements with the same measure and balance, the same manner of combination and mixture, and the same influence of other beings, exactly the same man existed then as now. This is evident and not worth debating. A thousand million years hence, if these elements of man are gathered together and arranged in this special proportion, and if the elements are combined according to the same method, and if they are affected by the same influence of other beings, exactly the same man will exist.[275]

The point of 'Abdu'l-Bahá's argument in this passage seems to be that once the appropriate composition needed for a species to manifest itself in the world is realized, and the right environmental conditions, it does not evolve into another species because its essential perfection, as determined by its essence, is already present. A species essence will not allow its biological counterpart to exceed its own potentialities. In this case, as 'Abdu'l-Bahá explains, if the same elements are combined again a thousand million years from now in the same manner and under the same influence of other beings (i.e., under the same environmental conditions), exactly the same kind of biological being will be realized. This is because the species essence which allows the composition to exist is time invariant. It is a natural law, universally valid for all times and all places. Hence, the human species could not have evolved by chance from another species, since each is a unique creation in the divine intelligible order.

In one of his letters, 'Abdu'l-Bahá gives an argument which was also given by Cuvier (see Section 1.3) as evidence for the generally long-term invariability of biological species:

The species and essences of all things are permanent and established. Only within the limits of each species do progress and decline occur.

For example, the human species and essence has always been and will remain preserved and inviolable. As can be seen from the ancient, dried, and embalmed bodies which have been exhumed from the pyramids of Egypt 5,000 years after their death, there is not the slightest change or variation, to the extent of a hair, from the human beings of today. Similarly, the [ancient] pictures of animals on the frescoes of Egypt are identical to present-day animals. . . . Man is man with his beautiful, radiant countenance. "There is no change in the creation of God" (Qur'an 30:30).[276]

'Abdu'l-Bahá is not implying that the form of a biological species at its first appearance on earth is created suddenly from nothing and then undergoes no substantial change, as the special creationists hold. The passage merely means that man in his present form hasn't changed for thousands, even tens of thousands of years. But there was a time when the material reflection of the human essence, due to the undeveloped nature of the planet, took on more primitive forms. When a new biological species appears for the first time in the matrix of the planet, it is complete but develops further perfections in a step-by-step fashion.

'Abdu'l-Bahá emphasizes in several places that nothing attains its full perfection at once: "When you consider this universal system, you see that there is not one of the beings which at its coming into existence has reached the limit of perfection. No, they gradually grow and develop, and then attain the degree of perfection."[277] In regard to the initial appearance of the human species, he clarifies:

It is evident and confirmed that the development and growth of man on this planet, until he reached his present perfection, resembles the growth and development of the embryo in the womb of the mother: by degrees it passed from condition to condition, from form to form, from one shape to another, for this is according to the requirement of the universal system and divine law. . . . Man's existence on this earth, from the beginning until it reaches this state, form, and condition, necessarily lasts a long time, and goes through many stages until it reaches this condition. But from the beginning of man's existence he has been a distinct species. . . . Now assuming that the traces of organs which have disappeared actually existed, this is not a proof of the lack of independence and nonoriginality of the species. At most it proves that the form, appearance, and organs of man have evolved.[278]

This passage clearly differentiates 'Abdu'l-Bahá from those classical essentialists who did not allow for any kind of evolution, and shows that his conception of a "species essence" contains more than just the ideal form of a species. It also must contain all of its possible evolutionary pathways from the most primitive to the most advanced. Such an essence, though permanent, cannot be regarded as fixed.

In addition to the above arguments against the transmutation of species, in Chapter 49 of *Some Answered Questions* 'Abdu'l-Bahá also presents the Darwinian argument for transmutation based on the presence of vestiges or rudimentary organs. He rebuts the Darwinian argument using the same types of essentialist arguments found in Section 1:

Certain European philosophers think that the species (*naw'*) evolves, and that even modification and transmutation are possible. One of the proofs that they give for this theory is that through the attentive study and verification of the science of geology it has become clear that the existence of the vegetable preceded that of the animal, and that of the animal preceded that of man. They believe that both vegetable and animal genera (*jins*) have changed, for in some of the strata of the earth they have discovered plants which existed in the past and are now extinct; in other words, they think these plants progressed and grew in strength, and that their form and appearance changed; and, therefore, the species has altered. In the same way, in the strata of the earth there are some species of animals which have changed and become modified. One of these animals is the serpent. There are indications that the serpent once had feet, but through the lapse of time those members have disappeared. In the same way, in the vertebral column of man there is a vestige which proves that man, like other animals, once had a tail. They believe that at one time that member was useful, but when man evolved, it was no longer of use; and, therefore, it gradually disappeared. As the serpent took refuge under the ground and became a creeping animal, it was no longer in need of feet, so they disappeared; but their traces survive. Their principal argument is this: the existence of traces of members proves that they once existed, and as now they are no longer of service, they have gradually disappeared, and there is no longer any benefit in or reason for these vestiges. Therefore, while the perfect and necessary members have remained, those which are unnecessary have gradually disappeared by the modification of the species, but the traces of them continue.

The first answer to this argument is the fact that the animal having preceded man is not a proof of the evolution, change, and transmutation of the species, nor that man was raised from the animal world to the human world. For while the creation of these different beings is certain, it is possible that man came into existence after the animal. So when we examine the vegetable kingdom, we see that the fruits of different trees do not all come into existence at the same time; on the contrary, some come first and others afterward. This priority does not prove that the latter fruit of one tree was produced from the earlier fruit of another tree.

Second, these slight signs and traces of members may have a great wisdom of which minds are not yet cognizant. How many things exist of which we do not yet know the reason! So the science of physiology—that is to say, the knowledge of the composition of the members—records that the reason and cause of the difference in the colors of animals, and of the hair of men, of the redness of the lips, and of the variety of the colors of birds, is still unknown; it is secret and hidden. But it is known that the pupil of the eye is black so as to attract the rays of the sun, for if it were another color—that is, uniformly white—it would not attract the rays of the sun. Therefore, as the reason of the things we have mentioned is unknown, it is possible that the reason and the purpose for these traces of members, whether they be in an animal or in man, are equally unknown. Certainly, there is a reason, even though it is not known.

Third, let us suppose [for the sake of argument] that there was a time when some animals, or even man, possessed some members which have now disappeared; this is not a sufficient proof of the transmutation and evolution of the species. For man, from the beginning of the embryonic period till he reaches the degree of maturity, goes through different forms and appearances. His aspect, his form, his appearance and color change; he passes from one form to another, and from one appearance to another. Nevertheless, from the beginning of the embryonic period he is of the species of man—that is to say, an embryo of a man and not of an animal; but this is not at first apparent, and only later does it become clear and evident. For example, let us suppose that man once resembled an animal, and that now he has evolved and changed. Supposing this to be true, it is still not a proof of the transmutation of the species. No, as mentioned before, it is merely like the change and modification of the embryo of man until it reaches the degree of reason and perfection. We will state it more clearly. Let us suppose that there was a time when man walked on his hands and feet, or had a tail; this change and alteration is like that of the fetus in the womb of the mother. Although it changes in all respects, and grows and develops until it reaches this perfect form, from the beginning it is a particular species. We also see in the vegetable kingdom that the original, separate species do not change and alter, but the form, color, and bulk may change and alter, and they may evolve within themselves.

To recapitulate: just as man in the womb of the mother passes from form to form, from shape to shape, changes and develops, and is still the human species from the beginning of the embryonic period—in the same way man, from the beginning of his formation in the matrix of the world, is also a distinct species—that is, man—and he has gradually passed from one form to another. Therefore, this change of appearance, this evolution of organs, this development and growth, does not prevent the originality of the species. This explanation is assuming assent to the evolution of species (pl. *anwá*). But the fact is that man, from the beginning, had this perfect form and composition, and possessed the potentiality and capacity for acquiring inner and outer perfections, and was the manifestation of these words, "We will make man in Our image and likeness." He has only become more pleasing, more beautiful, and more graceful. Civilization has brought him out of his wild state, just as the wild fruits which are cultivated by a gardener become finer, sweeter and acquire more freshness and delicacy. The gardeners of the world of humanity are the prophets of God.[279]

In his first rebuttal to the arguments of the Darwinists, 'Abdu'l-Bahá seeks to establish that the precedence of the animal kingdom to the human kingdom does not in itself prove that man has evolved from an animal species. All it proves is that the formation of man on this earth was completed after the formation of the animal. In the second rebuttal, 'Abdu'l-Bahá states that the existence of vestiges of organs that now apparently have no function is also not a proof of the transmutation of the species, since these vestiges may have a reason we do not yet understand. Abu al-Majd al-Iṣfahání and Ḥussein al-Jisr also made this argument (see Section 1.12).

'Abdu'l-Bahá's third rebuttal takes the track of assuming for the sake of argument that the species form has changed dramatically, such that man once walked on four legs and had a tail. He then says that if this were so, it would not prove the non-originality of the species, because although the form has changed it could still be the same species (i.e., under the influence of the same essence). He gives the example of how the human embryo does not at all resemble the state of a fully-developed human being, yet it still belongs to the human species and has not traversed from one species to another. 'Abdu'l-Bahá explains that this analogy is given for the sake of those who assent to the theory of the transmutation and evolution of species, meaning those who believe man descended from the animal.

In his talk on this subject at the Open Forum in San Francisco in 1912, 'Abdu'l-Bahá uses the same qualifying language while presenting the same argument, showing that he considers the idea that man's biological form descended from more primitive animal forms belonging to other species to be improbable. He says:

> The philosophers of the East say: If the human body was originally not in its present composition, but was gradually transferred from one stage to another until it appeared in its present form [as the philosophers of the West say], then we would postulate that although at one time it was a swimmer and later a crawler, still it was human, and its species has remained unchanged. . . . Provided that we assent [to this theory] that man was at one time a creature swimming in the sea and later became a four-legged, assuming this to be true, we still cannot say that man was an animal. Proof of this lies in the fact that in the stage of the embryo man resembles a worm. The embryo progresses from one form to another, until the human form appears. But even in the stage of the embryo he is still man and his species has remained unchanged.[280]

'Abdu'l-Bahá is so certain of this position that he asserts in this talk that the link assumed to be missing between man and the animal will never be found: "The link which they say is lost is itself a proof that man was never an animal. How is it possible to have all the links present and that important link absent? Though one spend this precious life searching for this link, it is certain that it will never be found."[281]

Although 'Abdu'l-Bahá does accept evolution and modification within a species, he consistently does not assent to the idea of inter-species evolution (i.e., the theory that one species can evolve into another solely through environmental forces), which was how the Darwinists understood the implications of modification.

'Abdu'l-Bahá concludes his argument above by saying that man has, in fact (*va ḥál án-ki*), always had "this perfect form and composition," which belongs to the human species, and that he "has only become more pleasing, more beautiful, and more graceful." By extension, the same would apply to all species.

Now a seeming dilemma arises here. How is this conclusion of 'Abdu'l-Bahá, that the human species has "from the beginning" had "this perfect form and composition" and "only become more pleasing, more beautiful, and more graceful," to be reconciled with this equally clear statement of his:

Man in the beginning of his existence in the matrix of this terrestrial globe, like the embryo in the womb of the mother, gradually grew and developed, and passed from one form to another, from one shape to another, until he appeared with this beauty and perfection, this force and this power. It is certain that in the beginning he had not this loveliness and grace and elegance, and that he only by degrees attained this shape, this form, this beauty and this grace. There is no doubt that the human embryo did not at once appear in this form; neither did it suddenly become the manifestation of the words "Blessed be God, the best of creators." . . . Thus it is evident and confirmed that the development and growth of man on this planet, until he reached his present perfection, corresponds to the growth and development of the embryo in the womb of the mother: by degrees it passed from condition to condition, from form to form, from one shape to another, for this is according to the requirement of the universal system and the Divine

Law. . . . And in the same way, man's existence on this earth, from the beginning until it reaches this state, form and condition, necessarily lasts a long time, and goes through many stages until it reaches this condition. But from the beginning of man's existence he has been a distinct species.[282]

The solution to this seeming contradiction lies in the realization that 'Abdu'l-Bahá's concept of evolution is very different from that of Darwin. To 'Abdu'l-Bahá "evolution" (*taraqqi*) means the "progress" of something from a primitive though perfect and complete seed state toward the state of fulfilling its innate potential or reason for being. For example, an acorn is perfect and complete in itself, but it has not yet realized its potential to become an oak tree. To become an oak tree, which will have the capacity to feed and shelter other creatures, it must pass through many stages of development over a long period of time. But from the beginning the acorn has the specific potential in its composition and configuration of elements to become an oak tree. It cannot become anything else; it stays within its species. In the same way, when 'Abdu'l-Bahá states that "man, from the beginning, had this perfect form and composition," he means this in the sense that a seed already has the perfect composition and configuration to become a tree, even though it will still change in outward form and pass through many stages of development.

This view has been designated by some Bahá'ís as "parallel evolution," and it appears to correspond roughly to the views of such thinkers as Augustine, Iṣfahání, and Leibniz (see sections 1.4, 1.12, and 3.3). According to this idea, a parallel but distinct path of evolution is maintained for each biological population from the time of its original formation on this planet. In the beginning stages, such as the single-celled stage and in other early stages, various species may have looked alike and even been nearly identical genetically, but they later gradually differentiated in appearance and continued to evolve new characteristics separately from each other. This is analogous to the way the nearly identical, undifferentiated cells of the blastula begin to specialize into particular types of cells, such as bone cells, blood cells, skin cells and so forth.

Although this type of evolution is designated "parallel," the source of parallelism is not in the biological forms themselves but in their corresponding essences. For this reason, the evolutionary pathway of all of earth's life will physically take the form of a tree with certain biological species appearing (because of physical similarity) to derive from or branch out of others, while, in reality, their essences are distinct. Outwardly, then, as a physical process, parallel evolution appears no different than Darwinian evolution. The critical difference resides in the source of speciation. To Darwin speciation is arbitrary and comes from the natural selection of favorable random variations; to 'Abdu'l-Bahá speciation is already determined and comes from timeless nonspatial essences.

4.6 A Model for Temporal Creation

If, as 'Abdu'l-Bahá proposes, "all beings, whether universal or particular, were created perfect and complete from the first, but their perfections appear in them by degrees,"[283] then how does the physical and temporal realization of this creation occur? In other words, how do you get the *first* human being on earth, the seed of the species, without reverting to literal biblical special creation? 'Abdu'l-Bahá's answer retains the idea of creation, but incorporates the role of evolution in realizing a species' potential. And of course what is formed at first is not the finished product of the species but only its most primitive form.

As explained in Section 4.2, 'Abdu'l-Bahá teaches that "the coming together of the various constituent elements of beings cannot be accidental" and "cannot be necessary," but arises from the Will of a supreme Being.[284] This Primal Will contains the species essences (i.e., the realities, the possibilities, the natural laws) of all things, which define the space of possible formations that can take place in the universe in accordance with God's perfect wisdom. As 'Abdu'l-Bahá explains:

> Each time that the isolated elements become combined in accordance with the divine universal system, one being among beings comes into the world. That is to say, that when certain elements are combined, a

vegetable existence is produced; when others are combined, it is an animal; again others become combined, and different creatures attain existence. In each case, the existence of things is the consequence of their realities.[285]

Before the elements became composed by God's Will into the first primitive forms of creatures, these elements themselves underwent a period of evolution in their formation. 'Abdu'l-Bahá says:

> Therefore, it is evident that in the beginning there was a single matter, and that one matter appeared in a particular form in each element. Thus various forms were produced, and these various forms as they were produced became independent, and each element was specialized. But this independence was not definite, and did not attain realization and perfect existence until after a very long time. Then these elements became composed, organized, and combined in infinite forms; in other words, from the composition and combination of these elements a limitless number of beings appeared.
>
> This composition and arrangement, through the wisdom of God and His preexistent might, were produced from one natural organization. As the world was composed and combined with the utmost perfection, conformable to wisdom, and according to a universal law, it is evident that it is the creation of God, and is not a fortuitous composition and arrangement.[286]

Given that all things at their first appearance in the temporal domain are formed as 'Abdu'l-Bahá has described, how might this look in practice? Before answering this with a tentative model, two general principles of 'Abdu'l-Bahá first need closer examination.

The first principle is that the biological manifestations of species are latent or potential (*kumún* or *bi'l-quwah*) on this earth and become manifested in stages: first inorganic structures of atomic and molecular organization appeared and then gradually more complex biological structures appeared, finally cumulating in the appearance of the animal and human kingdoms. 'Abdu'l-Bahá explains:

> For example, in this seed all the vegetable perfections exist, but not visibly; afterward, little by little, they will appear. So it is first the

shoot which appears from the seed, then the branches, leaves, blossoms, and fruits; but from the beginning of its formation all these
things exist in the seed potentially (*bi 'l-quwah*), though not outwardly
. . . . In the same way, the planet earth from the beginning was created
with all its elements, substances, minerals, parts, and organisms; but
these only appeared by degrees: first the mineral, then the plant, afterward the animal, and finally man. But from the first these genera and
species existed, although they were latent (*kumún*) in the terrestrial
globe. Later they gradually appeared.[287]

What is significant in this passage is 'Abdu'l-Bahá's use of the
words *kumún* and *bi 'l-quwah*, latency and potentiality. Something
can be latent or potential in two senses: either it can be potential in
a general sense, or it can be potential in a specific sense. If something is potential in a general sense, such as the potentiality of a pile
of bricks to become a house, or a group of atoms to become a horse,
not even a trace of the actual existence of the thing is present in the
bricks or the atoms. In other words, this pile of bricks or these atoms
at some future time might become configured as such, but they
could just as well become configured as something else. 'Abdu'l-
Bahá says every atom has the potentiality to be part of the composition of God's creatures in each of the kingdoms of nature; this is a
general potentiality. The house is not in the bricks in any form, nor
is the horse in the atoms. The form of the house only preexists in the
mind of the architect or builder; and the ideal form of the horse, as
a species essence, only preexists in God's created knowledge.
Therefore, when 'Abdu'l-Bahá says "from the first these genera and
species existed, although they were latent in the terrestrial globe," he
really means they were latent in what *causes* the forms in matter.
The potential is not in the clay; it is in the unseen essence. It is not
in the image, but in the object casting the image.

Unlike something that has a general potentiality, something that
has a specific potentiality can only become one thing. The seed of a
tree or the embryo of a human being, for example, can only become
one thing. The animal species that have appeared on this planet
since its inception could only have had a general potentiality in the
terrestrial globe in the early stages of its formation when the chem-

ical and biological constituents from which all organic life is composed were developing. During this period, not even a trace of the actual existence of plant and animal species was present. In this respect, 'Abdu'l-Bahá's analogy of the seed (above) should not be taken literally, since, in a sense, branches, blossoms, and fruit actually exist in the seed in its genetic code. The acorn can only become an oak tree, but we could not say that certain atoms or molecules can only become a horse.

The species essence can be compared with the intention to build a house. First there is nothing visible, only the intention and perhaps a preliminary design of it. Then it becomes a file of papers containing the drawings of the architect and the legal papers needed to construct a house. Then it becomes a pile of bricks or lumber. Gradually, you see the frame being raised, although the roof is still missing and the finishing touches remain to be done. Finally, everything is ready and you move in with your family. Only now is the house ready to serve its original purpose; only now can it really be called a house. But from the beginning it was planned to be a house for living.[288]

The steps for building other types of structures, such as libraries or factories, would not be very different. The same kind of preliminary planning would be necessary, the same kind of materials, the same workers. Only when a structure is finished does its original purpose, or essence, become fully realized. Prior to that it is only a potentiality. In the same way, the laws of formation, the biological materials, and the mutual influence of different beings must be in common for all biological species. Only when their biological structures become completed are their species essences (or plans) fully realized. But God's way of building living beings is more complex than this analogy can show, since He has built the tools by which He builds biological structures, such as DNA and genes, into the biological structures themselves.

The second relevant principle given by 'Abdu'l-Bahá is that the timeless divine emanations, which include the species essences of things, become manifested in the temporal domain whenever capacity has developed to receive them. In a talk to the Theosophical Society in New York 'Abdu'l-Bahá states: "The divine emanations (*fayúḍát-i illáhíyyih*) pervading all created beings have had no beginning and will have no end. That illimitable bounty becomes effective in every station whenever the capacity appears to receive it."[289] If this principle is applied to the idea of biological evolution, then each timeless species essence should begin manifesting its influence as soon as the environmental conditions are prepared to receive it.

With these two principles, and assuming a species essence for each unitary being, it is possible to give a tentative model for how temporal creation by formation and evolution occurs according to 'Abdu'l-Bahá. By a unitary being is meant any of God's creatures, each of which is a unity-multiplicity or self-contained system consisting of harmoniously interacting parts. Each atom, as a unitary being, has appeared, according to this view, under the influence of its own unique species essence and always remains under the influence of that species essence in its individual being. Once the kinds of atoms required for the composition of beings have appeared in their predetermined states, in which they are able to fulfill the functions for which they have been created, then another species essence, say the essence for water, allows two atoms of hydrogen and one of oxygen to combine together to form the molecule of water, provided the conditions are right for this transformation. The other molecules are also formed when their constituent elements are present and conditions are appropriate. The atoms have not changed in essence and evolved into molecules; they have simply been combined into a more complex structure under the influence of a different species essence, so that collectively they manifest entirely different properties.

Molecules, such as amino acids, are combined by the influence of new essences and the preparation of the environment into more complex substances, such as proteins. The amino acids themselves have not evolved into proteins, but in their new configurations they manifest properties different from their individual properties.

In the philosophical terminology of the ḥikmat philosophers, each new structure is *form* in relation to the less complex structure preceding it, and *matter* in relation to the more complex structure that follows (see Section 3.9-10). So molecules are form in relation to atoms, because they are configurations of atoms, but they are matter in relation to proteins, because the proteins configure them. According to the logic of this pattern, the components of living things do not evolve arbitrarily into each other, but some can act as building blocks for others. Each is the completed organization of less complex components and appears as soon as those components have attained their own perfection and environmental conditions (i.e., the influence of other beings) are right.

It is important to remember that, according to 'Abdu'l-Bahá's philosophy, the potential for all these things is not in the material forms themselves but in their species essences. All material things are composed (hence equivalent to matter) but what composes (i.e., gives form) is an immaterial power emanating from a higher realm. There is no dualism of spirit and matter in this view, only one reality (God's actional will) which through successive vertical emanations and corresponding horizontal manifestations expresses itself in infinite forms (cf. Section 3.10).

In general terms, plants began to appear as soon as atmospheric and geological conditions became appropriate and all the inorganic compounds necessary for their existence were present. Which species essences became manifested depended on the preparation of the environment. The latent potential of the plant species essences could now begin to be realized. These plants, in turn, were necessary to prepare the environment for the appearance of more complex organisms. The same can be said for the microscopic one-celled organisms. The one-celled organisms, in this view, did not evolve from plants or from any other individual entities, but were composed from less complex components under the influence of new species essences. In the same way, these one-celled organisms may have become combined in accordance with new essences into more complex biological structures, as soon as conditions were suitable.

This process of the combination of already existing materials in accordance with possible essences would then continue until the primitive "seeds" of all the species existing on earth today were formed. The seeds may not have been formed at the same time but at different times in accordance with the preparedness of the environment for certain essences. Once the seeds appeared, they would evolve independently according to their essences but harmoniously with each other (and perhaps indistinguishably from each other for a long time) according to their physical circumstances.

Not only must the required components for new, more complex structures be present, but the environment must possess the means for each newly manifested species to survive and hopefully flourish. This necessarily involves the appearance of many organisms simultaneously which mutually influence and assist each other. The environmental system as a whole is therefore more essential to the continuance of life than any of its individual members. As 'Abdu'l-Bahá describes it, "all beings are connected together like a chain; and reciprocal help, assistance and interaction belonging to the properties of things are the causes of the existence, development, and growth of created beings."[290] Thus, the environmental system of all life, like a single being, has grown and evolved, each part developing in relation to other parts, just as the diverse members of the human body all develop in coordinated harmony.

As the plant kingdom, in general, was necessary for the appearance of the animal kingdom, so was the animal kingdom, according to 'Abdu'l-Bahá, necessary for the appearance of the human kingdom. The human body itself "grows and develops through the animal spirit." As soon as conditions became right for the appearance of man, man appeared, but he did not evolve by chance from another species because his particular species essence has always existed. Only his biological form was molded from the biological materials already present and then continued to progress toward greater perfection.

4.7 Saltation

The following letter of 'Abdu'l-Bahá on the possibility of man having evolved from the animal summarizes his view well:

> O seeker of the truth! Man is the greatest member of the world of existence and the fruit of the tree of this visible universe. His species is eternal, and this eternal reality has no beginning and no end. That

which the philosophers of Europe have stated in regard to human evolution—that man came from the kingdom of the mineral, the vegetable, and then the animal, and by means of evolution reached this
station, is pure supposition, for his species has always existed. It may
be that on this globe of earth in the beginning he was in the stage of a
seed, and afterwards he evolved and attained the station of manifesting the words "Blessed be God, the best of creators!" But that seed
which evolved by degrees belonged to the human species, not an animal species. Therefore, this species is beyond time (*qadím*) and from
the outset was the noblest of creatures upon the earth. This is the truth,
and naught lies beyond the truth but evident error. God has ever existed while His creation renews itself continuously. Take for example the
sun and its rays. Without light it would be opaque darkness, and an
extinguished lamp is fit for the abode of the blind. The glory of glories
rest upon thee.[291]

'Abdu'l-Bahá is saying that the potentiality or reality of man (and
implicitly all other species) is eternal. No species is the arbitrary
product of another by the process of evolution, since each possible
kind exists timelessly in the divine intelligible order and is necessary
for the unfoldment of a harmonious cosmos of which man is the
fruit. Once a species essence, by reason of the preparedness of the
environment, connects to a biological "seed," that seed evolves or
progresses in parallel to other biological seeds under different
essences until it reaches its full potential perfection.

Now some questions arise: What is the nature of this seed? How
did the "seed" get there? Are we limited to the explanation given in
Section 4.6, that the seed came about through the *combination* of the
materials already present? Could the seed also have appeared
through *transmutation*?

If this seed came about through transmutation rather than by a
combination of elements, it would be easier to explain it in terms of
the presently accepted scientific theory of evolution. In this case the
seed would derive from a previously existing biological population
which jumped or "saltated" to a new essence. As long as that seed
develops under the human essence, it would develop in parallel to
other biological forms, because it belongs to the human species, not

an animal species. This view, called *saltation*, incorporates a component of parallel evolution as well (see Section 1.4).

Saltation is an alternative to maintaining 'Abdu'l-Bahá's essentialism without relying wholly upon parallel evolution or upon biblical special creation. Saltation allows temporal creation to occur via essences by using radical mutations that occur within the biological populations already existing. If the species space is very dense then each population would have a large number of closely related species to which it could jump. In practice, this would be hard to distinguish from the idea of slow gradual evolution proposed by Darwin. If, on the other hand, the species space is more sparce, a population would have a smaller chance of jumping over to another species.

Although 'Abdu'l-Bahá does not refer to the saltation theory, which was proposed by certain essentialists of his time, one of his letters on the subject of the transmutation of elements allows for its possibility. In that letter, he says:

> As for the question of the transmutation of copper into gold, this is possible and certain; that is to say, by means of the hidden science, which in this cycle is one of the special bounties of the Blessed Beauty. The materialistic philosophers of modern science believe that the metals are isolated elements incapable of transmutation into one another; in other words, they think that the essential qualities (*máhíyat*) of things cannot become transformed. But in the future, it will become manifest and clear that this is possible.[292]

Despite the fact that things have different essences, 'Abdu'l-Bahá is here saying that their transmutation is possible by external intervention. In the case of the metals mentioned above, he says they may be transmuted by means of the hidden science (i.e., alchemy), which itself contains an element of divine permission. It is impossible for copper to suddenly transmute into gold unless it saltates, or jumps, to the gold essence. By extending this principle to other species, it means that new biological populations could be produced by the transmutation (or mutation) of older ones if they jump to a new essence. This is what saltation means. (Of course, it may be that 'Abdu'l-Bahá does not intend to extend this principle of transmutation in alchemy to living forms.)

Despite these speculations there is no definite support for saltation in 'Abdu'l-Bahá's statements, whereas a parallel evolution model is more clearly supported.

4.8 The Question of Uniqueness

Is evolution as the temporal unfoldment of timeless essences bound to ever repeat the same physical forms? Does the concept of essences somehow limit the free and creative ability of life to express itself in endless original forms that delight our senses with their variety? One of the criticisms of classical biology was that a static cosmos of unchanging species created perfect from the beginning is incompatible not only with the appearance and extinction of countless unknown species in the fossil record, but also with the incredible variation of life and the continuous adaptation of organisms to their environment. Darwin praised his theory of evolution because it allowed for the continuous expression of uniqueness in nature. He said: "There is a grandeur in this view of life [wherein] . . . from so simple a beginning endless forms most beautiful and wonderful have been, and are being, evolved."[293]

Since timeless essences correspond to whatever structures and kinds of beings are possible in the universe, they are in no sense a limitation to the possible expressions of evolution. They only define what can and cannot exist and under what conditions, and what can exist is probably beyond the ability of our intelligence to grasp. Furthermore, the continuous need and ability of organisms to adapt to random environmental changes (what some call "chance") ensures that the varieties of the expressions of life are absolutely infinite.

'Abdu'l-Bahá affirms that uniqueness is a rule that applies to all things in the universe, whether individuals or populations, as a consequence of the uniqueness of the Creator. The possible individual, temporal expressions of species essences are endless. The factors of constantly changing environmental influences and the inheritance of genes from two different parents ensure that appearances are never exactly repeated and that endless diversity within the same species is possible. Even if an organism is cloned from another, they will never be exactly alike due to the differences of individual nurture and experience. On the other hand, similar environmental pressures, such as the need to move in water, can create very similar forms among populations with distinct essences.

On this subject, 'Abdu'l-Bahá says:

> Now observe that in the sensible world appearances are not repeated, for no being in any respect is identical with, nor the same as, another being. The sign of singleness is visible and apparent in all things. If all the granaries of the world were full of grain, you would not find two grains absolutely alike, the same and identical, without distinction. . . . As the proof of uniqueness exists in all things, and the oneness and unity of God is apparent in the realities of all things, the repetition of the same appearance is absolutely impossible.[294]

A similar sentiment is beautifully expressed in a prayer revealed by Bahá'u'lláh in support of the uniqueness and exquisiteness of every created thing:

> Blind is the eye that faileth to behold Thee seated upon the throne of Thy sovereignty, and that seeth Thee not exercising undisputed authority over all Thou hast created of the manifestations of Thy names and attributes. . . . Just as Thou hast assigned no partner to Thyself, in the same way, whatever Thou hast called into being hath no peer or equal, since Thou hast revealed Thyself in each thing through the effulgent light of Thy divine unity. . . . In truth, every thing that proceedeth from Thyself is the most excellent and most exquisite of all things that exist betwixt Thy heaven and Thy earth, and by it the tokens of Thy glorious sovereignty are revealed to Thy creatures, and Thy proof is perfected to all mankind.[295]

4.9 'Abdu'l-Bahá's Criticism of the "Struggle for Survival"

One of the things apparent in 'Abdu'l-Bahá's writings and talks on the subject of Darwinian evolution is that his criticisms, rather than attempting to judge its validity as a scientific theory, focus instead on the implications Darwin's theory will have in all the spheres of human thought and civilization. 'Abdu'l-Bahá was looking at the broad scheme of things and seeing how these ideas affected our ideas of God, purpose, and human progress in the future. He knew that they are only part of the picture as seen from a limited materialistic perspective, which recognizes no reality beyond what the senses can behold and no authority outside of science.

One of the ideas spawned from Darwinism by late nineteenth-century Victorian philosophers was that Darwin's principle of the "struggle for survival" should also be applied to the realm of human society. According to this idea, it is natural and desirable for one nation to behave aggressively toward another and to dominate it for its own benefit. As mentioned in Section 1, this materialistic philosophy was used as a justification for the horrors of World War I. 'Abdu'l-Bahá was fiercely opposed to this idea, and called it the greatest of all errors and the cause of utter ruin to humanity. The tragic events of the twentieth century justify his position. In a letter written to a society dedicated to the advancement of humanity, he wrote:

> Observe that the primary principle adhered to by every individual of the human species is to attract benefit to himself and to avoid injury. His aim is to secure his own tranquility and happiness. This is his sole desire in life, and he strives to distinguish himself from all others through the ease, wealth, and fame he has obtained. This is the goal of every individual of the human species. But, in truth, this is a base, dangerous, and inferior notion. If man advances a little in his thinking and his aspirations become nobler, he will realize that he should strive to benefit his whole family and to protect it from harm, for he perceives that by bringing comfort and affluence to the whole family, his own felicity and prosperity will increase. Should his thinking expand even more and his aspirations grow in depth, he will realize that he should endeavor to bring blessings to the children of his country and nation and to guard them from injury. Although this aspiration and thought are for his own sake and that of his family, all the children of the nation will benefit therefrom. But this aspiration will become the cause of

injury to other nations, for he then exerts the utmost effort to bring all the advantages of the human world to his own nation and the blessings of the earth to his own family, singling them out for the universal felicity of humankind. He imagines that the more other nations and neighboring countries decline, the more his own country and nation will advance, until by this means it surpasses and dominates the other nations in power, wealth, and influence.

However, a divine human being and a heavenly individual is sanctified from these limitations, and the expansion of his mind and the loftiness of his aspirations are in the utmost degree of perfection. The compass of his thinking is so vast that he recognizes in the gain of all mankind the basis of the prosperity of every individual member of his species. He considers the injury of any nation or state to be the same as injury to his own nation and state, indeed, the same as injury to his own family and to his own self. Therefore, he strives with heart and soul as much as possible to bring prosperity and blessings to the entire human race and to protect all nations from harm. He endeavors to promote the exaltation, illumination, and felicity of all peoples, and makes no distinctions among them, for he regards humanity as a single family and considers all nations to be the members of that family. Indeed, he sees the entire human social body as one individual and perceives each one of the nations to be one of the organs of that body. Man must raise his aspiration to this degree so that he may serve the cause of establishing universal virtues and become the cause of the glory of humankind.

At present the state of the world is the opposite of this. All the nations are thinking of how to advance their own interests while working against the best interests of other nations. They desire their own personal advantage while seeking to undermine affairs in other countries. They call this the "struggle for survival" (*tanázu'-i baqá*), and assert that it is innate to human nature. But this is a grievous error; nay, there is no error greater than this. Gracious God! Even in the animal kingdom cooperation and mutual assistance for survival are observed among some species, especially in the case of danger to the whole group. One day I was beside a small stream and noticed some young grasshoppers which had not yet developed wings seeking to cross to the other side in order to obtain food. To accomplish their goal, these wingless grasshoppers rushed forward into the water and vied with each other to form a bridge across the stream while the remaining grasshoppers crossed over on top of them. The grasshoppers were able to pass from one side of the stream to the other, but those insects which had formed the bridge in the water perished. Reflect how this incident illustrates cooperation for survival, not struggle for survival. Insofar as animals display such noble sentiments, how much more should man, who is the noblest of creatures; and how much more fitting it is in particular that, in view of the divine teachings and heavenly ordinances, man should be obliged to attain this excellence. . . .

All the divine teachings can be summarized as this: that these thoughts singling out advantages to one group may be banished from our midst, that human character may be improved, that equality and fellowship may be established amongst all mankind, until every individual is ready to sacrifice himself for the sake of his fellowman. This is the divine foundation. This is the law come down from heaven.[296]

Conclusion

Though I have tried to be thorough and objective in this study of 'Abdu'l-Bahá's response to nineteenth-century Darwinism, my analysis is necessarily influenced by the narrow compass of my specialized training in classical Greek and Islamic philosophy. Other writers trained in other disciplines may draw different conclusions. Let me therefore state plainly that although I deem the following conclusions sound and reasonable, in the character of a true scientific hypothesis, they are nevertheless tentative and subject to being either strengthened or weakened as additional research is undertaken on this subject.

In my paper I hold that 'Abdu'l-Bahá teaches a form of evolution that is congruent with a teleological worldview and which corresponds generally with certain philosophical concepts put forward by the Greek and Islamic philosophers whom he calls the "philosophers of the East." His ideas, however, should not be confused with the essentialism of classical Western biology, which promoted a static harmonious cosmos without evolution. As we saw in Section 1, many of 'Abdu'l-Bahá's Muslim contemporaries responded to Darwinism from a similar point of view.

The debate between 'Abdu'l-Bahá and "certain European philosophers" is not so much scientific, but philosophical. One of the main points of controversy is the question of whether the term "species" refers to merely the nominal classification of a biological population of mutually interbreeding individuals (the modern scientific definition), or to a reality transcending space and time by which a thing is what it is (the Platonic definition). In this essay such a reality is referred to as a "species essence" in order to distinguish the Platonic definition from the modern scientific definition.

The word "species," to 'Abdu'l-Bahá, refers primarily to such timeless realities, or laws, which are part of God's eternal creation. By "laws" here are meant "natural laws" by which God causes the universe to operate. In other words, a species is not just the biological form with which we are all familiar; rather it is also that by which such a biological form exists. A biological population is consequently both a changing reflection of the influences of its environment and a unique temporal manifestation of a timeless natural law. As 'Abdu'l-Bahá stated, "this question [of evolution] will be decided by determining whether species are original or not—that is to say, has the species of man been established from the beginning or was it afterward derived from the animal?"[297]

Another important point of controversy is the question of whether or not mechanical causes (random variation and natural selection) are sufficient to account for the evolution of complex order in the universe. 'Abdu'l-Bahá infers that mechanical causes are not sufficient to explain the origin of complex order, because these causes, too, require an explanation. Since the regress of causes and effects cannot be infinite, it must end in a self-sufficient First Cause at least as sophisticated as the order it creates and possessing the power and wisdom to call creation into being. The difference between these two views, if each is carried to its logical end, is the difference between biological populations that are purely self-created by blind environmental selection and evolve arbitrarily into new species, and biological populations that evolve according to designed laws created by a transcendent Creator.

'Abdu'l-Bahá supported the doctrine of creation and the independence of species, which was held in one way or another by all the essentialists studied in sections 1 and 3. But he certainly did not take the biblical story of genesis literally, requiring all living kinds to have been created fully formed in two day's time about 6,000 years ago. Like Abu al-Majd al-Iṣfahání, 'Abdu'l-Bahá held that religion and science must ultimately agree, and in his teachings, he has retained essential components from each. From the Holy Scriptures, he affirmed the concept of God as the Creator of species by His voluntary will; from science he accepted what had been categorically established, such as the great age of the earth and the fact that numerous biological populations have appeared and disappeared during the vast expanse of geologic time. He supported the idea of evolution, but in his own special way as progress and development "within the species itself."

As this essay has explained, evolution to 'Abdu'l-Bahá is goal-directed so that each temporal material reflection of a species essence progresses gradually towards its goal in a step-by-step fashion under (or "within") the boundaries set by its essence. The possibility of the retrogression and/or temporal extinction of a species is also accepted by 'Abdu'l-Bahá. But Darwinian or inter-species evolution, from this perspective, is considered to be an error.

'Abdu'l-Bahá, like most of his Muslim and Christian contemporaries and his predecessors in medieval Islamic philosophy, viewed the universe and its possible species as preexisting, in plan and in a general way, in the mind of the Creator. This "plan" eternally unfolds itself in the unique and endlessly diverse expressions of life in the cosmos.

To say that God has a "plan" and a "mind," of course, does not mean that we can know them or that they resemble anything with which we are familiar. The use of such terms reflects the limitations of the human condition, not the reality of God. This understanding of the universe intends to preserve for it a predetermined, non-arbitrary meaning and purpose. From this perspective, biological species and the relationships between them are the unfolding of preexisting potentials inherent by design in the universe. When and where these potentials become manifested varies by the needs and preparedness of the environments in which they appear.

NOTES

Preface

1. 'Abdu'l-Bahá, *Khiṭábát,* vol. 2, p. 299; *The Promulgation of Universal Peace,* p. 356, revised translation.
2. All of the revised translations of 'Abdu'l-Bahá's writings and talks contained in this essay are provisional and have not been authorized by the Universal House of Justice.

Section 1: The Historical Context

3. The description of the reception of Darwinism in Europe in this section depends heavily on two works: David L. Hull, *Darwin and His Critics: The Reception of Darwin's Theory of Evolution by the Scientific Community* (Cambridge: Harvard University Press, 1973), which is largely a collection of reviews of Darwin's published works by his peers; and Ernst Mayr's *The Growth of Biological Thought* (Harvard University Press, 1982).
4. Quoted in Ernst Mayr, *The Growth of Biological Thought. Diversity, Evolution, and Inheritance* (Cambridge: Harvard University Press, 1982) p 141.
5. A U.S. News poll conducted in 1994 indicated that 93% of Americans "believe in a benevolent God who hears prayers and is able to intervene in human events." (*U.S. News & World Report*, April 4, 1994, pp. 48-49) A Gallop poll conducted in 1993 found that 47% of Americans believe "God created humans pretty much in their present form at the same time within the last 10,000 years." (Raymo, *Skeptics and True Believers*, p. 122)
6. Quoted in Mayr, *Growth of Biological Thought*, p. 257.
7. Quoted in David L. Hull, *Darwin and His Critics: The Reception of Darwin's Theory of Evolution by the Scientific Community* (Cambridge: Harvard University Press, 1973) p. 89.
8. Quoted in Ashley Montagu, ed. *Science and Creationism* (Oxford: Oxford University Press, 1984) pp. 245, 247.
9. Mayr, *Growth of Biological Thought*, p. 376.
10. One of Darwin's critics, Richard Owen, noted that ancient species also could have disappeared for the same reasons species disappear today: not adapting to a changing environment, destruction by another species, etc. (Hull, *Darwin and His Critics*, p. 196)
11. Charles Darwin, *The Origin of Species by Means of Natural Selection*, 6th ed. (London: E. P. Dutton, 1928) p. 67.
12. Mayr, *Growth of Biological Thought*, p. 490.
13. Ibid., p. 491.
14. Thomas Kuhn, *The Structure of Scientific Revolutions*, 2nd ed. (Chicago: University of Chicago Press, 1970) pp. 171-172.
15. Darwin, *Origin of Species*, p. 463.
16. Darwin, May 22, 1860, *Life and Letters* (1887) vol. 2, no. 105; quoted in Hull, *Darwin and His Critics*, pp. 62, 65-66.

17. For an essentialist answer to this objection, see Section 1:4.
18. Hull, *Darwin and His Critics*, p. 71.
19. Today's biologists would add that the similarity continues down to the fundamental steps of biochemistry. The genetic code is the same in all organisms as well as the mechanism that translates the genetic message into proteins.
20. Darwin, *Origin of Species*, p. 422.
21. Ibid., p. 145.
22. Quoted in Hull, *Darwin and His Critics*, p. 299.
23. Extracts from Albertus Magnus, Thomas Aquinas, and Nicolaus Cusanus quoted in Arthur Lovejoy, *The Great Chain of Being* (Harvard University Press, 1964) pp. 79-80.
24. Francis Hitching relates that Ernst Mayr, one of Darwin's staunchest twentieth-century supporters, conducted an experiment on *Drosophila* which ironically supported Agassiz's point: "He selectively bred successive generations of flies to try to increase or decrease the number of bristles they grew, normally averaging thirty-six. He reached a lower limit, after thirty generations, of twenty-five bristles; and an upper limit, after twenty generations, of fifty-six bristles. After that the flies rapidly began to die out. Then, Mayr brought back nonselective breeding, letting nature take its course. Within five years, the bristle count was almost back to average." (*Neck of the Giraffe*, p. 41)
25. Quoted in Hull, *Darwin and His Critics*, pp. 436, 441.
26. Darwin, *Origin of Species*, p. 82.
27. Herschel (1861) 12; quoted in Hull, *Darwin and His Critics*, p. 61.
28. Quoted in Hull, *Darwin and His Critics*, p. 211.
29. Quoted in Hull, *Darwin and His Critics*, pp. 442-443.
30. Quoted in Mayr, *Growth of Biological Thought*, p. 368.
31. Mayr, *Growth of Biological Thought*, p. 365.
32. Darwin, *Origin of Species*, p. 293.
33. Quoted in Montagu, *Science and Creationism*, p. 123.
34. Quoted in Hull, *Darwin and His Critics*, p. 150.
35. Hull, *Darwin and His Critics*, p. 149.
36. Mayr, *Growth of Biological Thought*, p. 508.
37. Quoted in Hull, *Darwin and His Critics*, p. 318.
38. Quoted in Hull, *Darwin and His Critics*, p. 338.
39. Quoted in Mayr, *Growth of Biological Thought*, p. 324.
40. Ibid. pp. 129, 326-327.
41. Lovejoy, *Great Chain of Being*, p. 256.
42. Quoted in Hull, *Darwin and His Critics*, p. 135.
43. Quoted in Hull, *Darwin and His Critics*, p. 141.
44. John Locke, "An Essay Concerning Human Understanding," Book 3, Chapter 6, in *Classics of Western Philosophy* (Cambridge: Hackett, 1990) p. 673.
45. Mayr, *Growth of Biological Thought*, pp. 270, 458.
46. Although scientists today accept evolution as a fact, they are still engaged in scientifically healthy debate over exactly how species originate. For example, Darwinian gradualism and the role of natural selection are both being challenged. (See Augros, *New Biology*, Chapter 8.)
47. For the general Arab response to Darwinism, I have relied on Adel A. Ziadat,

Western Science in the Arab World: The Impact of Darwinism: 1860 - 1930 (New York: St. Martin's Press, 1986). For the details, I have referred to the original works of Arabic-speaking authors.

48. Adel A. Ziadat, *Western Science in the Arab World: The Impact of Darwinism: 1860 - 1930* (New York: St. Martin's Press, 1986) pp. 13-14.
49. R. al-Barbárí, "*Fí Aṣl al-Insán*" (On the Origin of Man), *al-Muqtataf*, vol. 1 (Beirut 1876), pp. 242-244, 279-280.
50. Ibid., p. 242.
51. Ibid., p. 243.
52. Ibid., p. 279.
53. Ibid., p. 280.
54. Ziadat, *Western Science*, p. 23.
55. Y. Sarruf, "*al-Madhhab al-Darwiní*" (Darwinism), *al-Muqtataf*, vol. 7 (1882) 65-72; 121-27; J. Denis, 7 (1882-1883) 233-236; Edwin Lewis, 7 (1882-1883) 287-290; Y. al-Ḥá'ik, 7:290-292.
56. This idea of a fixed chain of being dominated biological thinking until Darwin. Aristotle had no concept of evolution. Cf. Section 3.1.
57. Y. Sarruf, "*al-Madhab al-Darwiní*," *al-Muqtataf*, vol. 7 (1882) p. 65.
58. Ibid., p. 66.
59. Ibid., pp. 66-67.
60. Ibid., p. 67.
61. Ibid.
62. Ibid., pp. 67-68.
63. Ibid., p. 68.
64. Ibid., p. 69.
65. Ibid.
66. Ibid.
67. Ibid., p. 71.
68. Ibid., pp. 121-122.
69. Ibid., pp. 122-123.
70. Ibid., p. 124.
71. Ibid., p. 125.
72. Ibid., p. 126.
73. Ibid., p. 127.
74. J. Denis, *al-Muqtataf*, vol. 7 (1882-1883), p. 235.
75. Ibid.
76. Ibid.
77. Ibid., p. 236.
78. Edwin Lewis, *al-Muqtataf*, vol. 7 (1882-1883), p. 288.
79. Ibid., p. 289.
80. Ibid., p. 290.
81. Y. al-Ḥá'ik, *al-Muqtataf*, vol. 7 (1882-1883) p. 290.
82. Ibid., p. 291.
83. The full title is *Sechs Vorlesungen über die Darwin'sche Theorie von der Verwandlung der Arten und die erste Entstehung der Organismenwelt* (Six Lessons on Darwin's Theory of the Transmutation of Species and the First Origin of the World of Living Things) 3rd ed. Leipzig: Thomas, 1872.

122 ᴥ KEVEN BROWN

84. Quoted in Shiblí Shumayyil, "Lesson Two," *Falsafat al-Nushú' wa'l-Irtiqá'* (The Theory of Evolution) (Cairo 1910) p. 129.
85. Shumayyil, *Falsafat al-Nushú'*, pp. 39-40.
86. Shumayyil explains that the modern concept of "ether" is identical to the idea of matter: "Whether we call the original substance of the universe ether or matter, and the forces which are its transformations energy or motion, the meaning is the same." (*Falsafat al-Nushú'*, p. 35)
87. Shumayyil, *Falsafat al-Nushú'*, p. 33.
88. Ibid., pp. 40-41.
89. Ziadat, *Western Science*, p. 41.
90. *al-Muqtataf*, vol. 7 (1883), pp. 606-612.
91. Ibid., p. 606.
92. Ibid., p. 609.
93. *al-Muqtataf*, vol. 48 (1916) pp. 299-300; 397-399.
94. *al-Hilal*, vol. 23 (1925) pp. 464-468; cited in Ziadat, *Western Science*, pp. 57-58.
95. *al-Usur*, vol. 2 (1928) pp. 678-680; cited in Ziadat, *Western Science*, p. 60. Contemporary authors Robert Augros and George Stanciu present convincing evidence that Darwinian struggle for survival does not characterize the relationship between species in the natural state, but rather harmony and cooperation is the norm. See *The New Biology*, chapters 4 and 5.
96. *al-Mashriq*, vol. 9 (1913) pp. 694-695; quoted in Ziadat, *Western Science*, p. 79.
97. Ziadat, *Western Science*, p. 81.
98. Jamál al-Dín Afghání, *al-Radd 'ala'l-Dahriyín*, trans. Nikki Keddie in *An Islamic Response to Imperialism* (Berkeley: University of California Press, 1968) p. 133.
99. Ibid., p. 135.
100. Ibid., p. 136.
101. Ibid., p. 137.
102. Hussein al-Jisr, *Al-Risála al-ḥamidíya fí ḥaqíqa al-Diyána al-Islámíya wa ḥaqqíya al-Sharí'a al-Muḥammadíya* (The Praiseworthy Epistle on the Truth of Islam and Islamic Canon Law) (Beirut, 1887) pp. 293, 300.
103. Ibid., p. 297.
104. Ibid., p. 303.
105. Ibid., pp. 310-311.
106. Ibid., p. 314.
107. Ibid., p. 311.
108. Ibid., pp. 316-317.
109. Ibid., pp. 311-312.
110. Ibid., p. 318.
111. Ibid., p. 319.
112. Ibid., p. 323.
113. Abu al-Majd al-Isfahání, *Naqd Falsafah Darwin* (Critique of Darwin's Philosophy). 2 vols, (Baghdad, 1914) vol. 1, pp. 16-17.
114. Ibid., p. 19.
115. Ibid., p. 39.
116. Ibid., pp. 39-40.

117. Ibid., p. 49.
118. Ibid., p. 51.
119. Quoted in Iṣfahání, *Naqd Falsafah Darwin*, vol. 1, p. 53.
120. Iṣfahání, *Naqd Falsafah Darwin*, p. 54.
121. Ibid., p. 66.
122. Ibid., p. 69.
123. Ibid., pp. 71-72.
124. Ibid., pp. 73-74.
125. Ibid., pp. 76-77.
126. Ibid., p. 98.
127. Ibid., pp. 101-102.
128. Ibid., p. 102.
129. The difference in understanding between the essentialists and the Darwinists on the role of variation illustrates precisely the point at issue between teleological and population thinking.
130. Iṣfahání, *Naqd Falsafah Darwin*, pp. 133-134.
131. Ibid., vol. 2, p. 33.
132. Ibid., vol. 1, p. 135.
133. Quoted in Iṣfahání, *Naqd Falsafah Darwin*, pp. 135-136.
134. Iṣfahání, *Naqd Falsafah Darwin*, p. 136.
135. Ibid., p. 144.
136. Ibid., p. 147. Elsewhere Iṣfahání notes that Darwin has the eye evolve gradually from a light-sensitive spot through limitless transformations solely by natural selection. He is amazed at this view and asks: "How can it be hidden from them that these organs are among the greatest proof of the existence of a Creator and His wisdom and providence. . . . Eternal Providence prepares organs for animals over a long period of time, according to their needs, then He completes their creation and they become capable of performing their function." (*Naqd Falsafah Darwin*, vol. 2, p. 40)
137. Ibid., p. 179.
138. Ibid., p. 221.
139. Ibid., p. 180.
140. Ibid., p. 225.
141. Ibid., vol. 2, pp. 30-31.
142. Personal communication with Professor Amin Banani, Department of Near Eastern Languages and Cultures, University of California, Los Angeles, June 1996.

Section 2: The Originality of Species

143. This book, known in Persian as *Mufávadát*, is Laura Clifford Barney's collection of the table talks that 'Abdu'l-Bahá gave in 'Akká' between the years 1904-1906. It was later corrected by 'Abdu'l-Bahá and he encouraged Miss Barney to publish it.
144. 'Abdu'l-Bahá, *Má'idiy-i Ásmání* (The Heavenly Bread) (New Delhi: Bahá'í Publishing Trust, 1984). Reprint of vols. 2, 5, and 9 formerly published in Tehran. Vol. 2, p. 69.

145. 'Abdu'l-Bahá, *Mufávadát* (Table Talks) (New Delhi: Bahá'í Publishing Trust, 1984) pp. 135-136; *Some Answered Questions* [*SAQ*] (Wilmette, Ill.: Bahá'í Publishing Trust, 1981) p. 191, revised translation.

146. 'Abdu'l-Bahá, *Mufávadát*, pp.130-131; *SAQ*, p.184, revised translation.

147. 'Abdu'l-Bahá, *Má'idiy-i Ásmání*, vol. 9, p. 27.

148. For example, he says: "The species existing on this planet had a beginning, for it is established that there was a time when these species did not exist on the surface of the earth. Moreover, the planet earth has not always existed, but the world of existence has always been, for the universe is not limited to this terrestrial globe." (*Mufávadát*, p. 107; *SAQ*, p. 151, revised translation)

149. Toshihiko Izutsu, *Concept and Reality of Existence* (Tokyo: The Keio Institute of Cultural and Linguistic Studies, 1971) p. 101.

150. Fazlur Rahman, *The Philosophy of Mullá Ṣadrá* (Albany: State University of New York Press, 1975) pp. 29, 47.

151. William Chittick, *The Sufi Path of Love. The Spiritual Teachings of Rumi* (Albany: University of New York Press, 1983) p. 84.

152. Mullá Ṣadrá, *Al-Ḥikmat al-Muta'áliya fi'l-Asfár al-'Aqlíya al-Arba'a* (The Sublime Wisdom in Four Journeys of Reason), 9 vols. (Qum 1368 - 1379 A.H.) vol. 2, pp. 56-57.

153. Ibid., vol. 6, pp. 256-257.

154. 'Abdu'l-Bahá, *Mufávadát*, p. 203; *SAQ*, p. 292, revised translation.

155. 'Abdu'l-Bahá, *Má'idiy-i Ásmání*, vol. 9, p. 27.

156. Montagu, *Science and Creationism*, p. 120.

Section 3: Species, Essence, and Becoming: The Views of the "Philosophers of the East"

157. Mayr, *Growth of Biological Thought*, p. 88.

158. Aristotle, *Categories*, 1b.35, 2b.6.

159. Ibid., 2b.8-12.

160. Ibid., 3b.10-18.

161. Aristotle, *Metaphysics*, vii.13, 1038b - 1039a.

162. Ibid., vii.8, 1034a; cf. xii.3, 1070a.25.

163. Ibid., xii.7, 1073a.

164. Ibid., xii.7, 1072a.20 - 1072b.30.

165. Plato, *Timaeus* 28a - 29a, 52d - 53a. The Greek *eidé*, translated here as "Form," or "Idea," is the same word used to translate "species."

166. Plato, *Republic*, v.479d - 480.

167. Ibid., 508e; 509b.

168. Plato, *Phaedo*, 97c.

169. Plato, *Timaeus*, 52d -53c.

170. Proclus, *Commentary on Plato's Parmenides*, trans. Glenn Morrow and John Dillon (Princeton: Princeton University Press, 1987) 2, iv, 735.

171. Some of Aristotle's objections to Plato's Forms can be read in the *Metaphysics*, i.9, 990b - 993a; vii.14, 1039a.25 - 1039b.15. The whole of Aristotle's *Metaphysics* is really a critique of the theory of separate Forms, and an attempt to set up an alternate theory based on the idea of immanent forms.

172. The Ideas of species are not one in an absolute sense; rather they are one as unity-multiplicities. The Idea "Man himself" would include the Ideas of "animal," "two-legged," "rational," etc.

173. Plato, *Timaeus*, 27d.

174. Ibid., 48e.

175. For a fuller discussion of how Plato understood the relation between the separate Form and its concrete images, see Keven Brown, "A Bahá'í Perspective on the Origin of Matter," *The Journal of Bahá'í Studies* 2.3 (1989-1990) pp. 30-35.

176. Albinus, *Didaskalos*, ix.1 and 3 cited by Harry A. Wolfson, "Extradeical and Intradeical Interpretations of Platonic Ideas." *Journal of the History of Ideas*, vol. 22 (January-March 1961) pp. 4-5.

177. Thanks to Aly Kassam Khan for reminding me of Augustine's seminal reasons without which this section would have been missing a critical idea in the development of pre-Darwinian philosophical concepts.

178. Frederick Copleston, *A History of Philosophy*, vols. 1-3 (New York: Doubleday, 1985) vol. 1, p. 389.

179. Ibid., vol. 2, p. 77.

180. Quoted in Copleston, *A History of Philosophy*, vol. 2, p. 73.

181. Mayr, *Growth of Biological Thought*, pp. 129, 264.

182. See *Pseudo-Aristotle in the Middle Ages: The Theology and Other Texts*, eds. J. Kraye, W. F. Ryan, and C. B. Schmitt (London: University of London, 1986) for an extensive discussion of this book.

183. Alfarabi, *Mabádi'Ará' Ahl al-Madína al-Fádila*, trans. Richard Walzer as *Al-Farabi on the Perfect State* (Oxford: Clarendon Press, 1985) p. 137; revised translation.

184. Ibid., pp. 139-141.

185. Avicenna, *Naját*, quoted in A. M. Goichon, *Lexique de la Langue Philosophique d'Ibn Síná* (Paris: Desclée de Brouwer, 1938) p. 405.

186. Ibid., p. 386.

187. Ibid., p. 257.

188. *Hikmat* is a term referring to a form of wisdom combining the esoteric teachings of the Shí'ah Imams, the illuminationist knowledge of Suhrawardí, the teachings of Ibn 'Arabí and other Sufis, and the heritage of the Greek philosophers. For more on this see Seyyed Hossein Nasr, "The School of Ispahán" *A History of Muslim Philosophy*, vol. 2, M. M. Sharif ed. (Wiesbaden: Otto Harrassowitz, 1966) pp. 907-908.

189. Avicenna, *Dánish Náma-i 'alá'í*, trans. Parviz Morewedge as *The Metaphysica of Avicenna*. (New York: Columbia University Press, 1973) p 33.

190. Ibid., p. 61.

191. Avicenna, "On the Proof of Prophecies" in *Medieval Political Philosophy*, eds. Ralph Lerner and Muhsin Mahdi (Ithaca: Cornell University Press, 1972) pp.117- 118.

192. Avicenna, *Shifá': Iláhiyyát*, ed. Ibrahim Madkour (Cairo 1960) pp. 402 - 409.

193. Etienne Gilson, *History of Christian Philosophy in the Middle Ages* (New York: Random House, 1955) p. 482.

194. Herbert A. Davidson, *Alfarabi, Avicenna, and Averroes, on Intellect* (New York: Oxford University Press, 1992) pp. 227-228.

195. Ibid., p. 250.
196. Suhrawardí, *Kitáb Ḥikmat al-Ishráq* (*The Philosophy of Illumination*). Typed manuscript belonging to John Walbridge and Hossein Ziai, dated May 30, 1996; pp. 144-145.
197. Ibid., p. 146, revised translation.
198. Ibid., p. 156.
199. Ibid., p. 155.
200. Ibid., p. 152.
201. Fazlur Rahman, *The Philosophy of Mullá Ṣadrá* (Albany: State University of New York Press, 1975) p. 96.
202. Ibid., p. 97.
203. Mullá Ṣadrá, *Al-Ḥikmat al-Muta'álíya fi'l-Asfár al-'Aqlíya al-Arba'a* (The Sublime Wisdom in Four Journeys of Reason), 9 vols, (Qum 1368 - 1379 A.H.) vol. 6, pp. 256-257.
204. Rahman, *Philosophy of Mullá Ṣadrá*, p. 77.
205. Mullá Ṣadrá, *Asfár*, vol. 2, pp. 56-57.
206. Ibid., vol. 6, p. 234.
207. Rahman, *Philosophy of Mullá Ṣadrá*, p. 97.
208. The reader is referred to "The Metaphysics and Cosmology of Process According to Shaykh Aḥmad al-Ahsá'í" by Idris Hamid (Dissertation, State University of New York, Buffalo, 1998) for an excellent and comprehensive treatment of Shaykh Aḥmad's philosophy.
209. Quoted in Idris Samawi Hamid, "The Metaphysics and Cosmology of Process According to Shaykh Aḥmad al-Ahsá'í: "Critical Edition, Translation, and Analysis of Observations in Wisdom", (Dissertation: State University of New York at Buffalo, 1998) p. 166.
210. Shaykh Aḥmad Ahsá'í, *Sharh 'al-Mashá'ir* (Tabriz 1278 A.H.) p. 25.
211. Hamid, "Metaphysics and Cosmology of Process", p. 136.
212. Shaykh Aḥmad, *Sharh 'al-Mashá'ir*, p. 204.
213. Hamid, "Metaphysics and Cosmology of Process", p. 253.
214. Shaykh Aḥmad, *Sharh 'al-Mashá'ir*, p. 16.
215. Hamid, "Metaphysics and Cosmology of Process", p. 134.
216. Shaykh Aḥmad, *Sharh 'al-Mashá'ir*, p. 17.
217. Ibid., pp. 182, 185.
218. Quoted in Hamid, "Metaphysics and Cosmology of Process", pp. 169, 345.
219. Shaykh Aḥmad, *Sharh 'al-Mashá'ir*, p. 53.
220. Ibid., pp. 16, 38.
221. Ibid., pp. 200-201.
222. Ibid., p. 153.
223. Ibid., p. 128.
224. By "appointed time" (*ajal*) is meant a creature's lifespan.
225. Shaykh Aḥmad, *Sharh 'al-Mashá'ir*, p. 57.
226. Ibid., p. 67.
227. Ibid. p. 124.
228. Hamid, "Metaphysics and Cosmology of Process", p. 258.
229. This is the basis of Shaykh Aḥmad's doctrine of the resurrection body, selected writings of which have been translated by Henry Corbin in *Spiritual Body and Celestial Earth* (Princeton 1977) pp. 180-221. So at death the elements of

man's physical body are dispersed but the elements of the spiritual body at the next higher level still subsist. It is in this next dimension, sometimes called the autonomous world of forms and images (*'álam al-mithál*), that the events of the resurrection take place. According to Shaykh Aḥmad, *'álam al-mithál* is one stage below the world of the Kingdom (*malakút*). The same I-spirit speaks through the body at each level and is itself inseparable from the most essential body. Shaykh Aḥmad says, for example: "Zayd is the one who speaks, but his soul which speaks to you in this cage [of the body] is not at this moment in the domain of time; his soul is only generated in time through its connection to the body which it administers. . . . The sanctified intellects are free in themselves from the mixtures of the material substances, temporal duration, and geometrical shapes, but they are not free from matter, form, and extension absolutely as most recent thinkers have imagined. Nay, they have luminous matters, atemporal duration, and subtle forms." (*Sharḥ 'al-Mashá'ir* 228)

230. Shaykh Aḥmad, *Sharḥ 'al-Mashá'ir*, pp. 37, 53, 109.
231. Hamid, "Metaphysics and Cosmology of Process", p. 122.
232. Ibid., p. 123.
233. Quoted in Hamid, "Metaphysics and Cosmology of Process" (*Fá'idah* 18) p. 373.
234. Hamid, p. 243.
235. Quoted in Hamid, "Metaphysics and Cosmology of Process" (*Fá'idah* 12) p. 346.

Section 4: 'Abdu'l-Bahá's Response to Darwinism

236. 'Abdu'l-Bahá, *Promulgation of Universal Peace*, p. 307.
237. 'Abdu'l-Bahá, *Some Answered Questions [SAQ]*, p. 244.
238. 'Abdu'l-Bahá, *Tablet to Forel* published in John Paul Vader, *For the Good of Mankind, August Forel and the Bahá'í Faith* (Oxford: George Ronald, 1984) pp. 75-76.
239. For a full and excellent discussion of Aristotle's proof and other proofs for the existence of God in medieval philosophy, see Herbert A. Davidson, *Proofs for Eternity, Creation and the Existence of God in Medieval Islamic and Jewish Philosophy* (Oxford University Press 1987).
240. 'Abdu'l-Bahá, *Mufávadát*, pp. 4-5; *SAQ*, p. 6, revised translation.
241. *Ilzámí*, as a philosophical term, is translated consistently here as "necessary" for the sake of clarity. In Shoghi Effendi's translation above, he had translated the first appearance of *ilzámí* as "necessary" and the second as "compulsory."
242. 'Abdu'l-Bahá, *Tablet to Forel*, p. 75.
243. 'Abdu'l-Bahá, *Promulgation of Universal Peace*, p. 424.
244. 'Abdu'l-Bahá, *SAQ*, p. 3.
245. Ibid., p. 244.
246. 'Abdu'l-Bahá, *Má'idiy-i Ásmání*, vol. 2, p. 70.
247. 'Abdu'l-Bahá, *Makátíb* (Collected Letters) (Cairo 1912), vol. 2, p. 38.
248. A similar statement is found in the writings of the Báb: "He [God] knows the dispositions of all things, and through the dispositions of all, He creates all, giving each one a portion according to its disposition. . . . Were He to create something other than in accord with the state of its own receptivity, this would be an injustice to it." (*Amr va Khalq*, vol. 1, p. 76)
249. 'Abdu'l-Bahá, *Mufávadát*, p. 144; *SAQ*, p. 203, revised translation.

250. 'Abdu'l-Bahá, *Min Makátíb*, vol. 1, p. 275.
251. I.e., the divine intelligible order in God's mind or will.
252. 'Abdu'l-Bahá, *Mufávadát*, p. 204; *SAQ*, p. 292, revised translation.
253. 'Abdu'l-Bahá, *Mufávadát*, p. 141; *SAQ*, p. 199, revised translation.
254. 'Abdu'l-Bahá, *Muntakhabát az Makátíb-i Ḥaḍrat-i 'Abdu'l-Bahá* (Wilmette: Bahá'í Publishing Trust, 1979) p. 154; *Selections from the Writings of 'Abdu'l-Bahá*, p. 157, revised translation.
255. 'Abdu'l-Bahá, *Promulgation of Universal Peace*, p. 140.
256. 'Abdu'l-Bahá, *Má'idiy-i Ásmání*, vol. 2, p. 69.
257. Ibid., pp. 68-69.
258. The Arabic word translated here as "gradually" (*bitadríj*) literally means "step by step" or "by degrees."
259. 'Abdu'l-Bahá, *Mufávadát*, p. 129; *SAQ*, p. 182, revised translation.
260. This statement: "the formation of man in the matrix of the world was in the beginning like [the development of] the embryo" should not necessarily be interpreted to mean the two processes are equivalent. Rather, they have an analogical resemblance.
261. 'Abdu'l-Bahá, *Mufávadát*, p. 141; *SAQ*, pp. 198-199, revised translation.
262. 'Abdu'l-Bahá, *Kitábát*, vol. 2, pp. 170-171; *Promulgation of Universal Peace*, pp. 225-226, revised translation.
263. See, for example, William Chittick's explanation of the arcs of ascent and descent in the poetry of Rúmí in *The Sufi Path of Love* (Albany: SUNY, 1983) pp. 72-82.
264. Chittick, *Sufi Path of Love*, p. 72.
265. 'Abdu'l-Bahá, *SAQ*, p. 283; *Promulgation of Universal Peace*, p. 270.
266. 'Abdu'l-Bahá, *Makátíb*, vol. 3, p. 172.
267. 'Abdu'l-Bahá, *Mufávadát*, pp. 124-125; *SAQ*, pp. 177-178, revised translation.
268. 'Abdu'l-Bahá, *Mufávadát*, p. 64; *SAQ*, p. 88, revised translation.
269. 'Abdu'l-Bahá, *SAQ*, pp. 143-144.
270. "Perfect man" is a technical term used by Ibn 'Arabí and his followers to refer to human individuals who reflect in perfect equilibrium all the names and attributes of God, though in their specific functions (as determined by time and place) they may display only certain names. All of the prophets and saints are "perfect men," and as such they are exemplars to the rest of humanity and reveal the fullness of what other men possess only potentially. Ibn 'Arabí says: "The highest cosmic level is...'poverty toward all things.' This is the level of perfect man, for everything was created for him and for his sake and subjected to him" (qtd. in Chittick, *Sufi Path of Knowledge* 46).
271. 'Abdu'l-Bahá, *Mufávadát*, pp. 139-140; *SAQ*, pp. 195-197, revised translation.
272. 'Abdu'l-Bahá, *SAQ*, p. 201.
273. 'Abdu'l-Bahá, *Mufávadát*, p. 94; *SAQ*, p. 129, revised translation.
274. In a paper by Aly-khan Kassam called "Matter, Spirit, and Complexity," posted on the newsgroup Talisman on December 18, 1996, he explains cogently 'Abdu'l-Bahá's understanding of the relation of spirit to matter. By "spirit" here is meant an emergent property of matter that is dependent on particular kinds of compositions of constituent elements. In other words, spirit, in this case, is not

the same as a species essence, which guides the composition; rather, it is a manifestation of a species essence realized through a particular arrangement of constituent elements. The whole of a composition, being more than just the sum of its parts, "attracts" a spirit to itself. "It adds," Kassam explains, "another dimension which cannot be inferred by simply examining the constituent parts." So "a collection of elements when arranged according to a specific pattern will attract an ordained level of spirit to the group, which is then manifested in the group by certain properties or behavior in the physical world. The spirit thus attracted will not be attributable to any part of the group, and if the group is broken up the spirit vanishes." All spirits realized in this manner are perishable, except for the human spirit. According to 'Abdu'l-Bahá, once the human spirit, i.e. the rational soul, comes into existence, it continues forever (SAQ, p. 151). But the other spirits, such as the plant and animal spirits, are perishable (SAQ p. 143). The point of Kassam's paper is that all complex systems, which can be anything from a group of cells in the body to a rain forest or a galaxy, exhibit just such emergent properties, which are "associated with the system as a whole and not any part of it."

275. 'Abdu'l-Bahá, *Mufávadát*, p. 126; *SAQ*, pp. 178-179, revised translation.

276. 'Abdu'l-Bahá, *Má'idiy-i Ásmání*, vol. 9, pp. 27-28.

277. 'Abdu'l-Bahá, *SAQ*, p. 199.

278. 'Abdu'l-Bahá, *Mufávadát*, p. 130; *SAQ*, pp. 183-184, revised translation.

279. 'Abdu'l-Bahá, *Mufávadát*, pp. 136-138; *SAQ*, pp. 191-194, revised translation.

280. 'Abdu'l-Bahá, *Kitábát*, vol. 2, p. 303; *Promulgation of Universal Peace*, pp. 358-359, revised translation.

281. Ibid., pp. 303-304; *Promulgation of Universal Peace*, p. 359, revised translation.

282. 'Abdu'l-Bahá, *Mufávadát*, pp. 129-130; *SAQ*, p. 183-184, revised translation.

283. 'Abdu'l-Bahá, *Mufávadát*, p. 141; *SAQ*, p. 199, revised translation.

284. 'Abdu'l-Bahá, *Tablet to Forel*, p. 75.

285. 'Abdu'l-Bahá, *Mufávadát*, p. 204; *SAQ*, p. 292, revised translation.

286. 'Abdu'l-Bahá, *Mufávadát*, p. 128; *SAQ*, p. 181, revised translation. Shaykh Aḥmad proposes in his *Sharḥ al-Masha'ir* that the concept of "unity of existence," if we are not referring to the special meaning of this expression used by the leaders of the Sufis, can only refer to the unity between a whole and its parts. He says: "Unity of existence is inconceivable except between a whole and its parts. For example, man is a single existent by the existence of his parts" (228). In the same manner, 'Abdu'l-Bahá says that the true meaning of "unity of existence," at the level of physical things, is to be found in the elements or atoms from which all things are composed, because every atom is capable of becoming part of the constitution of any being in the universe and consequently expressing the properties of that level of organization (*Promulgation*, p. 286).

287. 'Abdu'l-Bahá, *Mufávadát*, pp. 141-142; *SQA*, p. 199, revised translation.

288. I owe this analogy to Eberhard von Kitzing, who shared it with me in one our many email correspondences.

289. 'Abdu'l-Bahá, *Kitábát*, vol. 2, p. 106; *Promulgation of Universal Peace*, p. 160, revised translation.

290. 'Abdu'l-Bahá, *Mufávadát*, p. 126; *SQA*, pp. 178-179, revised translation.

291. 'Abdu'l-Bahá, *Makátíb*, vol. 3, p. 257.
292. 'Abdu'l-Bahá, letter 440 of a collection sent to author from the Bahá'í World Center, 12 July 1998.
293. Darwin, *Origin of Species*, p. 463.
294. 'Abdu'l-Bahá, *Mufávadát*, p. 197; *SAQ*, p. 283.
295. Bahá'u'lláh, *Tasbíh va Tahlíl*, pp. 88-89.
296. 'Abdu'l-Bahá, *Kitábát*, vol. 3, pp. 35-37.
297. 'Abdu'l-Bahá, *Mufávadát*, p. 136; *SAQ*, p. 191, revised translation.

BIBLIOGRAPHY

'Abdu'l-Bahá. *Khiṭábát* (Talks of 'Abdu'l-Bahá). Hofheim-Langenhain: Bahá'í Verlag, 1984. (Reprint of the 3 volume original edition published in Egypt in 1921, 1942/43, and in Tehran 1970/71.)

_____. *Má'idiy-i Ásmání* (The Heavenly Bread). Part 2. Comp. 'Abdu'l-Hamíd-i Ishráq Khávarí. New Delhi: Bahá'í Publishing Trust, 1984. (Reprint of vols. 2, 5, and 9 formerly published in Tehran.)

_____. *Makátíb-i 'Abdu'l-Bahá* (Collected Letters). Vol. 2 and Vol 3. Cairo 1912.

_____. *Min Makátíb-i 'Abdu'l-Bahá.* (From the Collected Letters). Vol. 1. Rio de Janeiro: Editora Bahá'í Brasil, 1982.

_____. *Mufávaḍát* (Table Talks). New Delhi: Bahá'í Publishing Trust, 1984. (Reprint of the 1920 Cairo edition.)

_____. *The Promulgation of Universal Peace.* Talks Delivered by 'Abdu'l-Bahá during His Visit to the United States and Canada in 1912. Comp. Howard MacNutt. Wilmette: Bahá'í Publishing Trust, 1982.

_____. *Some Answered Questions.* [=SAQ] Trans. Laura Clifford Barney. Wilmette: Bahá'í Publishing Trust, 1981.

_____. "Tablet from 'Abdu'l-Bahá to August Forel" in John Paul Vader. *For the Good of Mankind, August Forel and the Bahá'í Faith.* Oxford: George Ronald, 1984.

Afghání, Jamál al-Dín. *al-Radd 'ala al-Dahriyín* (The Refutation of the Materialists). Trans. Nikki Keddie in An Islamic Response to Imperialism. Berkeley: University of California Press, 1968.

Alfarabi. *Mabádi'Ará' Ahl al-Madína al-Fáḍila.* Trans. Richard Walzer as Al-Farabi on the Perfect State. Oxford: Clarendon Press, 1985.

Aristotle. *Metaphysics.* Trans. Hippocrates G. Apostle. Grinnell, Iowa: The Peripatetic Press, 1979.

_____. A New Aristotle Reader. Ed. J. L. Ackrill. Princeton: Princeton University Press, 1987.

Augros, Robert, and George Stanciu. *The New Biology: Discovering the Wisdom in Nature.* Boston: New Science Library, 1988.

Avicenna. "On the Proof of Prophecies." *Medieval Political Philosophy.* Eds. Ralph Lerner and Muhsin Mahdi. Ithaca: Cornell University Press, 1972.

_____. *Al-Shifá', al-Iláhiyyát.* Ed. Ibrahim Madkour. Cairo 1960.

_____. *Dánish Náma-i 'alá'í.* Trans. Parviz Morewedge as "The Metaphysica of Avicenna." New York: Columbia University Press, 1973.

Balínús. *Sirr al-Khalíqa wa Ṣan'at at-Ṭabí'at.* Ed. Ursula Weisser. Aleppo, Syria: University of Aleppo, 1979.

Chittick, William C. *The Sufi Path of Knowledge. Ibn al-'Arabí's Metaphysics of Imagination.* Albany: State University of New York Press, 1989.

_____. *The Sufi Path of Love. The Spiritual Teachings of Rumi.* Albany: University of New York Press, 1983.

Copleston, Frederick. *A History of Philosophy.* Vols. 1-3. New York: Doubleday, 1985.

Darwin, Charles. *The Origin of Species by Means of Natural Selection.* 6th ed. London: E. P. Dutton, 1928.

Davidson, Herbert A. *Alfarabi, Avicenna, and Averroes, on Intellect.* New York: Oxford University Press, 1992.

Gilson, Etienne. *History of Christian Philosophy in the Middle Ages.* New York: Random House, 1955.

Goichon, A. M. *Lexique de la Langue Philosophique d'Ibn Síná.* Paris: Desclée de Brouwer, 1938.

Hamid, Idris Samawi. "The Metaphysics and Cosmology of Process According to Shaykh Ahmad al-Ahsá'í: Critical Edition, Translation, and Analysis of Observations in Wisdom." Ph.D. Dissertation. State University of New York at Buffalo, 1998.

Hitching, Francis. *The Neck of the Giraffe: Darwin, Evolution, and the New Biology.* New York: New American Library, 1982.

Hull, David L. *Darwin and His Critics: The Reception of Darwin's Theory of Evolution by the Scientific Community.* Cambridge: Harvard University Press, 1973.

al-Isfahání, Abu al-Majd. *Naqd Fasafat Darwin* (Critique of Darwin's Philosophy). 2 vols. Baghdad, 1914.

Izutsu, Toshihiko. The Concept and Reality of Existence. Tokyo: The Keio Institute of Cultural and Linguistic Studies, 1971.

al-Jisr, Hussein. *Al-Risála al-Ḥamídíya fí Ḥaqíqa al-Diyána al-Islámíya wa Ḥaqqíya al-Sharí'a al-Muḥammadíya* (The Praiseworthy Epistle on the Truth of Islam and Islamic Canon Law) Beirut, 1887.

Kuhn, Thomas S. *The Structure of Scientific Revolutions.* 2nd ed. Chicago: University of Chicago Press, 1970.

Lovejoy, Arthur. *The Great Chain of Being.* Cambridge: Harvard University Press. 1964.

Mayr, Ernst. *The Growth of Biological Thought.* Diversity, Evolution, and Inheritance. Cambridge: Harvard University Press, 1982.

Montagu, Ashley, ed. *Science and Creationism.* Oxford: Oxford University Press, 1984.

Mullá Ṣadrá. *Al-Ḥikmat al-Muta'álíya fi'l-Asfár al-'Aqlíya al-Arba'a* (The Sublime Wisdom in Four Journeys of Reason). 9 vols. Qum 1368-1379 A.H.

al-Muqtaṭaf. Beirut and Cairo, 1876 - 1930.

Plato. *The Collected Dialogues.* Ed. Edith Hamilton and H. Cairns. Princeton: Princeton University Press, 1961.

_____. *Timaeus and Critias.* Trans. Desmond Lee. Baltimore: Penguin Books, 1971.

Proclus. *Commentary on Plato's Parmenides.* Trans. Glenn Morrow and John Dillon. Princeton University Press, 1987.

Rahman, Fazlur. *The Philosophy of Mullá Ṣadrá.* Albany: State University of New York Press, 1975.

Raymo, Chet. *Skeptics and True Believers.* New York: Walker and Company, 1998.

Shaykh Aḥmad Aḥsá'í. *Sharḥ al-Mashá'ir.* Tabriz 1278 A.H.

Shumayyil, Shiblí. Falsafat al-Nushú' wa'l-Irtiqá' (The Theory of Evolution and Progress). Cairo 1910.

Suhrawardí. *Kitáb Ḥikmat al-Ishráq* (The Philosophy of Illumination). Typed manuscript belonging to John Walbridge and Hossein Ziai, dated May 30, 1996.

Wolfson, Harry A. "Extradeical and Intradeical Interpretations of Platonic Ideas." *Journal of the History of Ideas,* vol. 22 (January-March 1961) pp. 3-32.

Ziadet, Adel A. *Western Science in the Arab World: The Impact of Darwinism: 1860 - 1930.* New York: St. Martin's Press, 1986.

PART TWO

The Origin of Complex Order in Biology: 'Abdu'l-Bahá's Concept of the "Originality of Species" Compared to Concepts in Modern Biology

by

Eberhard von Kitzing

Acknowledgments

The author would like to thank several people for their open discussion and valuable comments on the internet. Special contributions came from Ralph Chapman, Kamran Hakim, Roger Kingdon, Mark Towfiq, Gerhard Schweter, and Viktoria Sparks-Forrester.

The present essay owes a lot to Keven Brown's support. He made many constructive suggestions during the development of the essay, provided the provisional retranslations of the cited passages of *Some Answered Questions* and certain passages from *The Promulgation of Universal Peace*. Finally, he put this essay into readable form.

My discussions with Ron Somerby and Stephen Friberg clarified important points in this work.

'ABDU'L-BAHÁ

". . . we may acknowledge the fact that at one time man was an inmate of the sea, at another period an invertebrate, then a vertebrate and finally a human being standing erect. Though we admit these changes, we cannot say man is an animal."

Section 1

Evolution and Bahá'í Belief

1.1 Darwin's Challenge to the Classical Worldview

Today it is commonly accepted that the introduction of general relativity by Albert Einstein and quantum mechanics by Max Planck led to and still requires a reorganization of our philosophical concepts about the universe as a whole and our previous understanding of space, time, and matter.[1] That the consequences of modern biology may cause an even more drastic reformulation of our understanding of our existence is the central theme of Dennett's book *Darwin's Dangerous Idea*.[2] According to Ernst Mayr, Darwin changed not only the science of biology but our whole way of thinking:

> For no one has influenced our modern worldview—both within and beyond science—to a greater extent than has this extraordinary Victorian. We turn to his work again and again, because as a bold and intelligent thinker he raised some of the most profound questions about our origins that have been asked, and as a devoted and innovative scientist he provided brilliant, often world-shaking answers.[3]

Dawkins emphasizes the far-reaching, but often neglected, implications of natural selection for philosophy: "Today the theory of evolution is about as much open to doubt as the theory that the earth goes round the sun, but the full implications of Darwin's revolution have yet to be widely realized. . . . Philosophy and the subjects known as 'humanities' are still taught almost as if Darwin had never lived."[4]

When Darwin published his book *The Origin of Species* in 1859,[5] he presented the first consistent theory that explained the diversity of biological species by natural means. Until this date, the majority of naturalists, including the most illustrious ones, were convinced that God's special creation was the only reasonable explanation for the existence of the complex order of life.[6] The central theme of Darwin's theory is the "modification of species," which stands in sharp contrast to most previous theories in biology. Most biologists before Darwin thought of species as fixed, timeless entities.

According to Mayr, Darwin replaced voluntary design as the main origin of order with the concept of natural selection:

> It dealt with the *mechanism* of evolutionary change and, more particularly, how this mechanism could account for the seeming harmony and adaptation of the organic world. It attempted to provide a natural explanation in place of the supernatural one of natural theology. In that respect Darwin's theory was unique; there was nothing like it in the whole philosophical literature from the pre-Socratics to Descartes, Leibniz or Kant. It replaced teleology in nature with an essentially mechanical explanation.[7]

The main challenge of Darwin's new theory was not that it presented an alternative origin of the complex forms of life, but that it threatened the commonly accepted worldview. At least in biology, the picture of a God caring for His creatures was replaced by the mechanistic and aggressive concept of the survival of the fittest. If biological characteristics are subject to natural selection, one should expect the same for instincts and social behavior. If our reality is grounded in the unity of nature, the development of human society should not be contrary to the laws of nature. Rather, the same fundamental driving forces should operate in the evolution of life and in the formation of the social characteristics of humanity. From the late nineteenth century until today, many people have concluded that the concept of the survival of the fittest means that our universe is driven by a blind mechanism, and that no purpose, plan, or goal exists behind our universe.

Today, biological evolution is the model widely accepted to explain the appearance and development of life on this planet. Statements similar to the following ones are common place— Dawkins: "No serious biologist doubts the fact that evolution has happened nor that all living creatures are cousins of one another"[8]; Howells: "Evolutionary theory is now the center of the whole science of biology"[9]; and Mayr: "It is perhaps fair to state at the outset that no well-informed biologist doubts evolution any longer; in fact, many biologists consider evolution not a theory but a simple fact documented by the change of gene pools from generation to generation and by the changes in the sequence of fossils in the successive accurately dated geological strata."[10] Nevertheless, there are still objections to the theory of evolution, especially among fundamentalist Christian groups.[11]

1.2 The Seminal Nature of 'Abdu'l-Bahá's Statements on Evolution

During the second half of the nineteenth century, the consequences of Darwinism were not only heatedly discussed in the Occident but also in the Near East.[12] They were also considered by 'Abdu'l-Bahá, the son of the prophet-founder of the Bahá'í Faith, who devoted considerable attention to the subject of evolution. This fact indicates that he was aware of the far-reaching consequences of these new ideas about the origin of life. The opinions formulated in this essay are based on the assumption that the statements of 'Abdu'l-Bahá about evolution are not intended to be a detailed explanation of cosmogony and biological evolution. They are understood rather as seminal statements from which Bahá'í scholars may develop a relevant Bahá'í philosophy. Based on the cornerstones established by 'Abdu'l-Bahá, a later chapter will speculate on how a non-trivial origin of our universe may be formulated in the language of modern natural sciences. It is important to note that this essay does not address the question of the particular mechanisms of evolution as such.

Most of 'Abdu'l-Bahá's talks on evolution were given on two occasions: during the visit of Miss Barney to 'Akká between 1904-1906[13] and during his journey through the United States.[14] In his table talks with Miss Barney, published under the title *Some Answered Questions*, 'Abdu'l-Bahá explicitly mentions "some European philosophers" who believed in the "modification of the species" and the "evolution of beings." As 'Abdu'l-Bahá referred to the understanding of evolution discussed during the second half of the nineteenth century and at the beginning of the twentieth century, much attention is devoted in this essay to clarifying that understanding.

Because of the general nature of 'Abdu'l-Bahá's statements about evolution, it is assumed that he was not interested in the details of evolution biology, but in the philosophical consequences of Darwinism. He was one of the few great religious figures at the end of the nineteenth century who accepted the development of the biosphere as an evolutionary process. However, he severely criticized the philosophic concepts of purposelessness and atheism. Contrary to many contemporary scientists and philosophers, 'Abdu'l-Bahá understood evolution to support the existence of God.[15]

A second group of philosophers that 'Abdu'l-Bahá explicitly mentions in his talks about evolution are the "philosophers of the East," whose understanding of the origin and nature of species, similar to that of Western classical biology, were rooted in concepts formulated by Plato and Aristotle. The diverse species concepts of the Islamic philosophers are not further considered in this essay. The reader is referred to the accompanying essay by Keven Brown for a detailed discussion of these concepts.

1.3 About "Some European Philosophers"

In the Near East the evolution discussion addressed mainly philosophical and social issues. The early literature about evolution available in Arabic were translations of representations of Darwinism addressed to the general public by authors such as Ludwig Büchner and Ernst Haeckel, who wrote their books to spread a new worldview based entirely on the empirical sciences. They explained the theory of biological evolution as an atheistic, mechanistic philosophy. Those ideas were presented as a direct consequence of the new findings of modern science.

Because 'Abdu'l-Bahá explicitly refers to "some European philosophers," the views of Ludwig Büchner and Ernst Haeckel are presented and discussed in this essay. Ludwig Büchner (1824-1899) wrote many books and pamphlets about his philosophic ideas which were published in many languages. He popularized Darwinism together with a materialistic worldview in the West, but also in the Near East. He tried to base his worldview on natural sciences. The first edition of his famous and well-known book *Kraft und Stoff* (Force and Matter)[16] was published in 1855, four years before Darwin's *Origin of Species*.

As early as 1855, Büchner postulated the evolution of species following the teachings of Lamark. The book *Kraft und Stoff* appeared in twenty-one editions and was translated into fifteen languages. German and English editions were reprinted several times in North America, where he gave many lectures during his visit in the winter of 1872-1873. His book *Sechs Vorlesungen über die Darwin'sche Theorie* (Six Lessons on Darwinism)[17] was translated into Arabic by Shiblí Shumayyil and published in 1884. It soon became the center of a heated debate in the Near East over Darwinism, a debate that continued for a long time in the pages of Lebanese and Egyptian newspapers. Büchner severely criticized prevalent Christian beliefs as myths and childish ideas undermining the moral of society. He presented his worldview, which he claimed was based only on the facts and discoveries of modern science, as the reasonable alternative. Büchner taught that the golden rule is the foundation for all human moral behavior, and solidarity is the essence of human ethics. Of course, such a view, divorced from traditional religion, provoked the resistance of German conservative circles, including the churches. As a consequence, Büchner had to give up his position at Tübingen University.

When Haeckel published his *Welträtsel* (World's Mysteries) in 1899,[18] he was a famous scientist and professor of zoology at Jena University. He was one of the first supporters of Darwin's evolution theory. One of the main reasons he wrote *Welträtsel* was to overcome the "artificial and pernicious distinction between natural sciences and philosophy, between the results of experience and thinking." Haeckel insisted that empirical studies (natural sciences) must be guided by reason (philosophy): "An overemphasis on empiricism is just as dangerous an error as the opposite one of speculation. Both paths of understanding are mutually indispensable."[19]

According to Haeckel, revelation consists either of "fiction or deception and imposture."[20] He caricatured the Christian view of God as being extremely anthropomorphic: "This anthropomorphism results in the paradoxical view of God as a gaseous vertebrate."[21] His book further polarized the heated public debate about evolution. He not only promoted Darwinism, but also claimed that Christian dogma and evolution are incompatible. Haeckel tried to build a monistic religion on the classical ideals of truth, beauty, and goodness: "Within the pure cult of 'the true, the good, and the beautiful,' which is at the center of our monistic religion, we find sufficient reparation for the lost anthropomorphic ideals of 'God, freedom, and immortality.' "[22] He claimed that his monistic religion was based on experience and rational arguments: "This monistic religion and ethics differs from all others for it is exclusively based on pure reason, and its worldview is grounded in science, experience, and reasonable faith."[23]

1.4 Evolution Discussions in the Bahá'í Community

There are a growing number of books and articles dealing specifically with the question of evolution in Bahá'í literature. John Esslemont,[24] Anjam Khursheed[25] and B. Hoff Conow[26] understand 'Abdu'l-Bahá to propose a biologically distinct evolution of the human species parallel to the animal kingdom. Julio Savi[27] does not present specific interpretations of 'Abdu'l-Bahá's evolution statements. Craig Loehle[28] claims the compatibility of the Bahá'í writings with today's commonly used scientific model of the evolution of life on earth: "In conclusion, in the context of the Bahá'í teachings, it is possible to take both a religious view of evolution without altering science and an evolutionary view of religion without losing faith." A lively discussion about Loehle's article followed in succeeding issues of the *Journal of Bahá'í Studies*.[29] Keven Brown[30] proposes that 'Abdu'l-Bahá's statements about "man" in the context of evolution refer primarily to the archetype of the human species. More recently William Hatcher[31] presented "A Scientific Proof of the Existence of God" based on a short proof of the existence of God by 'Abdu'l-Bahá.

The repeated statements of 'Abdu'l-Bahá that "from the beginning of man's existence he is a distinct species," that the human species does not descend from the animal, and similar ones, have led many Bahá'ís to the conclusion that humanity developed biologically in parallel to the animal kingdom. This concept is designated in this essay as the *parallel evolution model*. Esslemont, Khursheed, Conow, and others assume that there was a separate biological line for the human race running in parallel to the vegetable and animal lines. The supporters of parallel evolution consider the line consisting of pre-human creatures to be biologically distinct from the animal world, but shaped like animal species. Esslemont formulates such a view in his introduction to the Bahá'í Faith, *Bahá'u'lláh and the New Era*:

> Each individual human body develops through such a series of stages, from a tiny round speck of jelly-like matter to the fully developed man. If this is true of the individual, as nobody denies, why should we consider it derogatory to human dignity to admit a similar development for the species? This is a very different thing from claiming that man is descended from a monkey. The human embryo may at one time resemble a fish with gill-slits and tail, but it is not a fish. It is a human embryo. So the human species may at various stages of its long development have resembled to the outward eye various species of lower animals, but it was still the human species, possessing the mysterious latent power of developing into man as we know him today, nay more, of developing in the future, we trust, into something far higher still.[32]

In a footnote, a remark about "species" is given: "The word 'species' is used here to explain the distinction which has always existed between men and animals, despite outward appearances. It should not be read with its current specialized biological meaning." Esslemont gives an analogy between human phylogeny and ontogeny that 'Abdu'l-Bahá used in a similar form.

Khursheed describes the same idea of parallel human evolution: "At one stage it may have resembled a fish, at another an ape, but all the way through its evolution it was a distinct species undergoing a process of design."[33] Conow expresses a similar interpretation: "Bahá'u'lláh and 'Abdu'l-Bahá say simply that the human being has always occupied a distinct evolutionary tier although his form and shape evolved and changed over millions of years . . . even though in his first stage man was aquatic, and in a later stage may have appeared ape-like."[34]

How one interprets the statements of 'Abdu'l-Bahá on evolution depends crucially on the meaning of the term "species" in those quotations. The definition of "species," however, has changed drastically during the last two-hundred years. Did 'Abdu'l-Bahá use this term in its modern sense which was formulated during the first half of the twentieth century? Or did he have a concept of species close to the one current at the beginning of the nineteenth century? Or did he have another definition of his own?

Section 2

"Species" and "Evolution" in Occidental Biology

The modification of species is an idea fundamental to the theories of biological evolution developed during the nineteenth century. The present chapter provides some background for understanding the arguments of 'Abdu'l-Bahá in favor of the originality of the humans species. It describes the development of the concepts of species and evolution in Europe before and after Darwin, giving special attention to the meaning of these terms during the last two centuries.

Sometime between the beginning of the nineteenth century and the middle of the twentieth century, the classical concept of a biological species was replaced by a modern definition. According to the classical species definition, the particular members of a population derive their outer form, that is their phenotype, from a timeless species essence. The species essence was thought to be like a blueprint in the Creator's mind. In modern biology, a biological species is defined by a population of particular individuals, i.e., by a gene pool common to a group of interbreeding organisms.

2.1 Classical Concepts of Species and Evolution

Plato and Aristotle initiated the discussion about how to understand the existence of distinct, stable biological populations. Because horses remain horses over many generations, these populations are stable. A cat can produce fertile offspring only with other cats, but not with dogs. This stability and distinction suggest that cats and dogs are separate universal entities. Plato was interested in discovering the order on which our cosmos is built. He was looking for unchanging realities behind all the constantly changing particular events. He proposed the existence of Ideas, or essences, to be the true timeless realities behind our everyday experiences. For Plato the prototypes of essences were geometric objects such as triangles, squares, tetrahedra, and cubes (i.e., the Platonic ideal bodies). These objects are clearly distinct, for there exists no "smooth" way to transform a triangle into a square, or a tetrahedron into a cube. Mayr describes this view:

> For Plato, the variable world of phenomena in an analogous manner was nothing but the reflection of a limited number of fixed and unchanging forms, *eide* (as Plato called them) or *essences* as they were called by the Thomists in the Middle Ages. These essences are what is real and important in this world. As ideas they can exist independent of any objects. Constancy and discontinuity are the points of special emphasis for the essentialists. Variation is attributed to the imperfect manifestation of the underlying essences.[35]

Because animals and plants form distinct classes, such as roses, cats, etc., Plato assumed the existence of essences for each of those classes, the species. These essences were believed to assure the stability of the species, i.e., that cats will always remain cats and not eventually become cows or birds. Plato assumed that such species essences are timeless realities existing independently of the biological populations of particular members.

In contrast to Plato, Aristotle was particularly interested in biology and invented many biological disciplines. He did not believe in the existence of essences in the sense that Plato did, but assumed that the existence of particular members of a biological population is sufficient to maintain the existence and the stability of its kind. Although Aristotle had a rather modern concept of the species as a population, he insisted on a purely static worldview. Mayr explains:

> Not so with Aristotle. He held too many other concepts irreconcilable with evolution. Movement in the organic world, from conception to birth to death, does not lead to permanent change, only a steady-state continuity. Constancy and perpetuity are thus reconcilable with movement and with the evanescence of individuals and individual phenomena. As a naturalist, he found everywhere well-defined species, fixed and unchanging, and in spite of all his stress on continuity in nature, this fixity of species and their forms (*eide*) had to be eternal. . . . There is order in nature, and everything in nature has its purpose. He stated clearly (*Gen. An.*, 2.1.731b35) that man and the genera of animals and plants are eternal; they can neither vanish nor have they been created. The idea that the universe could have evolved from an original chaos, or the higher organisms could have evolved from lower ones, was totally alien to Aristotle's thought. To repeat, Aristotle was opposed to evolution of any kind.[36]

Plato's concept of fixed essences and Aristotle's view of fixed biological populations laid the foundations of classical biology and philosophy. Today the progress of Western science is often presented as an emancipation from those concepts. Although modern biology has rejected the concept of essences, which was firmly established in nearly every branch of the sciences in the eighteenth and nineteenth centuries, physics today remains basically essentialistic.

2.1.1 *Essentialism in Physics and Chemistry.* The following statement by Isaac Newton about the relation between God and nature reflects the general belief of his time about the origin of complex order:

> We know Him only by His most wise and excellent contrivances of things, and final causes; we admire Him for His perfections; but we reverence and adore Him on account of His dominion; for we adore Him as His servants; and a God without dominion, providence, and

final causes, is nothing else but Fate and Nature. Blind metaphysical necessity, which is certainly the same always and everywhere, could produce no variety of things. All the diversity of natural things which we find, suited to different times and places, could arise from nothing but the ideas and will of a Being necessarily existing.[37]

Nature was understood to be a realization of God's ideas, an expression of His eternal plan. According to Newton, accidental and necessary forces cannot produce the diverse complex order found in biology, but can repeat only the same things again and again. The diversity found in nature, therefore, was assumed to require a Creator. This type of argument remained nearly unchallenged until the publication of Darwin's *Origins*.[38]

The concept of essences worked particularly well in physics and in chemistry. Originally, essences in physics were thought to be concrete, but today they have become rather abstract. After the discovery of the chemical elements, these elements were considered to be the expression of time-invariant essences. Chemical elements cannot be transmutated by chemical means. Within chemical reactions their properties can be modified, but one can always get them back afterwards completely unchanged. The smallest units of these elements are the atoms.[39] Later Rutherford discovered that the atoms themselves are composed of a nucleus and an electron shell. Nuclear physics revealed that the nucleus is composed of subatomic particles. For some time those subatomic particles were considered to be elemental, designated elemental particles, and regarded as the fundamental timeless units of our universe. The growing zoo of "elemental particles," however, and the possible transmutation of one type of particle into other ones brought into question their elementary status. At present, quarks are generally considered to be the elemental, timeless subunits of the physical world. All the higher levels of existence depend on and consist of them.

In his book *Das Teil und das Ganze* (The Part and the Whole), Werner Heisenberg explains how much his work in quantum physics owes to Plato's ideas. In his lectures, Friedrich Hund also frequently emphasized the close relation between Plato's ideal bodies and group theory in modern particle physics.[40] Nonetheless, modern physics is clearly distinguished from classical essentialism by its emphasis on continuity, unity of nature, and the wholeness of the universe.

In physics one often searches for conserved entities. In his famous treatise *Über die Erhaltung der Kraft*, published in 1847, Hermann Helmholtz (1821-1894) formulated the law of the conservation of energy. This discovery paralleled the earlier findings of Lavoisier on the conservation of mass and elements. Energy may change its form, but it is not created or eliminated in any physical process. Consequently, the search for timeless properties became essential in physics and dominates most of its branches. This is best expressed by the fundamental assumption that physics should be the same yesterday, today, and tomorrow. In other words, the general laws of physics are time-invariant.

In the nineteenth century, physics and physical chemistry concentrated mainly on equilibrium and close-to-equilibrium systems in thermodynamics. In mechanics, generally so-called integrable systems and closely related ones were carefully studied, that is, those systems for which an analytical solution can be formulated. In astronomy such methods were used to calculate the motion of the planets. Such systems often are sufficiently simple that their basic properties can be studied and the necessary mathematical instruments for their proper quantitative description derived. It was often assumed that this kind of simple behavior is typical for nature. However, because living systems exist far from equilibrium, nineteenth century concepts in physics and chemistry were generally inappropriate for the description of biological phenomena.[41] Therefore, repeated efforts to physicalize biology, as for instance attempted by Helmholtz, generally failed and provoked a counter reaction in biology resulting in the development of vitalistic theories.

At the end of the nineteenth century Henry Poincaré[42] analyzed the stability of the solar planetary system. He discovered that stability in a many particle system is more the exception than the rule. The

Russian scientist Lyapunov further developed these ideas, but they were then forgotten for some time. In recent years, this kind of instability has been shown to be typical for most dynamic systems, and has become popular under the name *chaos theory*. Thus, dynamic systems show a much richer behavior than originally thought during the nineteenth century. Only during the twentieth century have physics and chemistry become sufficiently developed to make the study of far-from-equilibrium systems possible.

2.1.2 Essentialism in Classical Biology. Darwin's idea of explaining biological evolution by means of natural selection led to a revolution in the philosophical concepts behind biology. In this sense, one must speak about a pre- and post-Darwinian biology, here referred to as *classical* and *modern* biology respectively.

Classical biology was dominated by two concepts originating from Plato: (1) that the phenotypes of the members of a population were determined by their species essence, and (2) that the origin and actual existence of a species required a creative force, a *demiurg*. In Christianity and Islam, the required creative force was equated with God. These ideas were still firmly rooted in the scientific community in the middle of the nineteenth century. The biologist Louis Agassiz stated that "it is the task of the philosopher to reveal the blueprint of the Creator."[43] The same author emphasized in his "Essay on Classification" published in 1857: "All organized beings exhibit in themselves all those categories of structure and of existence upon which a natural system may be founded, in such a manner that, in tracing it, the human mind is only translating into human language the Divine thoughts expressed in nature in living realities."[44] This credo was not a singular opinion of a somewhat obscure scientist; it represented the belief of a considerable number of his colleagues.

The famous Swedish naturalist Carl Linné, who made the first attempt to systematize the manifold forms of life in 1735, in his *Systema Naturae*, stated: "*Species tot sunt diversae, quot diversaes formas ab initio creavit infinitum ens.*" Translated into English: "There are as many species as originally created by the infinite being." The French biologist Georges Cuvier, who invented paleontology as a branch of biology, assumed that all particular members of a single species have their root in the first couple of their species created by God:

> We imagine that a species is the total descendence of the first couple created by God, almost as all men are represented as the children of Adam and Eve. What means have we, at this time, to rediscover the path of this genealogy? It is assuredly not in structural resemblance. There remains in reality only reproduction, and I maintain that this is the sole certain and even infallible character for the recognition of the species.[45]

Cuvier considered it to be impossible to trace the genealogy of a particular member of a population back to its original couple. However, because only members of the same species can interbreed, the ability to produce fertile offspring was in itself considered a sufficient proof that both parents belong to the same species. What Cuvier thought to be the consequence of God's creation today serves as a definition of a biological species, i.e., the ability of its members to interbreed.

Additionally, following Plato's concept of Ideas, each species was believed to be determined by a prototype, by a species essence. In his *Histoire Naturelle* Georges Louis Buffon explained:

> There exists in nature a general prototype of each species upon which all individuals are moulded. The individuals, however, are altered or improved, depending on the circumstances, in the process of realization. Relative to certain characteristics, then, there is an irregular appearance in the succession of individuals, yet at the same time there is a striking constancy in the species considered as a whole. The first animal, the first horse for example, was the exterior model and the internal mould from which all past, present, and future horses have been formed.[46]

The species essence was thought to be the unchanging idea in the mind of God of the ideal form of the members of a biological population. Because the particular members of a population were assumed to be the direct representations of their species essences, their phenotypes were also assumed to not change over time. Michel Adanson stated in 1769: "The transmutation of species [i.e., biological populations] does not happen among plants, no more than among animals, and there is not even direct proof of it among minerals, following the accepted principle that constancy is essential in the determination of a species."[47] The invariability of species according to classical biology is clearly stated by Mayr: "Each species had its own species-specific essence and thus it was impossible that it could change or evolve."[48] In classical biology, the biological population was believed to exactly mirror its species essence. These populations, therefore, were assumed not to change and to remain an exact and constant manifestation of their fixed species essences.

The combination of Plato's timeless essences, his idea of a perfect, harmonious universe, Aristotle's fixed populations, and biblical cosmology taken literally gave wide support to the concept of fixed species existing in a static world. In a world created from the beginning in its full perfection, there can exist, by definition, no process that increases this perfection. Any change could only decrease the degree of perfect harmony. To distinguish this kind of biological essentialism from the much more general form of Platonism current in physics, it is designated as *typological thinking* throughout this essay.

During the nineteenth century, accumulating fossil records, showing evidence of extinctions and the existence of species vastly different in appearance from those on earth today, increasingly brought into question the view of unchanging populations. New theories had to be developed to account for the findings of the fossil record. Early theories of biological evolution remained grounded in variants of the essentialistic species concept. For example, the evolution theory of Lamark maintained the idea of species essences. (See Section 2.1.4) For some early theorists, the appearance of a new biological form in the fossil record could only be explained by the creation of a new species essence. According to Mayr, all theories of biological change before Lamark were more or less variants of this idea. Because the invention of a new species in this concept is not gradual, such theories are designated *saltational evolution*. Thus Mayr explains:

> Saltational evolution is a necessary consequence of essentialism: if one believes in evolution and in constant types, only the sudden production of a new type can lead to evolutionary change. That such saltations can occur and indeed that their occurrence is a necessity are old beliefs. Almost all theories of evolution described by Osborn in his history of evolution, *From the Greeks to Darwin*, were saltational theories, that is, theories of the sudden origin of new kinds.[49]

Mayr summarizes the basic concepts of classical biology:

> It had two major theses. The first was the belief that the universe in every detail was designed by an intelligent creator. This together with the other one, the concept of a static, unchanging world of short duration, were so firmly entrenched in the Western mind by the end of the Middle Ages that it seemed quite inconceivable that they could ever be dislodged.[50]

According to Mayr, "real" theories of evolution could be developed only after the erosion of those ideas.

2.1.3 *The Mechanization of Biology.* With the publication of the *Principia* in 1687, Newton "unified" terrestrial with celestial mechanics. Newton's theory explains the falling of apples on earth as well as the path of the planet Venus around the sun. That apples falling to the ground should be subjected to the same kinds of forces as Venus circling around the sun was not at all self-evident at that time. This achievement and many others made mechanics a science *par excellence*. Until the beginning of the twentieth century, the quality of a science was often equated with the degree this science was based on mechanics.

In the Renaissance, the mechanization of nature generally had no atheistic tendencies, as shown in the quotation from Newton given above. But two opposing views about nature became established as a result. In the mechanistic view, the universe was created by God to run on the basis of a few natural laws,[51] (e.g., Newton's laws, with only minor interventions by the Creator). Living creatures were considered to be nothing but mechanisms. This mechanistic view, however, seemed at variance with the abundance of life. Natural theology, which arose as a reaction to such mechanization tendencies, considered nature to be the result of the direct and detailed providence of the Creator:

> Everything in the living world seemed to be so unpredictable, so special, and so unique that the observing naturalist found it necessary to invoke the Creator, his thought, and his activity in every detail of the life of every individual of every kind of organism. . . . John Ray's *The Wisdom of God Manifested in the Works of the Creation* (1691) is not only a powerful argument from design but also a very sound natural history. . . . Natural theology was a necessary development because design was really the only possible explanation for adaptation in a static "created" world. Any new finding in this early age of natural history was grist on the mill of natural theology. The supposedly idyllic life of the inhabitants of the tropics, in particular, was seen as evidence for the providential design by the Creator.[52]

In Britain natural theology was influential until the middle of the nineteenth century. No contradictions were found between biology and theology. The biosphere proved the glory of its Creator. At that time many British biologists were also theologians. In France and in Germany natural theology lost its importance much earlier, by around 1780. In Germany in the eighteenth and nineteenth centuries, various romantic movements determined the schools of thought. These movements were, in part, a reaction to mechanistic concepts. The names of Herder and Goethe are related to these schools, which culminated in the *Naturphilosphie* developed by Schelling, Oken, and Carus.

The nineteenth century experienced an explosive development of the natural sciences. Mechanics, as formulated by Newton and developed by Euler, Hamilton, Lagrange, Laplace, and Poincaré (to name only a few), was considered the basis of natural sciences. Important discoveries of modern science were the conservation of matter in 1789 by Lavoisier (1743-1794), and the conservation of energy in 1842 by Robert Mayer (1814-1878) and in 1847 by Helmholtz.

The high esteem for the physical sciences and the influence of vitalistic schools gave rise to a strongly reductionistic physicalism in physiology in the middle of the nineteenth century in Germany. A considerable number of prominent scientists expected any good science to explain its phenomena by mechanistic causes, at least in the long run. One of the most prominent advocates of the physicalization of physiology was the German physician and physicist Hermann Helmholtz. During the opening lecture at the meeting of German naturalists and physicians in Insbruck in 1869, he outlined his scientific program: "The ultimate objective of the natural sciences is to reduce all processes in nature to the movements that underlie them and to find their driving forces, that is, to reduce them to mechanics."[53] According to Büchner, such sciences reasonably prove "that macroscopic as well as microscopic beings in all aspects of their growth, life and decay follow only mechanical laws, grounded in the things themselves."[54] Haeckel also emphasized that living beings and evolution follow exclusively mechanical laws:

> This mechanical or monistic philosophy claims that all phenomena of human life as well as the rest of nature are ruled by rigid and unfaltering laws, that everywhere there exists a necessary, causal relation between all phenomena . . . and that all phenomena are brought forth by mechanical causes (*causae efficientes*), but not by thought and purposeful causes (*causae finales*).[55]

Consequently, the existence of independent higher qualities, like free will, were denied. Haeckel described free will as a dogmatic delusion: "Free will is not an object of scientific investigation, because as a mere dogma it is based on illusion and does not exist in reality."[56] The complexity of our universe, including all levels of life, was thought to emerge from the laws of physics and chemistry. Such ideas, popularized by Ludwig Büchner, Ernst Haeckel, Johannes Müller, Jacob Moleschott,[57] Wilhelm Ostwald, and Karl Vogt, became known as *positivism*. They should not be mistaken with the neopositivism of the Vienna School.[58] To develop and promote a scientific view of life, Büchner in 1881 co-founded the *Deutschen Freidenkerbund*, and until his death he was the head of this society. Haeckel established the *Monistenbund* in Jena in 1906. The central goal of such societies was to develop and promote a scientific worldview based upon a materialistic and atheistic philosophy.

2.1.4 *Orthogenetic Evolution.* Most early concepts of biological evolution were based on essentialism. Generally, they assumed a plan, or a purpose, in evolution "implemented" by a Creator. Such goal-directed evolution concepts are sometimes designated *orthogenetic evolution.* Many of the early philosophical approaches to evolution, such as those proposed by the German *Naturphilosophen*, were essentialistic and goal directed. They had, however, nearly nothing to do with biology. According to Mayr: "Teleological thinking was extremely widespread in the first half of the nineteenth century. For Agassiz and other progressionists the sequence of fossil faunas simply reflected the maturation of the plan of creation in the mind of the Creator."[59]

Jean Baptiste de Monet de Lamark (1744-1829) formulated the first systematic theory of biological evolution. From his studies of huge numbers of living and extinct molusks, he drew the revolutionary conclusion that all species, including man, are descended from earlier, less complex forms because of the ability of biological systems to accumulate complexity. In his *Philosophie Zoologique* published in 1809, fifty years before Darwin's *Origins*, he stated: "Nature, in successively producing all species of animals, beginning with the most imperfect of the simplest, and ending her work with the most perfect, has caused their organization to become more complex."[60] For Lamark the central force motivating evolution was the observation that organisms always strive to be in perfect harmony with their environments.[61] That such harmony can be discovered nearly everywhere in nature was always emphasized by natural theologians. Because the findings of geology documented drastic changes within the environment during geological history, Lamark concluded that animals must have evolved, that is, adapted to the new situation, simply to maintain their harmony with the environment and so became different in their species form.

During the first half of the nineteenth century, belief in orthogenetic evolution was widespread; that is, it was supposed that nature was following the plan and goals given it by a Creator. For instance, the embryologist von Baer stated in a review of Darwin's *Origin of Species*: "My goal is to defend teleology. . . . Natural forces must be coordinated or directed. Forces which are not directed— so-called blind forces—can never produce order. . . . If the higher forms of animal life stand in causal relationship to the lower, developing out of them, then how can we deny that nature has purposes or goals?"[62] Von Baer argued as Paley did in his watchmaker argument. Accidental influences cannot produce order.

Orthogenetic theories were defended until the middle of this century. A recent prominent advocate of orthogenetic evolution was Teilhard de Chardin[63] with his omega principle. He considers evolution to be a goal-directed process that will eventually lead to the unification of humankind. Most modern philosophies related to evolution biology, however, reject such directedness. Mayr describes this shift from accepting teleology, to rejecting it:

> From the Greeks on, there was a widespread belief that everything in nature and its processes has a purpose, a predetermined goal. And these processes would lead the world to ever greater perfection. Such a teleological worldview was held by many of the great philosophers. Modern science, however, has been unable to substantiate the existence of such a cosmic teleology. Nor have any mechanisms or laws been found that would permit the functioning of such a teleology. The conclusion of science has been that final causes of this type do not exist.[64]

Despite this, presentations of biological evolution to the general public often depict evolution as a directed process. Invertebrates are followed by fishes, which are followed by amphibians, which are followed by reptiles, which are followed by mammals, and finally *Homo sapiens*. The existence of evolution directed from the simple towards the complex would be a good argument in favor of orthogenetic theories. According to Gould, however, no directionality can be found in evolution, if studied in detail:

> Our impression that life evolves toward greater complexity is probably only a bias inspired by parochial focus on ourselves, and consequent overattention to complexifying creatures, while we ignore just as many lineages adapting equally well by becoming simpler in form. The morphologically degenerate parasite, safe within its host, has just as much prospect for evolutionary success as its gorgeously elaborate relative coping with the slings and arrows of outrageous fortune in a tough external world.[65]

2.2 Modern Concepts of Species and Evolution

Today, Darwinism is one of the central theories in biology. All concepts developed in modern biology have to be compatible with evolution. In 1973 Theodosius Dobzhansky stated this very clearly in *The American Biology Teacher*: "Nothing in biology makes sense except in the light of evolution."[66] The philosophical implications of Darwinism, of course, strongly influence the definitions of biological nomenclature. This is particularly true for the term "species." Before considering modern species concepts some background in neo-Darwinism is given.

2.2.1 The Neo-Darwinian Theory of Biological Evolution. The commonly proposed scientific model for the biological evolution of life on earth starts with the pre-biotic soup.[67] The soup is believed to have provided our planet with preliminary forms of life. The historical details of this process are largely unknown and may resist any attempt to become uncovered.[68] The oldest fossils are between two and four billion years old, originating from single celled organisms. Multicellular organisms appeared at the beginning of the Cambrium about 600 million years ago.[69]

According to neo-Darwinian theory, the target of evolution is the genome, or the *genotype*. It consists of a "program" containing the complete genetic constitution of an organism: how to run the cell, how to find food, how to react in difficult situations, how to interpret the program, etc., in short, its total potentiality. The actual properties an organism displays, as produced by interaction with the environment, is called the *phenotype*. The genotype is encoded in long polymer RNA chains for a few primitive organisms or in DNA chains for most primitive and all higher organisms. It consists only of four monomers, the elementary building blocks of DNA. The four elementary units, the nucleotides, are designated by the characters A, C, G and T (U for RNA). These four characters stand for the bases adenine, cytosine, guanine and thymine (uracil for RNA). The whole genome is made up of these four letters, and the precise sequence of these letters defines the genomic message and its translation-product, the phenotype, i.e., the particular living organism. The total chain length for bacteria is typically five million and for humans three billion nucleotides.[70] DNA and RNA are the genetic material common to all known living system on earth. Even the rules of translation into phenotype are exactly the same in all living cells with only rare exceptions.

For single-celled organisms reproduction means cell division, wherein a mother cell divides into two daughter cells. To provide both daughter cells with the necessary genetic information, the DNA must be copied. Although fidelity in gene-reproduction is very high,[71] occasionally errors occur. If a single letter is replaced by one of the three others, such a mutation is designated a point mutation. Deletions or insertions of parts of sequences are also possible. After cell division there is a certain probability that the genes of the two daughter cells will be different. Because the positions and directions of the mutations are unpredictable, they are considered to be random.

Many alterations in the genomic sequence will be lethal or will reduce the ability of the cell to face the needs of life. In rare cases, however, a mutation will improve the cell's capability to survive and to reproduce in its given or in a neighboring environment. Cells with the highest reproduction rates also have a good chance to spread their genes in the future. This rule is designated as *natural selection* or *the survival of the fittest*. Evolution in terms of neo-Darwinism can be considered the "diffusion" of the DNA sequences through the space of possible sequences using a four letter code accumulating increasingly potent genes. In principle, very similar rules apply for multicellular sexual reproduction.

2.2.2 Natural Selection as a Two-Step Process. Mayr and others describe natural selection as a two-step process. During the first step, mutations and recombination produce a wide range of variations. Random changes are, of course, a good way to achieve this goal. For example, after conception the male and female chromosomes mix to some extent. A few genes on the male chromosomes are randomly exchanged with those from the female chromosomes and vice versa. By this mechanism of *crossing over*, the different genes of a population reshuffle continuously.[72]

The second step consists in the selection of the most potent organisms that are best adapted for their particular environment. Mayr explains this view by contrasting it to typological thinking, to the static essentialistic species concept:

> Selection, for an essentialist, is a purely negative factor, a force which eliminates deleterious deviations from the norm. Darwin's opponents, therefore, insisted in the spirit of essentialism that selection could not create anything new. By saying this, they revealed that they have neither understood the two-step process of selection nor its populational nature. The first step is the production of an unlimited amount of new variation, that is, of new genotypes and phenotypes, particularly through genetic recombination rather than by mutation. The second step is the test to see which of the products of the first step are subjected to natural selection. Only those individuals that can pass this scrutiny become contributors to the gene pool of the next generation.[73]

Mayr breaks the process of evolution into two steps: (1) creating random variations in the genotypes, and (2) selecting phenotypes according to their ability to cope with the challenges of their environment. The question still remains how random changes in the genotype can lead to such "well-designed" adaptations as are found in nature.

The chances of obtaining the DNA sequence of an efficient enzyme within a few large mutation steps from scratch are by far too small. Such an event can practically be excluded by simple probabilistic estimates. Evolution becomes plausible only if it is possible to split up large evolutionary steps into many small gradual steps. Dawkins designates this concept as *cumulative selection*:

> We have seen that living things are too improbable and too beautifully 'designed' to have come into existence by chance. How, then, did they come into existence? The answer, Darwin's answer, is by gradual, step-by-step transformations from simple beginnings, from primordial entities sufficiently simple to have come into existence by chance. Each successive change in the gradual evolutionary process was simple enough, *relative to its predecessor*, to have arisen by chance. But the whole sequence of cumulative steps constitutes anything but a chance process, when you consider the complexity of the final end-product relative to the original starting point. The cumulative process is directed by nonrandom survival. The purpose of this chapter is to demonstrate the power of this *cumulative selection* as a fundamentally nonrandom process.[74]

Dawkins particularly emphasizes the cumulative character of evolution. The survival of DNA chains conserves small random favorable mutations. Each little improvement becomes subject to further gradual success.[75] Only if evolution can be decomposed into a sufficient number of small gradual progresses does neo-Darwinism become reasonable.[76]

2.2.3 *Relationships Between Species.* In classical biology the similarity between distinct species was understood to result from a unique "construction" plan of God resulting in the appearance of similar kinds of design several times in nature. The *scala naturae* was considered to represent a continuous spectrum of increasingly complex species. Although there was this scale of species, each species was seen to be distinct from all others from the very beginning, that is, from the time point of creation. Breeding was known to be possible only within species but not across species boundaries.

Because in classical biology the species is defined by its timeless essence, the resulting populations were likewise thought to be unchanging over time.

In the Darwinistic view, the situation is radically different. Here species do not depend on timeless essences, rather they are uniquely defined by their respective populations, and due to evolution populations change over time. If we go back in time, two closely related species that are clearly distinct today at some time merge in their common predecessor. The scale of originally distinct species of classical biology was replaced by a phylogenetic tree in Darwinian evolution. At branch points species split up into two separate populations to become distinct in the future.

Because most predecessors of modern species became extinct, we are not in the position to directly follow the tree of evolution down to its roots. How then can we infer the degree of biological relationship between putative cousin species? There are several ways to estimate the biological "distance" between species. The classical method is to compare the morphology. A similar form and constitution, and the presence of similar organs, often indicate a relationship. For the parts of a body preserved in the fossil record, such a comparison can be made throughout its history. Darwin's theory was based on this kind of data. Comparing modern and ancient species relics, Darwin arrived at a treelike relationship. Species can also be compared at the level of cellular organization.[77]

The most quantitative measure of biological relationship is RNA, DNA, and protein sequence analysis. Different parts of the genome of an organism have very different mutation rates. Genes coding for fundamental processes inside the cell, such as translating the DNA into protein sequences, are generally well conserved. Because no cell can live without such fundamental processes, they must have evolved very early during evolution. They are very similar throughout all organisms. Such sequences are important for estimating "long distance" relationships. Parts of the genome subject to intermediate mutation rates indicate relationships of intermediate distances. For example, between *Homo sapiens* and chimpanzees about 98% of the DNA sequences are identical. This is commonly interpreted to mean that the higher primates and *Homo sapiens* share a common ancestor. There are biological essays available to estimate the distances among DNA or RNA sequences directly. According to such a measure of the degree of relationship, the closest living non-human relatives to *Homo sapiens* are the chimpanzees.[78] Other parts of the genome, such as mitochondrial DNA, have very high mutation rates. They reveal relationships within species, for example, between human races.[79]

Neo-Darwinism predicts a specific kind of relationship pattern between the species: the "relationship distances" should clearly form a tree. If the sequence distances of many sequences are compared, one can distinguish mathematically different topologies such as trees, stars, or networks. A starlike pattern, for example, would suggest that all sequences originated from a separate origin and since then developed independently in parallel to other sequences. An arbitrary network would indicate no evolutionary relationship at all between the sequences. The comparison of t-RNA, RNA, DNA, or other protein sequences generally leads to a treelike relationship between distantly related species.[80] There exist examples where we can study evolution "at work." The analysis of viral DNA, where the mutation rates are sufficiently large to make evolution visible, favors the treelike relationship.[81] This treelike form of sequence distances is a strong argument in favor of neo-Darwinism.

2.2.4 *Population Thinking as the Basis for Modern Species Definitions.* A major distinction between classical and modern definitions of biological species is the complete rejection of essentialistic species concepts, (i.e., of typological thinking) in modern views. According to Mayr: "Essentialism was not the only ideology Darwin had to overcome."[82] Consequently, a new fundament for a species definition was adopted which does account for evolution:

> The old species concept, based on the metaphysical concept of an essence, is so fundamentally different from the biological concept of a reproductively isolated population that a gradual changeover from one into the other was not possible. What was required was a conscious rejection of the essentialist concept. . . . The first [difficulty with

applying essentialistic concepts to life] was that no evidence could be found for the existence of an underlying essence of "form" responsible for the sharply defined discontinuities in nature. In other words, there is no way of determining the essence of a species, hence no way of using the essence as a yardstick in doubtful cases. The second difficulty was posed by conspicuous polymorphism, that is, the occurrence of strikingly different individuals in nature which nevertheless, by their breeding habits or life histories, could be shown to belong to a single reproductive community. The third difficulty was the reverse of the second one, that is the occurrence in nature of "forms" which clearly differed in their biology (behavior, ecology) and were reproductively isolated from each other yet could not be distinguished morphologically.[83]

For the classification of the different life forms, no clear-cut features could be discovered that define a species and that necessarily distinguish it from all others. Such features should define a species uniquely, not only compared to present populations, but also in relation to the ancestors of the present ones. In contrast, one can clearly give a set of characteristics that uniquely define an electron. If all those characteristics are found for a certain particle, one can be sure that it is an electron. These characteristics are timeless. They would have applied a billion years ago and will be the same in another billion years. Such unchanging characteristics, however, do not exist in living systems. This situation becomes even more complicated by the existence of species where members show extreme variability in their appearance. There are also populations of morphologically indistinguishable individuals belonging to different reproductive communities, that is, to different species!

A characteristic of important physical features of the universe is their time invariance. A typical example is the law of the conservation of energy. In contrast, most important biological characteristics are the product of a long history. The physicist Max Delbrück states: "A mature physicist, acquainting himself for the first time with the problems of biology, is puzzled by the circumstance that there are no 'absolute phenomena' in biology. Everything is time-bound and space-bound. The animal or plant or micro-organism he is working with is but a link in an evolutionary chain of changing forms, none of which has any permanent validity."[84] Such a dependence of populations on their own particular history is alien to the idea of a static world. Species in classical biology were assumed to have been perfectly created by means of a first original couple, and thereafter to have no history of change. They were perfect from the beginning, living in a harmonious, perfect, static universe. Only minor adaptations within a population were allowed in this view.

The *historicity* of the fauna and flora clearly distinguishes most fields of biology from physics and chemistry.[85] In biology, references to an organism's history is the rule and not the exception:

> There is hardly any structure or function in an organism that can be fully understood unless it is studied against this historical background. To find causes for the existing characteristics, and particularly adaptations, of organisms is the main preoccupation of the evolutionary biologist. He is impressed by the enormous diversity as well as the pathway by which it has been achieved. He studies the forces that bring about changes in faunas and floras (as in part documented by paleontology), and he studies the steps by which have evolved the miraculous adaptations so characteristic of every aspect of the organic world.[86]

This explicit dependence of life on its history makes it impossible to apply the classical concept of essences as it was applied in classical biology, which assumes that the form of a particular cat is defined only by a timeless reality considered to be independent of the details of the particular history of the ancestors of this cat.

Instead of referring to a timeless species essence, the concept of species in modern biology is related to actually existing populations. A species is defined by an existing community of interbreeding individuals. Only recently it was recognized that this concept of species has much in common with the respective ideas of Aristotle. According to Mayr the major difference between essentialistic species concepts and those based on populations is the emphasis on the individual:

> Population thinkers stress the uniqueness of everything in the organic

world. What is important for them is the individual, not the type. They emphasize that every individual in sexually reproducing species is uniquely different from all others, with much individuality even existing in uniparentally reproducing ones. There is no "typical" individual, and mean values are abstractions. Much of what in the past has been designated in biology as "classes" are populations consisting of unique individuals.[87]

Modern definitions of a species are based on a group of individuals being able to produce common fertile offspring. Mayr defines a "species" as follows: "A species is a reproductive community of populations (reproductively isolated from others) that occupies a specific niche in nature."[88] There also exist other modern species definitions, but their particular differences are irrelevant to the purpose of this essay.

2.3 Summary

In classical biology species were thought to be defined and maintained by their species essence. The species present today were assumed to be the offsprings of the first couples originated by a Creator. In this view, only an intelligent Creator could have produced such a diversity of purposely well-adapted organisms. Typological thinking remained widely accepted into the second half of the nineteenth century. Biologists such as Cuvier (1769-1832) easily won disputes against evolution in favor of this classical understanding of biology.[89]

Because of the findings made in biology and paleontology, the classical concept of species became increasingly questionable. The biological populations inhabiting the earth were not always the same. They changed drastically during the geological history of this planet. The increasing number of facts pointing toward the evolution of life and toward the historical development of the characteristics of various populations made it more and more clear that the classical concept of fixed species essences corresponding to unchanging biological populations was unfeasible.

This situation led to a complete rejection of the classical concept of species essences. Typological thinking was replaced by population thinking. Today, species are defined as reproductively isolated populations occupying an ecological niche. The ability to interbreed and produce fertile offspring is a necessary condition to include two members of different sex in the same species. The particular characteristics of a species are thought to be entirely defined by its gene pool and to be maintained by the high fidelity of gene reproduction. According to this modern definition, species have no timeless, independent essence. They are names used by human scientists to classify an interbreeding population. Thus, Darwin's theory of evolution not only changed the theory of the origin of the different organisms on earth, but by replacing essentialism with a nominalistic school of thought, it modified the whole philosophy of biology.

A VICTORIAN CARTOON (C. 1890)

Satirizes the theory of evolution by depicting the development of lower forms of life into apes. Note that one ape looses his tail when it is bitten off by the one behind. Birds develop from flying fish. Evolution culminates with a figure of Darwin himself.

Section 3

The Origin of Complex Order in Our Universe

One of the central questions in philosophy and religion has ever been the question of the origin of the universe in general and that of the complex order of life in particular. The nearly perfect adaptedness of living systems to their environment, their expediency and complexity cries for an explanation. Dawkins in one of his books has the aim of impressing "the reader with the power of the illusion of design." He continues: "We shall look at a particular example and shall conclude that, when it comes to complexity and beauty of design, Paley[91] hardly even began to state the case."[90] For instance, the hawk's eye is able to see from a long distance a little mouse moving in the fields, bees can determine the position of the sun, even in the presence of clouds, to relocate flowers rich with nectar, and some crabs in the deep sea are able to detect single photons. One can fill a series of books with examples where "nature" has found marvelous solutions for survival under extreme conditions or in special situations.

It is an everyday experience that all kinds of order have the tendency to disperse. Books, marbles, and tools are only seldom at places we expect them to be! Keeping a certain level of order requires our attention, time, and energy. This tendency of order toward corruption is very general; it holds for our desk as well as for nearly every aspect of life. In physics, this tendency has been formulated as a fundamental law of nature: the second law of thermodynamics. Consequently, the origin, existence, and maintenance of order requires an explanation, a cause.

3.1 Explaining Complex Order

What does it mean to "explain" something and what is meant by the term "complex order." Does explaining always imply that the explained may be grounded in something else? But this would lead to an infinite chain of explanations! Are there things or events which are self-evident without need of an explanation? Complex order is particularly evident in biology and in human artifacts. How can we distinguish complex order, such as that found in living organisms, from trivial order?

Three possible causes of the origin of order are generally accepted: (1) accident, (2) necessity, and (3) voluntary design. Keith Ward describes these three kinds of explanations for the origin of complex order: "There are three main possible answers to these questions. One is that there is simply no explanation. The universe just came into existence by chance, for no reason, and that is that. Another is that it all happened by necessity. There was no alternative. A third is that the universe is created by God for a particular purpose."[92] The origin of order by chance is called a *bottom-up* process. The order is assumed to come from nothing. Necessary causation is regarded as a *horizontal* process: only those events can occur which are necessary all along. Nothing is added, nothing escapes. In contrast to these, voluntary design is a *top-down* process in which complex order is created by a Creator at least as "complex" as His creation.

3.1.1 *Explaining Things.* It is one of the central messages of Dawkins' book *The Blind Watchmaker* that life is complex and that this intricate order, so characteristic for living organisms, is in need of an explanation: "The complexity of living organisms is matched by the elegant efficiency of their apparent design. If anyone doesn't agree that this amount of complex design cries out for an explanation, I give up."[93] "Explaining" a particular event generally means to tell what causes that event to have occurred at that time. Apples fall to the ground because the wind shakes the tree. Such kinds of explanations often lead to a chain of explanations, to an infinite regression, because one can extend the question to what causes the wind to blow and shake the apple tree, and what causes that, and what causes . . . and so on.

"Explanation" can also mean that particular events are explainable by general rules. For instance, Newtonian mechanics explains the paths of the planets and the falling of apples on earth by the same law of gravitation. But this second kind of explanation may also lead to a chain because Einstein's general theory of relativity "explains" Newton's particular theory. The temporal regression leads to the question of a First Cause, and the hierarchical regression leads to the question of the most general theory.[94]

Of course, by stating the need for an explanation one, implicitly assumes that such an explanation exists. All natural sciences depend essentially on such an assumption. Science would make no sense in a reality that has no structure allowing for explanations, i.e., for a clear relation between cause and effect. A universe in which events have no (or only weak) relations, in which everything occurs accidentally, cannot be explained. The Bahá'í writings explicitly propose that our universe follows strong cause and effect relations. In the Lawḥ-i Ḥikmát, Bahá'u'lláh states:

> Every thing must needs have an origin and every building a builder . . . Nature in its essence is the embodiment of My Name, the Maker, the Creator. Its manifestations are diversified by varying causes, and in this diversity there are signs for men of discernment. Nature is God's Will and is its expression in and through the contingent world. It is a dispensation of Providence ordained by the Ordainer, the All-Wise.[95]

In this passage, Bahá'u'lláh clearly states the necessity of cause and effect relations by claiming an "origin" for "every thing" and a "builder" for "every building." Such cause and effect relations are not only applied to individual instances, (e.g. the sun as the cause and its rays as the effect) but are used on a general level. God's Will is stated to be the general cause of our universe, which is the effect. "Nature" is considered to be the effect of the creative force of God's name "the Creator" and the expression of God's Will "in and through the contingent world." 'Abdu'l-Bahá likewise emphasized the significance of cause and effect: "Every cause is followed by an effect and vice versa; there could be no effect without a cause preceding it."[96] According to this statement, every effect requires a cause, and nothing may happen without a cause. A substantially complex outcome requires a respectively complex origin. This argument is analogous to the second law of thermodynamics. Only disorder occurs on its own; complex order needs a non-trivial origin.

3.1.2 *Complex Order.* The origin of our universe as well as the origin of life is closely related to the question of the origin of complex order. According to modern physics, matter is made up of a combination of a few types of quarks. The different forms of matter, therefore, show various kinds of order of those quarks. The existence of quarks as such is not sufficient to produce multiple kinds of matter, so the order among the quarks is crucial.

One can distinguish two kinds of order: (1) regular patterns as in crystals, and (2) meaningful messages as in a text (e.g., hopefully this essay). The first kind of order is that of physics; its measure is entropy. It is subject to the second law of thermodynamics.[97] The second kind of order, related to the meaning of a message, depends on a specific context. In this case, the order of the letters is not important, but the message those letters convey. Outside a specific context, the order becomes meaningless. For most Europeans, a Sanskrit or Arabic text would not contain much information. The entropy measure does not apply to such kinds of order.

A possible measure of complex order is the degree by which a system deviates from randomness. A repetitive pattern, for instance, deviates from randomness. The design of functional watches as well as the precise amino acid sequence of an efficient enzyme are also clear deviations from randomness. Something showing all signs of good design we would not consider to be produced accidentally. Accordingly, Dawkins defines complex order as follows:

> A complex thing is something whose constituent parts are arranged in a way that is unlikely to have arisen by chance alone. . . . The minimum requirement for us to recognize an object as an animal or plant is that it should succeed in making a living *of some sort* (more precisely that it, or at least some members of its kind, should live long enough to reproduce). . . . The answer we have arrived at is that complicated things have some quality, specifiable in advance, that is highly unlikely to have been acquired by random chance alone.[98]

Dawkins here uses probability and functionality as criteria to define complex biological order. According to this understanding, something is complex if it is functional and the probability of forming it by chance alone is so small that its occurrence is unlikely during the existence of our universe.

'Abdu'l-Bahá presents a similar definition of complex order, but like Paley he concludes that complex order must be the result of design:

> Likewise every arrangement and formation that is not perfect in its order we designate as accidental, and that which is orderly, regular, perfect in its relations, and every part of which is in its proper place and is the essential requisite of the other constituent parts, this we call a composition formed through will and knowledge.[99]

Proper design constitutes a clear deviation from randomness. Because an accidental formation of such order is highly improbable, chance cannot explain complex order. The major difference between modern and classical explanations is that modern theories often try to base order on trivialities whereas classical concepts base it on voluntary design.

3.2 The Origin of Order in Modern Cosmologies

Modern explanations for the origin of complex order in this universe generally try to avoid getting trapped in the problem of an infinite regression. Such chains of causation are not satisfying because they always ask for further elements of the chain, for further even more fundamental explanations. Any explanation given at a certain level invites iteration to its metalevel, and again to its metalevel, and so forth. There is no obvious way to finish this regress.

3.2.1 *Physical Cosmologies.* The cosmological concepts of the nineteenth century were generally based on the laws of the conservation of energy and matter: energy cannot be created or destroyed but only changes in form. Haeckel wrote: "the conservation of energy and matter ruled at all times, as it applies today."[100] The universe was thought to be infinite in space and time. Haeckel understood the laws of conservation as a proof that this universe was not created: "All . . . forms of belief in creation are incompatible with the laws of the conservation of matter, which do not know a beginning of the world."[101]

Büchner believed that by means of such a concept he could escape the problem of an infinite regression: "What cannot be destroyed cannot be created. In other words, the world as such is without a cause; it is uncreated and everlasting."[102] Here, Aristotle's argument against an infinite regression is "solved" by assuming that the chain of temporal causes is infinite indeed and, therefore, does not need any "first" cause. Although the assumed eternity of the universe solves the problem of a temporal regression, the question of the hierarchical regress and the origin of order still remains. Consequently, Haeckel concluded that the only world mystery (German: *Welträtsel*) left unsolved by his monistic philosophy was the existence of matter as such: "This monistic philosophy accepts only a single, all-embracing mystery: the problem of matter."[103]

Today the situation in cosmology is fundamentally different. The universe is considered to be finite in space and time. Thus, temporal regression starts at the Big Bang. Particularly in cosmology, modern materialistic authors try to ground regression in self-evident states, claiming that complex order emerges from a trivial self-evident structure of matter. Atkins states:

There is nothing that cannot be understood, there is nothing that cannot be explained, and everything is extraordinarily simple. . . . A great deal of the universe does not need any explanation. Elephants, for instance. Once molecules have learned to compete and to create other molecules in their own image, elephants, and things resembling elephants, will in due course be found roaming through the country-side.[104]

In these concepts, the structure of our universe is claimed to be ultimately reducible to a self-evident level. Ward shows that the fundamental assumptions of Atkins are based purely on faith, not on facts or on science.

Wheeler proposes a trivial origin of the universe as a result of the concept that "the boundary of boundary is zero":

> So far as we can see today, the laws of physics cannot have existed from everlasting to everlasting. They must have come into being at the big bang. There were no gears and pinions, no Swiss watchmakers to put things together, not even a pre-existing plan. . . . Only a principle of organization which is no organization at all would seem to offer itself. In all of mathematics, nothing of this kind more obviously offers itself than the principle that "the boundary of boundary is zero."[105]

Here Wheeler refers to the fact that fundamental laws in physics are often formulated or can be transformed into conservation laws: the conservation of energy, the conservation of electric charge, etc. These laws can be stated to say that the change of the total energy of a whole system (or a respective conserved entity) is zero during any time interval. The laws of motion can also be formulated with respect to the conservation of momentum. Wheeler apparently identifies the zero on the left-hand side of those equations with nothing, which in turn gives rise to the complex theory on the right-hand side.[106] The complexity of the equation is not found in the "zero" but in the right-hand side, in the algebra of the equations which are, therefore, non-trivial.[107] Obviously, Wheeler only hides the problem of an infinite regression behind the phrase "the boundary of boundary is zero," but he does not solve it.

3.2.2 *Dennett's Darwinian Cosmology.* Dennett tries to escape the problem of an infinite regression not in a single step as Atkins or Wheeler do, but in many small gradual steps. Dennett proposes a kind of "Darwinian cosmology." As biological order is obtained via natural selection, he considers cosmological order to be generated by cosmological selection. He extends Darwin's concept of natural selection to cosmology and consciousness:

> Darwin's idea had been born as an answer to questions in biology, but it threatened to leak out, offering answers—welcome or not—to questions in cosmology (going in one direction) and psychology (going in the other direction). If *re*design could be a mindless, algorithmic process of evolution, why couldn't that whole process itself be the product of evolution, and so forth, *all the way down*? And if mindless evolution could account for the breathtakingly clever artifacts of the biosphere, how could the products of our own "real" minds be exempt from an evolutionary explanation? Darwin's idea thus also threatened to spread *all the way up*, dissolving the illusion of our own authorship, our own divine spark of creativity and understanding.[108]

In biology the concept of natural selection is explained by random variation of the genotype and selection by means of the survival or death of the phenotype. Dennett does not explain what is varied or what the criteria for selection are. In principle, his concept implies the existence of a meta-universe where meta-genotypes (the laws of the different cosmoses) are varied and meta-phenotypes (the different cosmoses themselves) survive or die according to the rules of meta-selection. Thus, Dennett only adds an element in the hierarchical regression without explaining the existence of the meta-universe and the origin of the meta-selection rules.

Dennett assumes that the existence of accidentally found cosmological order does not need any further explanation:

> What is left is what the process, shuffling through eternity, mindlessly finds (when it finds anything): a timeless Platonic possibility of order. That is indeed a thing of beauty, as mathematicians are forever exclaiming, but it is not itself something intelligent but, wonder of

wonders, something intelligible. Being abstract and outside of time, it is nothing with an *initiation* or *origin* in need of explanation.[109]

The only Platonic element which Dennett thinks his system requires is "a timeless Platonic possibility of order." All the rest of the order we discover in our universe is proposed to be found by the "mindless, algorithmic process of evolution." But does not "to find something" always mean that this "something" existed before it was found? And what does "to find something" mean in this context? To randomly sample some laws does not lead to cosmological order. Only if cosmological selection "knows" what to look for can order result!

Dennett does not explain why his "Platonic possibility of order" which is "abstract and outside of time" does not require "an *initiation* or *origin* in need of explanation." He simply takes its existence for granted. Apparently, Dennett proposes a set of self-creative laws of nature similar to what Monod envisioned for the self-creation of biological characteristics. (See Section 3.3.2) In this sense, the laws of nature are not preexistent but self-selected for during cosmology.

Dennett's approach parallels that of Wheeler who similarly assumes "a principle of organization which is no organization at all." According to Dennett, the laws ruling the existence and inter-action of elementary particles must have been selected for at some time, because the selection step always needs some time. The launching of the chemical laws must have taken place at a very early stage of the universe. Otherwise one would expect that the chem-istry of the early phase of the universe would have been different from today. If the form of the laws are not predetermined by any kind of timeless abstract order, one would expect different chemistries in different parts of the universe. In addition, without time-invariant laws of nature, new self-creations could change them at any time point and at any place within our universe. Dennett would have to explain why the chemical laws are apparently the same everywhere and all the time in the known universe.[110]

Atkins and Dennett as well as Wheeler propose a bottom-up version of cosmogony, for the origin of complex order within our universe.

Each of them claim to have reduced this origin to some self-evident principle, to "primeval simplicity." Atkins and Wheeler principally assume a timeless natural law which determines their cosmogony; that is, that order exists potentially from the beginning, but its unfolding requires time. Consequently, they really are suggesting a horizontal kind of evolution in which the actual order consists in the unfolding of a time-invariant potential order. Only Dennett appears to propose a genuine bottom-up cosmogony. However, as shown below, because he describes his model as an algorithmic process, his model is also at best horizontal. Thus, a more careful analysis of these cosmogonies shows that they assume the a priori existence of the complexity they claim to explain. The general cause and effect principle holds for these concepts: A complex outcome requires a complex origin.

3.3 The Origin of Order in Modern Biology

In cosmology the resulting order often appears to be a direct consequence of laws of nature with little room left for alternatives. In contrast, in biology complex order seems to be rather arbitrary with uncountable ways in which it could be different. In addition, the order in biology is always functional and generally extremely complex. How can such a complex biological order be explained; where does it come from? Is it the result of pure chance as proposed by Monod, or is it the outcome of a mindless algorithm as suggested by Dennett? What guides nature to select between efficient and inefficient forms of life? Such questions are analyzed below.

3.3.1 *Forces Deciding Life or Death.* If the process of evolution is able to produce and maintain the complex order of the biosphere, the particular process that creates this order has to be identified. As explained by Mayr, evolution consists of two steps: (1) creating random, undirected variations in the genotypes (that is, the DNA sequences), and (2) selecting the phenotypes (that is, the resulting organisms) according to their ability to cope with the odds of their environment. The random production of variability in the genetic information by means of mutations and recombinations needs no further explanation. It agrees with the second law of thermodynamics that the order stored in the DNA chains, as with any other kind of order, has the tendency to get corrupted.

In neo-Darwinism complex biological order is considered to be formed gradually by likely probabilistic causes (mutation and recombination) and accidental or necessary causes (natural selection). Because the unsuccessful genes quickly get lost, successful information is kept and reproduced; and the repeated cumulation of small improvements over a long time leads to the creation of complex biological order. According to Dawkins: "Cumulative selection, by slow and gradual degrees, is the explanation, the only workable explanation that has ever been proposed, for the existence of life's complex design."[111] Accidental improvements, however, cannot result in evolution as long as they are not selected for. Natural selection decides which individuals and, in the long run, which species survive. It is the "driving force" of evolution. It "preserves" successful genes and "rejects" defective ones. Consequently, to understand the origin of order in biology, this selection step must be understood.

What kind of force "selects" for survival? According to Mayr, there exists no particular external force which decides over life and death: "There is no particular selective force in nature, nor a definite selecting agent. There are many possible causes for the success of the few survivors. . . . It is not the environment that selects, but the organism that copes with the environment more or less successfully. There is no external selection force."[112] But where does complex order come from? In nature one finds that order sometimes appears spontaneously, as for instance, in the case of the Bénard instability.[113] But what is the origin of such a kind of order?

Systems almost always have the peculiarity that the characteristics of the whole cannot (not even in theory) be deduced from the most complete knowledge of the components, taken separately or in other partial combinations. The appearance of new characteristics in wholes has been designated *emergence*. Emergence has often been invoked in attempts to explain such difficult phenomena as life, mind, and consciousness. Actually, emergence is equally characteristic of inorganic systems.[114]

Today two major positions are held regarding the origin of genetic information, of where the "knowledge" to form wings and eyes comes from. The first position assumes the *ad hoc* origination of order, as for instance proposed by Monod. The information emerges, created *de novo* on the path of evolution. If the newly evolved characteristics are not the consequence of laws of nature, they must emerge as new *ad hoc* creations. The second position understands evolution as the unfolding of order inherent in laws of nature, as a process that makes implicit order visible, that transforms potential order into actual order. This understanding of the origin of complex biological order is closer to Plato's concept of essences.

Monod compares these two concepts of the origin of order in evolution. He designates the *ad hoc* emergence of order as *creation* and the unfolding of an inherent order of nature as *revelation*. For him, evolution consists in the emergence of absolutely new biological characteristics:

> Bergson, on s'en souvient, voyait dans l'évolution l'expression d'une force créatrice, *absolue* en ce sens qu'il ne la supposait pas tendue à une autre fin que la création en elle-même. En cela, il diffère radicalement des animistes (qu'il s'agisse d'Engels, de Teilhard ou des positivistes optimistes tels que Spencer) qui tous voient dans l'évolution le majestueux déroulement d'un programme inscrit dans la trame même de l'Univers. Pour eux, par conséquent, l'évolution n'est pas véritablement création, mais uniquement *révélation* des intentions jusque-là inexprimées de la nature. D'où la tendance à voir dans le développement embryonnaire une émergence de même orde que l'émergence évolutive. Selon la théorie moderne, la notion de *révélation* s'applique au développement épigénétique, mais non, bien entendu, à l'émergence évolutive qui, grâce précisément au fait qu'elle prend sa source dans l'imprévisible essentiel, est créatrice de nouveauté *absolue*.[115]

Monod explains Bergson's ideas, for whom evolution is the expression of a life-giving force, of an *élane vital*, whose only purpose is creation as such. He transforms this concept, which for Bergson was a vitalistic one, into a materialistic one, making absolutely new characteristics emerge during evolution as *de novo* creations. Monod compares the view of the "animists" with ontogenesis, that is, with the development of the embryo. The fertilized cell starts to repeatedly divide itself. The daughter cells then specialize and organize according to their genetic plan. In this case, the potential order encoded in the assembly of genes originating from the sperm and the egg cell, the genotype, is transformed into the actual order of the organism, the phenotype. Just as embryonic development consists in the actualization of the information stored in its genome, evolution based on the existence of a potential order "reveals" the implicit order encoded in fundamental laws of nature.

3.3.2 *Evolution as Ad Hoc Self-Creation*. Monod claims that evolution is mainly based on chance.[116] He bases this conclusion on his discovery that DNA sequences appear to be largely random; in other words, DNA sequences show only a weak pattern of statistical order: "Lessage qui, par tous les critères possibles, semble avoir été écrit au hasard. . . . D'un jeu totalement aveugle, tout, par définition, peut sortir, y compris la vision elle-même."[117] According to Monod, the apparent randomness of DNA sequences excludes the possibility that life is the reflection of laws inherent in nature. He then concludes that the appearance of life on earth as well as on other planets is an extremely unlikely event. He expects that terrestrial life is singular in our universe:

> L'hypothèse n'est pas exclue, au contraire, par la structure actuelle da la biosphère, que l'événement décisif ne se soit produit *qu'une seule fois*. Ce qui signifierait que sa probabilité *a priori* était quasi nulle. . . . Nous n'avons, à l'heure actuelle, pas le droit d'affirmer, ni celui de nier que la vie soit apparue *une seule fois* sur la Terre, et que, par conséquent, avant qu'elle ne fût, ses chances d'être étaient quasi nulles.[118]

Because of the gigantic improbability of the result of evolution by chance, today chance as the primary source of complex life is generally rejected. Most modern evolution biologists would agree that pure chance cannot explain the complex order of life: "The essence of life is statistical improbability on a colossal scale. Whatever is the explanation for life, therefore, it cannot be chance. The true explanation for the existence of life must embody the very antithesis of chance."[119] Using the results of modern molecular biology, it is clear that the diverse complex order present in the biosphere cannot have originated by pure chance. Such a view can be excluded by means of a simple probabilistic argument.[120] Consequently, a purely accidental origin of life can be excluded.

Thus, Monod claims a bottom-up process in which order appears by chance as an *ad hoc* self-creation. It is not clear what Monod meant by "créatrice de nouveauté absolue." Does he claim that a certain protein molecule can catalyze certain reactions today that it could not have done yesterday? For instance, since when could myoglobin bind oxygen and what function did it have before, if it had any? Only with such an understanding of evolution can one speak of an "absolutely new creation." The alternative view that the protein function existed as a potential function before its first realization, but was not yet disclosed, would depict evolution as the unfolding of inherent potentials, a view rejected by Monod. Thus, Monod's concept of the creation of absolutely new characteristics raises severe problems for studying evolution. We would have nearly no means to reconstruct the past from the present. We would not know which of the biological laws relevant today are applicable to past organisms. For those rules that did change we would not know their "ancient" forms.[121] In such a world, palaeontology would be rather difficult, if not impossible.

With Monod's concept of self-creative evolution, a scientific theory of evolution is impossible. Essential unpredictability cannot be the foundation for formulating laws that predict certain outcomes. An irreproducible reality does not allow the formulation of statements about reproducible experiments, which are essential requirements for modern scientific theories.[122] Evolution as *ad hoc* self-creation thus implies that a scientific explanation for the existence of complex biological order does not exist![123]

3.3.3 *Evolution as Cumulative Selection.* Whereas Monod considers life to be the result of pure chance, for Dawkins evolution is the very opposite of chance. According to his view, life evolves in a necessary manner by cumulative selection:

There is the familiar, and I have to say rather irritating, confusion of natural selection with "randomness." Mutation is random; natural selection is the very opposite of random. . . . This belief, that Darwinian evolution is "random," is not merely false. It is the exact opposite of the truth. Chance is a minor ingredient in the Darwinian recipe, but the most important ingredient is cumulative selection which is quintessentially *non*random.[124]

According to Dawkins, cumulative natural selection necessarily leads to the evolution of a complex biosphere. Thus, cumulative selection appears to present a mechanism which produces complex order nearly out of nothing, by means of a long, long series of very likely little accidents: "It took a very large leap of the imagination for Darwin and Wallace to see that, contrary to all intuition, there is another way and, once you have understood it, a far more plausible way, for complex 'design' to arise out of primeval simplicity."[125]

Dawkins' explanation of order emerging from a trivial origin is that death is a trivial event:

In nature, the usual selecting agent is direct, stark and simple. It is the grim reaper. Of course, the *reasons* for survival are anything but simple—this is why natural selection can build animals and plants of such formidable complexity. But there is something very crude and simple about death itself. And nonrandom death is all it takes to select phenotypes, and hence the genes that they contain, in nature.[126]

Apparently, Dawkins considers the lack of virtues of those who die in the battle of evolution to be more important than the virtues of those who survive, who are the "fittest." But of course, evolution is driven by the biological characteristics of those who survive and not of those who die. Analogously, the excellence of those who pass an examination cannot be evaluated by the lack of knowledge of those who fail. Although Dawkins claims a bottom-up process for his evolution concept (where order emerges "out of primival simplicity"), he still does not explain where the order ultimately comes from.

As pointed out correctly by Ward, the gradual appearance of order begs the same level of explanation as its sudden emergence:

> It is false to suggest that it is somehow less puzzling to have a long step-by-step building up of complexity than to have an instantaneous origin of complexity. If lots of bits of metal slowly assemble themselves on my doorstep by simple stages into an automobile engine, that is just as puzzling as the sudden appearance of an automobile engine on my doorstep. . . . If complexity needs explaining, it needs explaining, however long it took to get there![127]

The concept of cumulative selection solves the problem of probability, but it does not solve the problem of selection. It only shifts the problem to the question, how does "selection know" what to select? Although natural selection is generally assumed to "choose" all those well-adapted organisms against the rest of lesser qualified competitors, many evolution biologists assume that the selection step requires no further explanation, and that no particular *selective force* is necessary to explain evolution. If this step is trivial, selection would be an elegant name for the tautology of the *survival of the survivor*. If this step is non-trivial, as indicated by mathematical evolution models,[128] then this selection step needs further explanation.

3.3.4 Evolution as Algorithm. Dennett recently elaborated on evolution in his book *Darwin's Dangerous Idea*: "Darwin described how a Nonintelligent Artificer could produce those adaptions over vast amounts of time, and proved that many of the intermediate stages that would be needed by that proposed process have indeed occurred."[129] After reformulating the process of evolution as an algorithmic process, he states:

> It is hard to believe that something as mindless and mechanical as an algorithm could produce such wonderful things. No matter how impressive the products of an algorithm, the underlying process always consists of nothing but a set of individually mindless steps succeeding each other without the help of any intelligent supervision. . . . Can it [the actual biosphere] really be the outcome of nothing but a cascade of algorithmic processes feeding on chance? And if so, who designed that cascade? Nobody. It is itself the product of a blind, algorithmic process.[130]

Dennett describes biological evolution as an *ad hoc* process of the origin of order. The complex forms of life are created by a mindless algorithm. Life has no purpose, no goal. According to him, we are merely "the product of a blind, algorithmic process." However, only for utterly simple algorithms one might expect that no further explanation is needed. But what are the characteristics of "simple" algorithms? It is certainly the opposite of complex! So what is the complexity of an algorithm? At present, there exists no generally accepted definition for complexity. A reasonable, however not optimal, definition for measuring the degree of complexity is Kolmogorov's algorithmic complexity.[131] Because Dennett describes evolution as an algorithm, this measure of complexity is particularly applicable for his approach.[132] According to this measure, Dennett's evolution algorithm cannot be simple.[133] The claim that a simple algorithm without need of explanation can produce complex results is, therefore, self-contradictory. Consequently, although Dennett claims to describe a bottom-up mechanism of evolution without "need of explanation," his formulation of evolution as an algorithmic process actually places his concept into the category of horizontal evolution.

3.3.5 *Evolution as the Unfolding of Inherent Potentials.* In the second view about the origin of order, emergent properties represent inherent properties of the system. The emergent properties are assumed to "reveal" an inherent potential order encoded in timeless laws of nature, often completely unexpected.[134] Mathematical biologists generally support this second concept of evolution, since the self-creation of essentially new, unpredictable, and irreproducible characteristics cannot be modeled mathematically.

Interestingly, Dawkins proposes a similar idea. He speaks about the DNA sequence space as a mathematical space which potentially contains all possible forms of life: "There is another mathematical space filled . . . with flesh and blood animals made of billions of cells, each containing tens of thousands of genes. . . . The actual animals that have ever lived on Earth are a tiny subset of the theoretical animals that *could* exist."[135] Dawkins states here that there exists a space of all possible DNA sequences that define all possible forms of life. If all possible life forms exists a priori in the form of an abstract timeless DNA (RNA) sequence space, then, in principle, the universe is complex a priori. All potential forms of life are pre-existent. Mutations, recombinations, and natural selection provide the dynamics within this sequence space. In a stochastic sense, they determine the time points of the appearance of the different populations, and they unfold the potential forms of life into actually existing biological organisms.

In practice, the fitness related to a particular DNA sequence, its capacity for survival, can be estimated only for extremely simplified systems.[136] The fitness function directly reflects the reproduction rate, that is, the ability of a system to produce as many qualified offsprings as possible. In evolution models based on an abstract timeless order, the genotype is selected according to criteria which are at least in principle objective and reproducible. Consequently, this kind of evolution is the unfolding of potential forms of life preexistent in the known or unknown laws of nature. These laws are assumed to be the ultimate causes and are not explainable themselves. Because this kind of evolution describes the unfolding of something already potentially existing, it is called horizontal evolution. Thus, actual order reflects a potential complexity that exists from the very beginning. According to such a view, during cosmogony, and during the development of life, nothing happens that, at least in principle, could not have happened at any other place and time, given the necessary environment.

3.4 Summary

Monod called his famous book *Chance and Necessity*. This title reflects the two steps of evolution explained by Dawkins and Mayr. Often the selection step is considered to be trivial in that one has only to look for the survivors. But the survivors are the products of selection and, consequently, need an explanation. The selection step can be compared with the final examination of students at a university. The selection between better and lesser qualified students requires skillful examiners and cannot be done by a "blind, mindless algorithm."[137] The examiners must encompass the students in knowledge if they want to give a fair judgment, if the outcome is supposed to reflect the student's knowledge.

Analogously, the selection for complex biological order requires a respectively complex fitness function. Biological evolution is possible not because many die, but because particular complex assemblies of chemical elements which form well-adapted, complex organisms exist.[138] In other words, evolution can be described as the revelation of this complex order defined by time-invariant laws of nature. The fitness function is only a consequence of the preexisting order. Thus, at a fundamental level, the appearance of biological order is not a problem of probability, as discussed by Hatcher[139] or Ward, but a question of the genuine source of this order.

A major advantage of concepts of *ad hoc* evolution is that they apparently solve the problem of an infinite regression. In such bottom-up models of evolution, complex order appears as an absolute, new creation, or, in the words of Monod, as a "créatrice de nouveauté *absolue*." But as shown above, the origin of small gains of order is not explained in those theories; it is simply assumed to exist. In contrast to *ad hoc* evolution models, concepts of evolution based on an abstract timeless order explain the appearance of order on a certain level, but they shift the problem of the origin of order to the assumed potential order. In principle, Dennett proposes such a concept by describing evolution as an algorithmic process. A typical mathematical evolution algorithm consists in a mutation step (chance) and in a selection step where the members of populations are selected according to predefined fitness functions (necessity).

Dawkins' model of cumulative selection by means of a sequence space or fitness function containing all possible forms of life also refers to such an evolution model. But the question of the origin of this fitness function, of the "expertise" to distinguish between fruitful and fruitless phenotypes, is not answered. Because a First Cause is not included in this second type of evolution model, it suffers from the problem of an infinite regression, and from Gödel's incompleteness theorem. (See Section 4.1 for more on these problems.)

CHARLES ROBERT DARWIN, LL.D., F.R.S.

In his *Descent of Man* he brought his own Species down as low as possible—*i.e.*, to "A Hairy Quadruped furnished with a Tail and Pointed Ears, and probably *Arboreal* in its habits"—which is a reason for the very general Interest in a "Family Tree." He has lately been turning his attention to the "Politic Worm."

A PUNCH CARTOON (C. 1880)
lampoons Darwin and his theory of Evolution.

Section 4

Top Down Evolution: Assuming a Voluntary Origin of Order

In the previous chapter it was shown that true bottom up concepts of evolution assume the non-existence of a scientific explanation for evolution. In contrast, in horizontal evolution models scientific explanations are possible and explain the details of evolution quite well. However, these models suffer from the problem of an infinite regress and the principle of incompleteness. In this chapter, a top down concept of evolution is presented, based on the Bahá'í scriptures, which overcomes the problem of an infinite regress of causes and incompleteness.

4.1 Three Possible Causes of Formation: A Proof for Voluntary Design

'Abdu'l-Bahá, in his Letter to Forel, formulates a proof for the existence of a Creator by analyzing the three possible causes of the formation of things.

> Now, formation is of three kinds and of three kinds only: accidental, necessary and voluntary. The coming together of the various con-

stituent elements of beings cannot be accidental, for unto every effect there must be a cause. It cannot be necessary, for then the formation must be an inherent property of the constituent parts and the inherent property of a thing can in no wise be dissociated from it. . . . The third formation remaineth and that is the voluntary one, that is, an unseen force described as the Ancient Power, causeth these elements to come together, every formation giving rise to a distinct being.[140]

In this argument, 'Abdu'l-Bahá considers the three possible origins of the complex order found in this world: accident, necessity, and voluntary design. These three possible causes of formation correspond to the three possible models of evolution introduced above: the bottom up, horizonal, and top down concepts of the origin of order. Accident (or chance) is not considered a real possible cause, because it is a non-explanation. It is like saying something happens without a cause. As shown above, complex order, the "effect," requires an explanation, a "cause." The origin of complex order by chance alone is too improbable for such a possibility to be taken seriously.

4.1.1 *Evolution as a Necessary Process.* 'Abdu'l-Bahá refutes the evolution-by-necessity model by two arguments. By saying necessary formation means "formation must be an inherent property of the constituent parts," he is implying that one should see only upward development in evolution. According to Gould,[141] such unidirectionality is not seen in nature. Thus, 'Abdu'l-Bahá rejects trivial forms of orthogenetic evolution frequently assumed at the time he wrote that letter. His other argument against necessary formation is based on the hierarchical version of an infinite regression. The complexity of the set of laws which is able to produce the particular universe we live in is certainly not less complex than the complex order it produces. Now the question for the origin is iterated one level. What is the origin of the natural laws ruling our universe and implicitly coding for the complex order produced by these laws? In principle, one can assume a set of meta-laws which rule the origin of all possible universes and which once originated the particular laws ruling our universe. Because these meta-laws have to be more general, more encompassing than the laws of our universe, which they ground, they cannot be less complex. In other words, the iteration from laws to meta-laws to additional meta-laws, etc. simply does not solve the problem of the origin of the universe and the order therein. Such an iteration only "shifts" the problem of the origin from one meta-level to another, where this problem does not become simpler but becomes even more complex, a dilemma posed by Gödel's incompleteness theorem. This kind of argument applies not only to deterministic laws, but to stochastic theories as well.

In principle, stochastic models of evolution (e.g., diffusion in a fitness landscape) show the behavior found in evolution, if the fitness function is sufficiently well behaved.[142] Stochastic models of evolution combine random elements (mutation) and necessary elements (the fitness function). The argument against an infinite regression of causes, however, which is given by 'Abdu'l-Bahá in the same letter to Forel, applies also to the origin of the fitness function as a representative of horizontal evolution. Thus, although stochastic evolution models explain evolution on a scientific level, they do not explain the origin of order as such, because the existence of the fitness function as the implicit source of complex order has to be assumed to exist a priori. Again, the model is trapped by the problem of infinite regress.

But how can the problem of an infinite regress be resolved? If each effect depends on a previous or more general cause, that likewise should be the effect of still another cause. At what point does an explanation start?

The origin, the possible starting points for chains of explanations have been studied throughout human history. Early answers for such a question are found in ancient creation myths. The Greeks addressed this problem by rational means. That a regression of causes cannot extend to infinity was first postulated by Aristotle in *Metaphysics* II.2.[143] In a letter to the Swiss scientist Auguste Forel, 'Abdu'l-Bahá uses this kind of argument to establish the need of a voluntary First Cause:

> As we, however, reflect with broad minds upon this infinite universe, we observe that motion without a motive force, and an effect without a cause are both impossible; that every being hath come to exist under numerous influences and continually undergoeth reaction. These influences, too, are formed under the action of still other influences. . . . Such process of causation goes on, and to maintain that this process goes on indefinitely is manifestly absurd. Thus such a chain of causation must of necessity lead eventually to Him who is the Ever-Living, the All-Powerful, who is Self-Dependent and the Ultimate Cause.[144]

Here 'Abdu'l-Bahá proposes the need of a voluntary First Cause to avoid the problem of an infinite regression of causes. The First Cause is a special kind of meta-cause with the ability to create new chains of causation without requiring a predecessor. For 'Abdu'l-Bahá the regression of causes and effects, a problem of all horizontal evolution models, automatically implies the existence of an uncaused reality where the chain of causation stops, because an infinite regression makes no sense.

In the light of modern mathematics, this argument to initiate the universe by the voluntary acts of a First Cause is a reasonable way to escape the incompleteness theorem formulated by the Austrian mathematician Gödel.[145] Formal systems are essentially incomplete, that is, there are always true statements regarding the formal system which cannot be proven to be true within the system, but require a meta-system. Because the same incompleteness theorem applies to the meta-system, any formal system is necessarily incomplete. This purely mathematical theorem implies that there exists no complete formal theory to explain our universe. Because of the essential incompleteness of formal systems, it is certainly not unreasonable to go beyond formal systems and postulate "free will" as the primary entity of causation.

4.1.2 *Voluntary Design.* A famous statement in favor of the design of nature by an intelligent Creator is the watchmaker argument.[146] William Paley in his book *Natural Theology*, published in 1805, compares the fact that all life forms have a complex functional order with the design of a watch. Suppose that someone finds a watch.

From the purposefulness of the design and the high workmanship, the finder would naturally conclude that the watch was made by a watchmaker and cannot have been assembled by accident. Paley then argues that it is also very unlikely that the complex order of life occurred by accident, and that it is much more reasonable to assume purposeful design by a Creator. Such an argument in favor of voluntary design was generally understood as a powerful proof against evolution by chance.

'Abdu'l-Bahá's statement in favor of a Creator can be formulated in the language of a modernized watchmaker argument. Paley, in agreement with most evolution biologists, assumes that complex biological order requires an explanation, just as the existence of a watch requires an explanation which points to a watchmaker. The evolutionist could respond to Paley's argument that modern watches are not produced by watchmakers but by an automatic appliance. This appliance would be able not only to produce watches automatically, but would contain a mechanism to improve the design and function of the produced watches. This appliance certainly would have to be much more complicated than the individual watches it produces. But who made this appliance? It would require designers more skillful than common watchmakers. In a similar way, one can argue that the natural laws which can produce highly complex systems are more complex than the particular complex structures they produce and are in just as much need of an explanation.

4.1.3 Creation. A Reflection of the Names and Attributes of God: Virtually every religion provides a picture of the origin of the world we inhabit. For instance in Judaic, Christian, and Muslim traditions the origin of complex order is believed to result from a creative act of God. It owes its existence to a divine order which is complex beyond human comprehension. This is the kind of origin of order accepted in classical biology, particularly in natural theology. As correctly stated by Dawkins,[147] in such concepts complex order is not explained to result from a few simple principles, but complexity is assumed to exist from the very beginning. Many passages in the Bahá'í scriptures place the Bahá'í Faith within this tradition.

Bahá'u'lláh writes:

> A drop of the billowing ocean of His endless mercy hath adorned all
> creation with the ornament of existence, and a breath wafted from His
> peerless Paradise hath invested all beings with the robe of His sancti-
> ty and glory. A sprinkling from the unfathomed deep of His sovereign
> and all-pervasive Will hath, out of utter nothingness, called into being
> a creation which is infinite in its range and deathless in its duration.
> The wonders of His bounty can never cease, and the stream of His
> merciful grace can never be arrested. The process of His creation hath
> had no beginning, and can have no end. . . . From time immemorial He
> hath been veiled in the ineffable sanctity of His exalted Self, and will
> everlastingly continue to be wrapt in the impenetrable mystery of His
> unknowable Essence. Every attempt to attain to an understanding of
> His inaccessible Reality hath ended in complete bewilderment, and
> every effort to approach His exalted Self and envisage His Essence
> hath resulted in hopelessness and failure.[148]

Although our Creator reigns above human comprehension, this
universe reveals the signs of His creative force and discloses the
traces of His revelation. Bahá'u'lláh describes creation as a mirror
reflecting the names and attributes of God:

> Know thou that every created thing is a sign of the revelation of God.
> Each, according to its capacity, is, and will ever remain, a token of the
> Almighty. Inasmuch as He, the sovereign Lord of all, hath willed to
> reveal His sovereignty in the kingdom of names and attributes, each
> and every created thing hath, through the act of the Divine Will, been
> made a sign of His glory. So pervasive and general is this revelation
> that nothing whatsoever in the whole universe can be discovered that
> doth not reflect His splendor.[149]

According to this statement, each created thing in the universe is
able to reflect the Light of God and to mirror forth His names and
attributes to a certain prescribed degree. The creation as a whole is
considered a revelation of God's sovereignty. Nothing exists which
does not reflect His splendor. Bahá'u'lláh defines humanity as the
most complete reflection of God's bounty:

Upon the inmost reality of each and every created thing He hath shed the light of one of His names, and made it a recipient of the glory of one of His attributes. Upon the reality of man, however, He hath focused the radiance of all of His names and attributes, and made it a mirror of His own self. Alone of all created things man hath been singled out for so great a favor, so enduring a bounty.[150]

This ability to potentially reflect all the names and attributes of God is used in the Bahá'í writings to define human beings. It is an ability not necessarily limited, however, to the human species on this planet (*Homo sapiens*), since other humanlike beings may exist on other planets.

According to 'Abdu'l-Bahá, God and His names and attributes are independent from time:

Consequently, just as the reality of Divinity never had a beginning— that is, God has ever been a Creator, God has ever been a Provider, God has ever been a Quickener, God has ever been a Bestower—so there never has been a time when the attributes of God have not had expression. . . . So, likewise, if we say there was a time when God had no creation or created beings, a time when there were no recipients of His bounties and that His names and attributes had not been manifested, this would be equivalent to a complete denial of Divinity, for it would mean that Divinity is accidental.[151]

This argument complements Plato's argument for a perfectly harmonious universe subsisting by timeless essences, where the universe is assumed to be perfect from the beginning. The eternal names and attributes of God are the ultimate origins of all existing things in our universe and the source of complex order. The natural theologians likewise thought that nature everywhere reflects the presence of a benevolent Creator. Studying nature was the same as studying the plan of God.

4.2 Linking Voluntary Design and Modern Sciences

Many approaches to the origin of our universe based on physics try to reduce the fundament of this world to a few, apparently self evident, trivial rules. In the Bahá'í writings, however, the origin and foundation of this world is assumed to be substantially non-trivial, complex from its very beginning. If this assumed non-trivial origin of order in our cosmos and in biology is thought to correspond to reality, one should expect practical consequences for our physical world. The kingdoms of nature introduced by Aristotle, and restated in the writings and talks of 'Abdu'l-Bahá, may serve as a model of how reality may have a non-trivial origin without being in conflict with the laws of modern physics.[152] In the present section, a concept of a hierarchical order is outlined where the more complex levels are not the result of the complicated interactions of more simple levels but, on the contrary, the complex levels represent a framework within which the simple ones can exist.

4.2.1 *'Abdu'l-Bahá's Concept of the Kingdoms.* 'Abdu'l-Bahá describes the structure of this world in the form of a hierarchy. In his letter to Auguste Forel, 'Abdu'l-Bahá wrote:

> As to the existence of spirit in the mineral: it is indubitable that minerals are endowed with a spirit and life according to the requirements of that stage. . . . In the vegetable world, too, there is the power of growth, and that power of growth is the spirit. In the animal world there is the sense of feeling, but in the human world there is an all-embracing power. In all preceding stages the power of reason is absent, but the soul existeth and revealeth itself. The sense of feeling understandeth not the soul, whereas the reasoning power of the mind proveth the existence thereof.[153]

Here, 'Abdu'l-Bahá distinguishes between four levels of "spirit": the mineral, the vegetable, the animal, and the human kingdoms. In modern biology the kingdoms, originally introduced by Aristotle, are today used in a taxonomic sense; they designate distinct classes of organisms. 'Abdu'l-Bahá is obviously not concerned with a taxonomic distinction of biological classes, but with a hierarchy of increasingly complex faculties. Each higher level includes all the lower ones, but not those above.

This hierarchical understanding of the kingdoms is explained in

another passage of the letter to Forel, where 'Abdu'l-Bahá emphasizes the interrelation between the kingdoms:

> All divine philosophers and men of wisdom and understanding, when
> observing these endless beings, have considered that in this great and
> infinite universe all things end in the mineral kingdom, that the out-
> come of the mineral kingdom is the vegetable kingdom, the outcome
> of the vegetable kingdom is the animal kingdom, and the outcome of
> the animal kingdom the world of man.[154]

Thus, in this context, the "kingdoms" do not designate taxonomi-
cally distinct classes but hierarchical levels. 'Abdu'l-Bahá describes
this hierarchy phenomenologically, by the essential characteristics
related to each level: by "growth," the "sense of feeling," and "reason."[155] But how are these levels distinguished in practice? Is there
something added at each level, a kind of *élan vitale*? 'Abdu'l-Bahá
gives a rather atomistic view of those levels:

> In its ceaseless progression and journeyings the atom becomes imbued
> with the virtues and powers of each degree or kingdom it traverses. In
> the degree of the mineral it possessed mineral affinities; in the king-
> dom of the vegetable it manifested the virtue augmentative, or power
> of growth; in the animal organism it reflected the intelligence of that
> degree, and in the kingdom of man it was qualified with human attrib-
> utes or virtues. . . . No atom is bereft or deprived of this opportunity or
> right of expression. Nor can it be said of a given atom that it is denied
> equal opportunities with other atoms; nay, all are privileged to possess
> the virtues existent in these kingdoms and to reflect the attributes of
> their organisms.[156]

According to 'Abdu'l-Bahá, "no atom is bereft" of the ability to
reflect the respective names and attributes of God at the different
levels. The emergence of more complex characteristics, however,
requires an appropriate environment, certain necessary boundary
conditions, and a sufficiently complex organization.

4.2.2 *Hierarchical Levels of Information Processing.* A possible
interpretation of these "kingdoms" compatible with findings of mod-

ern science relates them to hierarchical levels of information processing. This understanding is supported by the ideas of Wheeler and Weizsäcker, who propose basing physics not on energy, as is the case today, but on information.[157] With information as the fundamental entity of our universe, and energy and matter only its derivatives, the concept of the kingdoms provides a model for a non-trivial, hierarchical order of our universe. Whereas today's physics refer mainly to the level of the mineral kingdom, the "influence" of the higher levels of the hierarchy would become detectable only in complex biological systems.[158]

The lowest kingdom is the mineral kingdom showing no information processing at all. It describes an organization level of atoms found in stones, water, air, etc. The second level is the vegetable kingdom, represented by the plants. As explained by 'Abdu'l-Bahá, there are no special mineral atoms or vegetable atoms, but the same atoms travel through all the kingdoms of life and observe the same laws of chemistry and physics. But the vegetable kingdom shows attributes not found in the mineral kingdom: growth, metabolism, and replication.

Ernst Mayr stresses the complexity of biological systems, the existence of a genetic plan, and the ability to perform purposeful actions:

> It is now widely admitted not only that the complexity of biological systems is of a different order of magnitude, but also that the existence of historically evolved programs is unknown in the inanimate world. Teleonomic processes and adapted systems, made possible by these programs, are unknown in physical systems.[159]

Biological cells are able to reproduce themselves because of their genetic plan. The vegetable kingdom represents information processing on the molecular level; the genetic plan regulates the molecular organization in the cell. Replication transfers the knowledge encoded in the genes from one generation to the next. The process of natural selection results in adaptations to the environment, to "learning" on a molecular level.

The third level in this hierarchy is occupied by the animal king-dom. The special properties of this level are the senses, mediated by a sufficiently complex neural network (i.e., the central nervous sys-tem), which receives input from the environment and allows animals to react instantaneously to this external input. This ability distin-guishes the animal kingdom from the vegetable kingdom. The animal kingdom encompasses both the mineral and vegetable kingdoms insofar as it depends, at its own level, on incorporating the structural and qualitative complexity of the kingdoms preceding it. At this level, one finds information processing on the intra-cellular level; the neural network enables the animal to take advantage of the sensual input and to react to it. It also provides the means for learning and simple forms of tradition.

The fourth stage is the human kingdom. The main attribute distin-guishing human beings from the lower kingdoms is the human intel-lect. This does not mean that other species do not show intelligence. But no other species has the capacity to develop speech, technology, culture, and civilization to the extent found with *Homo sapiens*. Individuals of the human species share many attributes in common with the animal world, though cooperation among human beings is stronger than in most other species. The human mind constructs an intellectual model of the surrounding environment. Speech provides the means to live and work in large, complex human societies. Knowledge is not only stored on the cellular level in the genes (veg-etable kingdom), or in the pattern of neuronal connectivity (animal kingdom), it becomes largely independent of its individual biological carriers in the form of stories and myths, and more recently in the form of published literature, films, and disks. The human intellect supports sophisticated interactions among individuals resulting in a complex global society.

Each higher level in the hierarchy encompasses the lower ones, but it is not the trivial outcome of them. The characteristics of each level are emergent properties in the best sense of the word. By the "spirit of growth" of the plant, 'Abdu'l-Bahá refers to more than the effect of a complex grouping of atoms. 'Abdu'l-Bahá makes this clear in the case of the human spirit:

> Moreover, these members, these elements, this composition, which are found in the organism of man, are an attraction and magnet for the spirit; it is certain that the spirit will appear in it. . . . When these existing elements are gathered together according to the natural order, and with perfect strength, they become a magnet for the spirit, and the spirit will become manifest in them with all its perfections.[160]

The human spirit (i.e., the essence of humanity) is not the result of a particular composition of the atoms. Rather the spirit is preexistent and only appears when the corresponding complexity in the atomic composition is obtained. Using Monod's terminology, the human spirit is not "created" during evolution, but it is revealed, or made manifest.

In contrast to the taxonomic understanding of distinct kingdoms in modern biology, 'Abdu'l-Bahá uses the concept of kingdoms to describe the complex order of the biosphere in the form of a hierarchy. These levels represent degrees of increasingly complex reflections of the names and attributes of God. Each higher level includes the lower ones, but not vice versa.

4.3 Hatcher's Interpretation of the "Three Causes of Formation"

In *The Journal of Bahá'í Studies* and in a recently published book, William Hatcher presents an article entitled "A Scientific Proof of the Existence of God."[161] He derives his proof from 'Abdu'l-Bahá's argument of the three possible causes of formation, and he provides a translation of this argument into the language of modern science. Hatcher bases his proof on two premises: (1) because complex biological order is not random it cannot be accidental, and (2) the nonrandomness of life requires a particular evolutionary force which he identifies with God.

4.3.1 *Complex Biological Order is Non-Random.* As shown above, complex biological order is certainly non-random. According to the second law of thermodynamics, closed systems on the average tend to evolve from more probable toward less probable states. Hatcher states that the appearance of order requires the input of free energy, such as sunlight in the case of plant growth, and an external ordering force in the case of human artifacts: "Those that exhibit evolution from more probable to less probable states cannot be the result of a random process. The cause of such growth patterns can only be some observable input of energy (e.g., plant growth on earth that is fueled by solar energy) or else some nonobservable (invisible) force."[162]

But this list of possible sources for the emergence of ordered patterns is incomplete. There exists also inherent order in nature. If steam is cooled, it first becomes fluid; then at or below the freezing point of water, it forms ice crystals, as in the case of snow. Despite their beauty, snow crystals only represent an inanimate form of order. Protein folding is an example much closer to the situation of evolution. Protein folding reveals implicit order encoded in a particular sequence of amino acids. Even so, the folding does not imply the transition from a probable (unfolded protein) to an improbable state (folded protein). Because of the chemical interactions between the amino acids within a certain environment, the folded protein (e.g., an active enzyme) represents the more probable state, the state of lowest free energy.

Hatcher adds the observation that the evolution of life is an example of a development from more simple towards more complex life forms:

> All these sedimentary layers show the same basic configuration, namely, that higher, more complex forms of life followed simpler, less complex forms. In other words, the process of evolution was a process of complexification, of moving from relative simplicity and disorder towards relative complexity and order. It was therefore a process of moving from more probable configurations towards less probable configurations.[163]

From this movement of evolution uphill (i.e., against the direction which would be adopted automatically by nature), Hatcher concludes that there must be a special kind of force which causes this complexification during the evolution of life on earth. Most evolutionists can follow Hatcher's reasoning in this conclusion. Dawkins, for instance, uses a similar probabilistic argument to show that "the essence of life is statistical improbability on a colossal scale."

4.3.2 *The Evolutionary Force:* Most evolution biologists will, however, generally not accept Hatcher's identification of this evolutionary force with "God" in a non-trivial sense: "It seems reasonable to call this force 'God,' but anyone uncomfortable with that name can simply call it 'the evolutionary force' (or, more precisely, 'the force that produced evolution and thus produced the human being')."[164] Mayr, for instance, explicitly rejects the existence of a particular evolutionary force.

Hatcher's rejection of the more conventional explanations of evolution may be influenced by his particular understanding of evolution: "This is why the currently accepted theory of evolution attempts to explain the upward movement (the movement towards greater order) in evolution as the fortunate coincidence of two random phenomena: the action of natural selection (essentially random environmental impact) on random mutations (spontaneous genetic change)."[165]

Although most evolutionists will agree that the mutation step is random, most of them will disagree that the selection step is random as well. Dawkins, for instance, emphatically emphasizes that evolution is not the result of pure chance; rather it "is the very opposite of random." Hatcher's understanding of the selection step applies to bottom-up models of evolution. There, order is assumed to originate *ad hoc*, resulting from unpredictable and quasi-random new creations.

In mathematical biology, the selection step is determined by a fitness function. In such theories, selection is not random but, on the long run, occurs according to the fitness values of the individuals. In this case, the complexity found in life represents the unfolding of the potential complexity inherent in laws of nature. This is similar to the protein-folding example. In his response to Gordon Dicks' comments about his article,[166] Hatcher claims that neo-Darwinism cannot explain evolution:

> Clearly and indisputably, this (narrow) process of natural selection could never, even theoretically, account for the progressive complexification of life forms in the evolutionary process. . . . In any case, under the neo-Darwinian assumption, mutations favorable to increased complexity would, at best, only be *sporadic* (or *sparse*), i.e., insufficiently frequent to allow for any significant process of convergence.[167]

Hatcher apparently assumes that this kind of evolution can be rejected on the basis of 'Abdu'l-Bahá's statement that evolution "cannot be necessary, for then the formation must be an inherent property of the constituent parts and the inherent property of a thing can in no wise be dissociated from it."[168] Hatcher concludes that "the clearly random element involved in the process of evolution utterly refutes the 'inherent necessity' objection to the classical design argument."[169]

'Abdu'l-Bahá's rejection of a necessary cause as the origin of complex biological order in his argument of the three causes certainly applies to the models of evolution assumed in the second half of the nineteenth century, where only necessary causes were considered and the element of chance was explicitly excluded.[170] The dynamics of matter were believed to follow Newton's laws exclusively, laws which are entirely deterministic. According to Büchner, nature can produce "only the results of strictest necessity."[171] Modern mathematical evolution theories explicitly include the "clearly random element involved in the process of evolution." According to those studies, not every fitness function leads to evolution, but some do.[172] Consequently, Hatcher's argument does not apply to evolution theories where a suitable, objective fitness function exists.

4.3.3 *God's Will in Evolution.* Hatcher envisions a kind of temporal regression where chains of causation important for evolution are initiated by God's voluntary intervention: "The evolution-based argument thus establishes not only the existence of God but also provides at least one clear instance when God has intervened in (or interacted with) the ongoing process of the world."[173] Such an intervention by God is likewise proposed by Loehle: "I postulate (the Bahá'í writings do not specify this) that divine Will may have operated at times to help guide the process towards humanity; it was God's intention from the beginning that humanity should arise."[174]

Ward made a similar suggestion. According to him, the physical laws of our universe represent idealizations which do not rule out the possibility of God's actions: "The element of indeterminism involved in the 'freedom hypothesis' is simply that not everything that happens is the result solely of the operation of a general law, or combination of general laws, upon some previous physical state. Such indeterminism, or at least the appearance of it, is commonplace in ordinary human affairs."[175] He discusses the proposed goal-directedness in terms of human values, addressing the question of socio-biology (i.e., the source of human values): "Its biological origins would be a natural consequence of the grounding of the whole evolutionary process in a divine plan."[176]

Although there are differences in the details of the arguments of Hatcher, Ward, Loehle, and the author of this essay, they agree in the conclusion that God's will is necessary to explain the origin of the complex order of life.

4.4 Does Evolution Have a Goal

The Bahá'í writings describe the universe and particularly humanity as mirrors of the names and attributes of God. These names and attributes can be considered as the "eternal building blocks," the "elementary units" of our universe. According to Bahá'u'lláh, this universe is a mirror image of the world of eternal reality and depends on the emanation of God's grace: "There can be no doubt whatever that if for one moment the tide of His mercy and grace were to be withheld from the world, it would completely perish."[177] From this perspective the fundamental order of this universe is complex from the very beginning. Cosmological and biological evolution are the realization of this preexisting order. In this view, evolution means the unfolding of possible complex order (building on the names and attributes of God) into actual complex order.

'Abdu'l-Bahá describes the order in this material universe in the form of a hierarchy, consisting of the mineral, vegetable, animal, and human kingdoms. The higher kingdoms build upon the lower ones. In this essay, a concept is proposed that relates the kingdoms, as they are used by 'Abdu'l-Bahá, to hierarchical levels of information processing. This interpretation shows how a spiritual view of our universe can include the results of modern sciences without insisting on a dualism that would divide our universe into an (evil) material world and a (divine) spiritual realm. But do not the conclusions of modern biology imply that evolution is undirected, without purpose or goal? Are those claims based on strict science and reason, or do they merely reflect the personal metaphysical views of their promoters?

4.4.1 *Can the Randomness of Evolution be Proven?* Now the question is considered whether or not the known body of biological data definitely implies a random direction in evolution and, therefore, excludes any kind of goal-directed evolution. During the second-half of the nineteenth and the first-half of the twentieth century in Germany, authors such as Büchner, Haeckel, and Oswald successfully popularized the view that a scientific worldview (i.e., the acceptance evolution) implies a materialistic world which per se excludes the existence of a higher purpose and destiny. Similar views were put forward in Britain by Huxley, Spencer, and others. Even today, the concept of teleological evolution is generally considered to be incompatible with the known facts of biology and the evolution of life. This is one of the central messages of Monod's famous book *Le Hazard et la Necessité*: that evolution has no purpose, no goal: "Message qui, par tous les critères possibles, semble avoir été écrit au hasard. . . . D'un jeu *totalement* aveugle, tout, par définition, peut sortir, y compris la vision elle-même."[178] This leads him to his conclusion that life is a strange phenomena in our universe and we are the strangers:

S'il accepte ce message dans son entière signification, il faut bien que l'Homme enfin se réveille de son rêve millénaire pour découvrir sa totale solitude, son étrangeté radicale. Il sait maintenant que, comme un Tzigane, il est en marge de l'univers où il doit vivre. Univers sourd à sa musique, indifférent à ses espoirs comme à ses suffrances ou à ses crimes.[179]

Gould proposes that in the evolution of individual species no directionality in its development can be detected. One finds complexification as well as drastic simplifications (e.g., in the case of some parasites). Dawkins suggests that evolution is absolutely blind, without any final goal. He formulates this position rather drastically in his *Blind Watchmaker*:

> Evolution has no long-term goal. There is no long-distance target, no final perfection to serve as a criterion for selection, although human vanity cherishes the absurd notion that our species is the final goal of evolution. In real life, the criterion for selection is always short-term, either simple survival or, more generally, reproductive success. . . . The 'watchmaker' that is cumulative natural selection is blind to the future and has no long-term goal.[180]

These statements propose that there is no obvious trend in evolution, no final goal which is necessarily discernable by our biological knowledge. Consequently, there is no obvious need to introduce final causes into biology. Deterministic and probabilistic processes (necessity and chance) appear sufficient to model all those aspects of reality which are known with a reasonable degree of precision.

Now the question is asked whether or not the absence of clear directionality implies that evolution definitely excludes any directionality or any finality which could represent a Creator's purpose. How can we determine whether sequences of events are directed by some inherent plan or not? A precondition for undirectedness would be the randomness of those events. The apparent randomness of a sequence of numbers does not imply that they are created randomly.[181] This fact makes any conclusion questionable that deduces from the apparent randomness of evolution that evolution as a whole must be random and without any direction.

Even if each mutation step is fully random, the directionality of evolution as a whole cannot be excluded. An illustrative counter-example is the diffusion of a spoon of crystalline sugar from the bottom to the top in a glass of tea[182] Here the random thermal motion directs sugar molecules towards the upper part of the glass. Another excellent example for directed evolution is the refolding of denaturated proteins into their native state. The thermal motion of the folding protein is restricted by the form of the conformational free energies to only a very small subspace of the whole conformational space. The important aspect of protein folding in this discussion is that even random driving forces can effectively result in directedness if there is an additional guiding force (e.g., the free energy of folding). In the case of evolution, random mutations and recombinations may be guided by the structure of the selectivity of the mutations, by the landscape of the fitness functions.

The question of whether or not cosmogony and evolution follow a pregiven plan may be further obscured by the problem of how to evaluate such directedness. To detect a direction in evolution one needs a measure for directionality, some kind of "compass." For instance, increasing complexity could be a possible direction of evolution. But what does complexity mean in terms of a clear unique definition? Is it the number of nucleic acids required to code for the organism? Is it the degree of adaptedness of an organism to a certain environment? As noted by Gould, in general, complexification increases simply due to the fact that non-artificial inanimate systems are generally simpler than living systems and consequently they can evolve only towards complexity. Such "diffusion" into "empty" complex regions, however, requires that those "regions" actually exist and that complex organisms may be at least as well equipped to face the needs of our world as the simpler ones.

4.4.2 *Finality in Evolution.* Of course, the philosophical compatibility between evolution and purpose as such does not prove that a purpose really exists. But what means do we have to decipher the purpose of our universe? How difficult is it to grasp "simpler" aspects of our universe, such as the laws ruling the physical realm. Why do we expect that understanding the purpose of the universe should be simpler than, for instance, learning quantum electro-dynamics? Why should a general purpose of our universe be easy to detect? What happens if the purpose of our universe is something completely beyond our imagination? Are we sure that we understand the "language of nature"? Why should our ideas of progress have any resemblance to the direction our universe may possibly be designed to follow? What measures do we have to evaluate progress if we do not know the final purpose of this universe, or even if such a purpose exists? Perhaps we will discover some intermediate achievements obtained during evolution still far away from the intended far-end goal.

Complex finality in evolution is rather unlikely if one assumes a trivial self-creative origin. If the origin is assumed to be essentially complex, the situation is different. The "complexity" of the origin of our universe may, for instance, by far exceed any level of complexity obtained by any particular organism or civilization at any time during evolution. Such a situation is stated in the Bahá'í writings:

> For whatever such strivings may accomplish, they never can hope to transcend the limitations imposed upon Thy creatures. . . . The loftiest sentiments which the holiest of saints can express in praise of Thee, and the deepest wisdom which the most learned of men can utter in their attempts to comprehend Thy nature, all revolve around that Center Which is wholly subjected to Thy sovereignty, Which adoreth Thy Beauty, and is propelled through the movement of Thy Pen.[183]

The complexity of the final goal of evolution may simply surpass the imagination of all evolving civilizations. In such a situation, directionality in cosmogony, evolution, and even history might remain undetectable for humanity because we have no measure to evaluate the direction of the development and to detect possible progress. Of course, this line of argument does not prove that finality exists in our universe, but it shows that the claim for the absence of directionality is not well founded. It is a statement of faith.

4.5 Summary

The cause of order, particularly the complex order of our biosphere, is by no means self evident. It needs an explanation. Three different kinds of origin of order are generally considered: (1) chance, (2) order as a necessary result of laws of nature, and (3) order as a result of voluntary design. These three kinds of causes correlate with the three fundamental concepts of the origin of the complex order of life: evolution as a bottom-up, horizontal, or top-down process.

Chance as the origin of order, a bottom-up concept, can be excluded by simple probabilistic arguments. (See Section 3.3.2) Evolution models describing the origin of order as a necessary outcome of laws of nature, as the unfolding of a hidden potential order, are horizontal concepts. Such models suffer from the problem of an infinite regression and incompleteness. (See Sections 3.4 and 4.1) If the existent order is the result of laws of nature, what causes the existence of the laws of nature? Popular presentations of modern cosmologies generally tend to hide this regression behind an apparently self-evident origin, claimed to be without need of a further explanation. Alternatively, some modern evolution biologists propose a stochastic process as the origin of order, a combination of chance and necessity. The problem of the "colossal improbability" of pure chance is claimed to be solved by cumulative selection. If selection is quasi-random, as in models of *ad hoc* origination, the problem of the "colossal improbability" remains and Hatcher's argument applies. If selection is based on an (in principle) objective and reproducible fitness function defining the fitnesses of all sequences of the DNA sequence space, the origin of this fitness function must be explained. This, again, leads to the problem of an infinite regression.

In a letter to Forel, 'Abdu'l-Bahá uses this situation to conclude that only the third alternative of three possible causes of order is satisfactory: the origin of order by voluntary design (i.e., evolution as a top-down process). This is really the same as extending the horizontal model to a top-down model by adding to it a voluntary "First Mover," who is identified as the Creator of our universe and the fashioner of the laws of nature. In this model the universe has a goal and a purpose, and is considered to manifest the eternal names and attributes of God.

A FOREST IN BORNEO, WITH MAMMALS
A plate from Wallace's *Geographical Distribution of Animals* (1876) intended to show differences between animals of the Oriental and Australian regions. Note a tarsier (top left), a tree shrew (center left), and a tapir (center right).

Section 5

Evolution and the Originality of Species

In talks on several occasions given to Western audiences, 'Abdu'l-Bahá criticized the theory of evolution of "some European philosophers." In this chapter, the arguments of 'Abdu'l-Bahá are presented, analyzed, and related to modern concepts of evolution.

At the beginning of this chapter a methodological issue must be raised. Why did 'Abdu'l-Bahá devote so much attention to the subject of evolution? As a non-scientist, he was not concerned with the biological details of evolution, such as whether or not chimpanzees are biologically more closely related to gorillas or to orangutans, or whether or not mice, rabbits, and guinea pigs belong to the same taxonomic family. Very few of his statements can be reasonably interpreted as addressing biological issues. His particular interest was in the social and religious consequences of Darwinism as it was interpreted by "some European philosophers." This was the focus of the interest of most of 'Abdu'l-Bahá's Near Eastern contemporaries who addressed the subject of evolution.[184]

According to Bahá'u'lláh, the purpose of religion is to educate mankind: "God's purpose in sending His prophets unto men is twofold. The first is to liberate the children of men from the darkness of ignorance, and guide them to the light of true understanding. The second is to ensure the peace and tranquillity of mankind, and provide all the means by which they can be established."[185] In *Miracles and Metaphors*, Mírzá Abu'l-Faḍl Gulpáygání argues that the prophets who come to fulfill such a purpose are not meant to be authorities in such areas as history, philosophy, and science as well: "It is clear that the prophets and Manifestations of the Cause of God were sent to guide the nations, to improve their characters, and to bring the people nearer to their Source and ultimate Goal. They were not sent as historians, astronomers, philosophers, or natural scientists."[186]

Consequently, 'Abdu'l-Bahá's main concern was the "education of mankind." He presented a view of evolution which, on the one hand, agreed with the facts of contemporary science, and which, on the other hand, preserved the purpose of religion. Most of the few biological statements of 'Abdu'l-Bahá can be understood primarily as analogies used to establish spiritual truths and principles supportive of a teleological worldview.

In the talks and writings of 'Abdu'l-Bahá, the principle of the originality of species (*aṣálat-i naw'*) forms a cornerstone for his conception of the origin of complex biological order and the evolution of life. Most secondary Bahá'í literature covering the subject of evolution emphasizes such a concept. In several chapters of *Some Answered Questions* and in one talk given in the United States, 'Abdu'l-Bahá claims the originality of species. He contrasts the principle of the originality of species with the theories of "some European philosophers" who claim the human species is derived from the animal kingdom:

> We have now come to the question of the modification of species . . . that is to say, to the point of inquiring whether man's descent is from the animal. This theory has found credence in the minds of some European philosophers, and it is now very difficult to make its falseness understood, but in the future it will become evident and clear, and the European philosophers will themselves realize its untruth.[187]

But what particular aspect of the theory of the European philosophers is really the object of 'Abdu'l-Bahá's criticism here? As the spiritual leader of the Bahá'í community, and as the authoritative interpreter of the Bahá'í scriptures, which claim the creation of the universe by God and a special purpose for humanity, the social and spiritual consequences of Darwinism, as taught by "some European philosophers" (such as Büchner, Haeckel, and Spencer) constituted the real challenge to the new Faith. If the concept that complex biological order originates from a mindless, mechanical process, and does not follow ancient God-given laws, could be applied to the biosphere, it could be applied to the human social world as well. If the biological order is largely accidental, the principles ruling human society would also be arbitrary. Such an idea was certainly unacceptable to 'Abdu'l-Bahá.

Another reason 'Abdu'l-Bahá had to address the question of evolution is the central Bahá'í teaching of the unity of science and religion. This principle contradicts the explicit claim made by Büchner and Haeckel that evolution and creation are two mutually exclusive worldviews. 'Abdu'l-Bahá's formulation of a concept of evolution agreeable with the known biological and paleontological facts, and compatible with the teachings of his father, gave evidence of the progressive nature of the new faith in the West. The principle of the harmony of science and religion was 'Abdu'l-Bahá's answer to atheistic movements (such as the German monists) and to materialistic interpretations of Darwinism, which were receiving wide attention at the time.

5.1 The Theory of "Some European Philosophers"

During her table talks with 'Abdu'l-Bahá in 'Akká, Miss Laura Clifford Barney asked concerning the theory of biological evolution: "What do you say with regard to the theory of the evolution of beings held by some European philosophers?"[188] 'Abdu'l-Bahá reformulated the question and expressed the problem as an alternative between arbitrarily derived and non-arbitrarily created species: "Briefly, this question will be decided by determining whether species are original or not—that is to say, has the species of man been established from the beginning, or was it afterward derived from the animal?"[189] 'Abdu'l-Bahá then presents the arguments of the European scientists which were used to support evolution:

Certain European philosophers think that the species evolve, and that even modification and transmutation are possible. One of the proofs that they give for this theory is that through the attentive study and verification of the science of geology it has become clear that the existence of the vegetable preceded that of the animal, and that of the animal preceded that of man. They believe that both vegetable and animal genera have changed, for in some of the strata of the earth they have discovered plants which existed in the past and are now extinct; in other words, they think these plants progressed and grew in strength, and that their form and appearance changed; and, therefore, the species has altered. In the same way, in the strata of the earth there are some species of animals which have changed and become modified. One of these animals is the serpent. There are indications that the serpent once had feet, but through the lapse of time those members have disappeared. In the same way, in the vertebral column of man there is a vestige which proves that man, like other animals, once had a tail. They believe that at one time that member was useful, but when man evolved, it was no longer of use; and, therefore, it gradually disappeared. As the serpent took refuge under the ground and became a creeping animal, it was no longer in need of feet, so they disappeared; but their traces survive. Their principal argument is this: the existence of traces of members proves that they once existed, and as now they are no longer of service, they have gradually disappeared, and there is no longer any benefit in or reason for these vestiges. Therefore, while the perfect and necessary members have remained, those which are unnecessary have gradually disappeared by the modification of the species, but the traces of them continue.[190]

At the time of 'Abdu'l-Bahá, these were two major lines of argument presented in favor of evolution: emphasizing fossil records and atrophic organs. Lamark's studies of the existing and extinct molusks showed clearly that their outer form changed throughout history. Some of them are now extinct; others still living today have a clear relationship to earlier forms. The famous French biologist Cuvier

. . . clearly demonstrated for the Tertiary strata of the Paris basin that each horizon had its particular mammalian fauna. More importantly, he showed that the lower a stratum was, the more different the fauna was from that of the present. It was he who proved extinction conclusively, since the extinct proboscidians (elephants) described by him could not possibly have remained unnoticed in some remote region of the world, as was postulated for marine organisms.[191]

These findings presented clear evidence that the biological populations living during earlier phases of our planet were different from those of today. Another argument in favor of evolution was the existence of atrophic organs, such as the blind eyes of the cave salamander or the relics of legs in the case of the serpent. Those organs very likely had a function in earlier times. Because they were no longer used, they became stunted. 'Abdu'l-Bahá does not deny the truth of those findings, but criticizes the philosophic interpretation of the data.

5.2 'Abdu'l-Bahá's Critique of the Theory of the European Philosophers

In *Some Answered Questions*, 'Abdu'l-Bahá formulates two arguments critical of the theory that the human species descended from the animal world. The first argument is based on Plato's concept that the whole universe is created in perfect harmony from the beginning. In the second argument, 'Abdu'l-Bahá grounds the originality of the human species on the time invariance and completeness of universal laws of nature.

5.2.1 *A Harmonious Universe.* In his argument based on the perfect harmony of the universe, 'Abdu'l-Bahá concludes that the missing of "humanity" during a certain period would imply a partly imperfect universe, which violates the principle of perfect harmony:

> When man looks at the beings with a penetrating regard, and attentively examines the condition of existents, and when he sees the state, organization, and perfection of the world, he will be convinced that in the contingent world there is nothing more wonderful than what

already exists. For all existing beings, terrestrial and celestial, as well as this limitless space and all that is in it, have been created and organized, composed, arranged, and perfected as they ought to be. The universe has no imperfection, so that if all beings became pure intelligence and reflected for ever and ever, it is impossible that they could imagine anything better than that which already exists.

If, however, the creation in the past had not been adorned with the utmost perfection, then existence would have been imperfect and meaningless, and in this case creation would have been incomplete. . . . Now, if we imagine a time when man belonged to the animal world, or when he was merely an animal, we shall find that existence would have been imperfect—that is to say, there would have been no man, and this chief member, which in the body of the world is like the brain and mind in man, would have been missing. The world would then have been quite imperfect. This is a categorical proof, because if there had been a time when man was in the animal kingdom, the perfection of existence would have been destroyed; for man is the greatest member of this world, and if this world were without its chief member, surely it would be imperfect.[192]

First, 'Abdu'l-Bahá describes our universe as a perfect, harmonious whole. Then the argument concludes that if there had been a time when the human species did not exist, or merely belonged to the animal kingdom, the harmony we see today would not have existed, and the universe would have been imperfect, since it would have been missing its chief member. The perfection and harmony of our universe, according to 'Abdu'l-Bahá, is founded on the eternal manifestation of the names and attributes of God. (As described in Section 4.1) 'Abdu'l-Bahá says: "The effulgence of the divine perfections appears in the reality of man, so he is the representative of God, the messenger of God. If man did not exist, the universe would be without result, for the object of existence is the appearance of the perfections of God."[193] Thus, the most perfect representative of God (i.e., humanity) needs to exist eternally.

5.2.2 *Time-Invariant Universal Laws.* In the second half of Chapter 46 of *Some Answered Questions*, 'Abdu'l-Baha augments Plato's classical argument of a harmonious universe with the idea of time-invariant laws, as proposed by modern physics, to substantiate the originality of the human species:

> In brief, the perfection of each individual being—that is to say, the perfection which you now see in man and apart from him, with regard to parts, organs, or faculties—is due to the composition of the elements, to their measure, to their balance, to the manner of their combination, and to the interaction and influence of other beings. In the case of man, when all these factors are gathered together, then man exists. As the perfection of man is entirely due to the composition of the elements, to their measure, to the manner of their combination, and to the interaction and influence of different beings—then, since man was produced ten or a hundred thousand years ago from these earthly elements with the same measure and balance, the same manner of combination and mixture, and the same influence of other beings, exactly the same man existed then as now. This is evident and not worth debating. A thousand million years hence, if these elements of man are gathered together and arranged in this special proportion, and if the elements are combined according to the same method, and if they are affected by the same influence of other beings, exactly the same man will exist.[194]

'Abdu'l-Bahá states that a certain composition of chemical elements leads to the same human being today, "ten or a hundred thousand years ago," or in "a thousand million years." Thus, in this argument, 'Abdu'l-Bahá derives the originality of the human species from the assumed existence of universal time-invariant laws of nature, which rule the interactions between the chemical elements and between other natural relationships. Because human beings would materialize whenever the required conditions are met, the "human species" is always potentially present in the universe, even if no particular biological population of human beings exists. This concept parallels Dawkins' idea that the space of DNA sequences defining all possible forms of life exists as an a priori potential.

'Abdu'l-Bahá considers the concept of time-invariant laws to be self evident: ". . . exactly the same man existed then as now. This is evident and not worth debating."[195] In a later part of the same quote,

'Abdu'l-Bahá uses the example of a lamp to illustrate the argument of the time invariance of the laws of nature: "For example, if after a hundred thousand years there is oil, fire, a wick, a lamp, and the lighter of the lamp—briefly, if there are all the necessary things which now exist, exactly the same lamp will be obtained."[196] According to this argument, the laws of nature that "ensure" the burning of the oil lamp were not created at some time point of cosmology, but they exist from the infinite beginning. And they will remain the same into the endless future.

That 'Abdu'l-Bahá applies this argument to human beings as well as to oil lamps indicates that 'Abdu'l-Bahá considers this argument a general one. It applies to salt crystals, oil lamps, computers, myoglobin molecules, viruses, bacteria, mice, human beings, and so on. According to this argument, whenever chemical elements are combined in the necessary order and under the right influence of other beings (environment), the respective result is obtained. This result is independent of the time point, if the respective boundary conditions are met (e.g., the necessary environment for viruses, bacteria, etc.). 'Abdu'l-Bahá concludes from this argument that the order to form salt crystals and all other things, exists a priori. It is not created *ad hoc* as proposed by Monod, but it reveals the inherent properties of nature.

'Abdu'l-Bahá distinguishes between natural (God-given) and accidental order:

> This composition and arrangement, through the wisdom of God and His preexistent might, were produced from one natural organization. As the world was composed and combined with the utmost perfection, conformable to wisdom, and according to a universal law, it is evident that it is the creation of God, and is not a fortuitous composition and arrangement. This is why from every natural composition a being can come into existence, but from an accidental composition no being can come into existence.[197]

Only when the composition and ordering of atoms follows the "natural organization" (i.e., the plan defined by the Creator) and forms stable assemblies of the chemical elements according to the laws of physics, will a living organism result. Only precise combinations of pinions and gears lead to functioning clockworks, but not arbitrary ones. In the language of evolution biology, this argument means that only those compositions of chemical elements and only those organisms which possess high fitness values can survive. Accidental assemblies of atoms, however, will produce no such stable complex structures as are found in the biosphere.

In a universe where evolution is real, not all possible forms of order are always realized. There has been a time in our universe without salt crystals or human beings. But 'Abdu'l-Bahá assumes that salt crystals and human beings are formed "automatically" with the appropriate combinations of the necessary chemical elements and the right environment. If this idea is correct, the structure found in salt crystals and human beings exists independently of actually existing salt crystals and human beings. This idea is contrary to Aristotle's concept of an immanent order and closely related to Plato's concept of transcendent essences.

According to 'Abdu'l-Bahá, the human species essence accounts for the ability of chemical elements to eventually form human beings. In this second argument, 'Abdu'l-Bahá refers to concepts of classical and modern physics also held by Büchner and Haeckel. According to them, matter, energy, and the laws of nature are not created but eternal. Modern physicists, likewise, generally assume the reality of a unique, universal set of time-invariant laws of nature. According to such a view, the root of the human species is an abstract timeless order where humanity has existed potentially from the very beginning of the universe, even though in the early phases of the universe the required environment for human life did not exist.

With the arguments of a harmonious universe and time-invariant, universal laws, 'Abdu'l-Bahá rejects theories which assume the completion of the laws of nature within time and the self-creation of absolutely new characteristics during evolution. These arguments reject the new generation of species considered by some naturalists, such as Maupertius, within the framework of classical biology,[198] as well as the *ad hoc* self-creation of new biological characteristics as proposed by Monod. According to 'Abdu'l-Bahá's arguments, all possible forms of life exist potentially from the "beginning" of our universe. Only predetermined assemblies of chemical elements produce living organisms; arbitrary compositions quickly disintegrate. 'Abdu'l-Bahá thus assumes a universe which has both a First Cause and potential complexity from its very origin. This is a top-down process.

5.3 The Compatibility of Evolution with an Abstract, Timeless Order

The question now arises: how can an abstract, timeless order be compatible with the evolution of the biosphere? Mayr, in his *Growth of Biological Thought*, explains that the concept of a harmonious universe was one of the major obstacles impeding the development of Darwin's theory of evolution.[199] The reason for this is that in classical biology, Plato's concept of a perfect universe was understood to mean that God had created the universe perfect from the beginning, both with respect to its essences and with respect to its outer form. In such an outwardly perfect world, evolution makes no sense because all organisms are perfect from the time point of their creation and cannot be improved. They can only vary within certain limits. In such a universe, natural selection would have the task of removing oddities which deviate too strongly from the perfect form dictated by its species essence. Classical biology was based on a static world view in which biological populations maintain a more or less fixed outer appearance. This interpretation of Plato's principle of a harmonious universe definitely excludes evolution. From this standpoint, Mayr's statement is correct that the idea of a perfect, harmonious universe constituted one of the major obstacles to the development of a theory of biological evolution.

'Abdu'l-Bahá, however, did not accept the classical worldview of a fixed and perfect cosmos. Instead, he combined the idea of a perfect cosmos with the idea of evolution. It is also important to know that not all neo-Platonic philosophies have the same view about the effect of timeless essences in the material world. Mullá Ṣadrá (c. 1571-1640) in Iran, for instance, formulated the concept of substantial motion (which allows for the temporalization of the effect of essences) before Leibniz (1646-1716) did in Europe. 'Abdu'l-Bahá corroborates the idea of substantial motion in one of his talks published in *Some Answered Questions*:

> Know that nothing which exists remains in a state of repose—that is to say, all things are in motion. Everything is either growing or declining; all things are either coming from nonexistence into being, or going from existence into nonexistence. So this flower, this hyacinth, during a certain period of time was coming from the world of nonexistence into being, and now it is going from being into nonexistence. This state of motion is said to be substantial (*jawharí*)—that is, natural; it cannot be separated from beings because it is their essential requirement, as it is the essential requirement of fire to burn.[200]

'Abdu'l-Bahá describes motion, and by implication change and evolution, as substantial in the world of being. The objects of this world grow, decline, and die. They are assembled by chemical elements, which are later redistributed again. These continuous changes are an essential aspect of this world. In another place, 'Abdu'l-Bahá explains that continuous change and transformation apply to all things save the realm of time-invariant essences:

> Physical bodies are transferred past one barrier after another, from one life to another, and all things are subject to transformation and change, save only the essence of existence itself—since it is constant and immutable, and upon it is founded the life of every species and kind, of every contingent reality throughout the whole of creation.[201]

5.3.1 *An Evolving Universe.* Evolution and transformation are not limited to particular individual objects. In the Bahá'í writings, the concept of transformation rules cosmogony and life as a whole. In this world all things, both wholes and parts, change and experience evolution. The elemental building blocks of animate and inanimate things—the atoms—are in constant motion and are constantly being transferred from one state to another, and from one form of life to another, so that the whole universe and its contents are undergoing endless transformations as new forms are unfolded from the timeless potential order.

Bahá'u'lláh presents cosmogony itself as an evolutionary process:

> God was, and His creation had ever existed beneath His shelter from the beginning that hath no beginning. . . . That which hath been in existence had existed before, but not in the form thou seest today. The world of existence came into being through the heat generated from the interaction between the active force and that which is its recipient.[202]

Only two parts of this statement are considered: (1) The creation as a whole is eternal (independent of time). It is an eternal reflection of the names and attributes of God, upon which the essences of our universe are based. (2) The universe as we know it today is the result of a long-lasting process; it is not static but dynamic. Although it is eternal as a whole, its particular states evolve and change within time and are subject to evolution.

'Abdu'l-Bahá gave the following interpretation of the second sentence of this quote from the Lawḥ-i Ḥikmát:

> From this blessed verse it is clear and evident that the universe is evolving. In the opinion of the philosophers and the wise this fact of the development and evolution of the world of existence is also established. This is to say, it is progressively transferred from one state to another.[203]

In interpreting the statement of Bahá'u'lláh given above, 'Abdu'l-Bahá explicates the dynamics of the universe. The terms "development and evolution" indicate that 'Abdu'l-Bahá assumes considerable changes in the unfoldment of the universe and not only minor adaptions. The cosmology 'Abdu'l-Bahá presents is essentially dynamic; changes are the rule and not the exception. In comparing the classical and modern views of biology, 'Abdu'l-Bahá's cosmology fits in much better with the concept of historicity emphasized in modern theories of the development of the universe, and found in the evolution of living systems, than with the static universe adopted by Aristotle and still by much of the scientific community during the nineteenth century (under the influence of scriptural fundamentalism).

'Abdu'l-Bahá explains that evolution applies to all levels of organization; even the atoms from which all physical things are composed underwent a period of development:

> It is necessary, therefore, that we should know what each of the great existents was in the beginning—for there is no doubt that in the beginning the origin was one: the origin of all numbers is one and not two. Then it is evident that in the beginning there was a single matter, and that one matter appeared in a particular form in each element. Thus various forms were produced, and these various forms as they were produced became independent, and each element was specialized. But this independence was not definite, and did not attain realization and perfect existence until after a very long time.[204]

This quote clearly indicates that, according to 'Abdu'l-Bahá, our universe underwent evolution over a very long period of time; it did not appear suddenly in its present form with all its beings simultaneously created in their present external forms. The whole material universe required an unimaginably long time (e.g., cosmological time scales of 10 to 30 billion years) to evolve to the state that we know today. During the development of the universe, matter, stars and planets appeared originating from a common origin.

5.3.2 Biological Evolution

'Abdu'l-Bahá's concept of evolution applies also to the biosphere. Life unfolds gradually in stages on earth:

> But it is clear that this terrestrial globe in its present form did not come into existence all at once, but that this universal existent gradually passed through different stages until it became adorned with its present perfection. . . . In the same manner, it is evident that this terrestrial globe, having once found existence, grew and developed in the matrix of the universe, and came forth in different forms and conditions, until gradually it attained this present perfection, and became adorned with innumerable beings, and appeared as a finished organization.[205]

The development of life on earth is explained as a long-lasting process (geological time scales of about 5 billion years). Life is not static or in a steady state as believed by Aristotle and the "classical" Christian world, but it continuously changes: "Similarly," continues 'Abdu'l-Bahá, "the terrestrial globe from the beginning was created with all its elements, substances, minerals, parts, and organisms; but these only appeared by degrees: first the mineral, then the plant, afterward the animal, and finally man."[206]

In brief, 'Abdu'l-Bahá emphasizes that the laws of nature for the formation of planets and for biological development are eternal and stable in relation to their objects. The unfolding realization of these potential realities, and of the eternal names and attributes of God, into actual existents, however, takes the form of evolution. After a very long time, the universe evolved to the state we see today. In the matrix of the universe, the terrestrial globe came into being and developed slowly until it attained its present form. Similarly, biological life evolved over a long period of time. Representatives of *Homo sapiens* appeared after plants and animals.

The general view of evolution presented by 'Abdu'l-Bahá agrees with the findings of modern science. This universe and all its subsystems are essentially dynamic.

5.3.3 *Phylogeny Resembles Ontogeny.* To establish both evolution and the concept of the originality of species, 'Abdu'l-Bahá had to argue against the conviction of most classical and modern biologists that species essences and evolution mutually exclude each other. This conviction is clearly stated by Mayr:

> Darwin was fully conscious of the fact that the change from one species into another one was the most fundamental problem of evolution. Indeed, evolution was, almost by definition, a change from one species into another one. The belief in constant, unchangeable species was the fortress of antievolutionism to be stormed and destroyed.[207]

Nevertheless, 'Abdu'l-Bahá clearly supported a form of evolution which he believed to be compatible with time-invariant laws of nature (i.e., species essences). To prove this compatibility, 'Abdu'l-

Bahá presented a particular biological argument: the analogy between human ontogeny (the development of the embryo) and phylogeny (human evolution on earth). There are several passages in *Some Answered Questions* and one talk in *The Promulgation of Universal Peace* where 'Abdu'l-Bahá presents the ontogeny-resembles-ontogeny argument.

> But it is clear that this terrestrial globe in its present form did not come into existence all at once, but that this universal existent gradually passed through different stages until it became adorned with its present perfection. Universal existents resemble and can be compared to particular existents, for both are subject to one natural system, one universal law, and one divine organization. So you will find that the smallest atoms in the universal system are similar to the greatest existents of the universe. It is clear that they come into existence from one laboratory of might under one natural system and one universal law; therefore, they are analogous to one another. Thus the embryo of man in the womb of the mother gradually grows and develops, and appears in different forms and conditions, until in the degree of perfect beauty it reaches maturity and appears in a perfect form with the utmost grace. And in the same way, the seed of this flower which you see was in the beginning an insignificant thing, and very small; and it grew and developed in the womb of the earth and, after appearing in various forms, came forth in this condition with perfect freshness and grace. In the same manner, it is evident that this terrestrial globe, having once found existence, grew and developed in the matrix of the universe, and came forth in different forms and conditions, until gradually it attained this present perfection, and became adorned with innumerable beings, and appeared as a finished organization.[208]

In this paragraph, 'Abdu'l-Bahá argues for the evolution of humanity on earth. First, 'Abdu'l-Bahá states that the planet earth once had a beginning and then developed. The situation we see today was obtained after a long evolution. Then 'Abdu'l-Bahá argues in three steps: (1) Because the universe is based on a single origin and is ruled by "one universal law," small and large systems are comparable. (2) The human embryo develops from the time point of conception and passes through many different stages. The same is true for the growth of plants from their seeds. (3) Because of the similarity between small and large systems, the phylogeny, or evolution, of life on earth follows rules analogous to the ontogeny of a particular human being in its mother's womb.

The relation between ontogeny and phylogeny has long been discussed in Occidental biology. Embryos of different biological species in their early phases of differentiation are often very similar. For instance, bird embryos and mammal embryos become morphologically distinct only at a certain stage of development. Both form gill arches during their early embryonic life which disappear later. In the above argument, 'Abdu'l-Bahá uses only a weak form of parallelism: an analogy. For the sake of the argument, only the development of the embryo as such is required. Particular concepts, such as the Meckel-Serrès law[209] or Haeckel's law of recapitulation[210] are not involved. The appeal to those well-known and widely accepted concepts, however, certainly helped to support 'Abdu'l-Bahá's argument.

In classical biology, species essences were thought to be directly responsible for the inner and outer appearance of their particular representatives. Only minor variations from the "ideal" were thought to be tolerable. Since this view is incompatible with any form of evolution, 'Abdu'l-Bahá's analogy between embryonic ontogeny and human phylogeny represents a way to bridge these differences. Starting from a single cell, the embryo passes through very different biological stages and forms, but all the way through it is human. Its development is determined by the same genome, by the same chromosomes, by the same DNA chains. Analogously, species essences (i.e., time-invariant laws of nature) can be assumed to guide evolution on earth and to rule its dynamics. Without the translation of the information stored in the genes, no complex living organism could develop. The same "unchanging" genome rules its development through these different forms.

Consequently, according to 'Abdu'l-Bahá's analogy, biological evolution does not imply that the species essence must change to allow for all the different stages and developments during evolution. On the contrary, the existence of the species essences ensure that development towards complex life forms is possible. Species essences define the "natural compositions," that is, the requirements to form a functional, dynamic living system that doesn't immediately desintegrate. As the constant genomic information regulates the development of an individual, the time-invariant species essences "guide" evolution as a whole. The species essences ensure that a certain composition of chemical elements always leads to the same result.

The analogy between human ontogeny and phylogeny may also be used to get a first impression of what 'Abdu'l-Bahá means by species essence. In classical biology, the essence was assumed to represent an ideal picture for the members of the species, for example, an ideal horse. Such an essence definition is certainly alien to evolution. Species essences which are assumed to guide evolution have to be more general. What characteristic of the embryo remains constant during ontogeny? At least the biological side of the embryo's development depends on the genetic information content. This is largely constant from the time point of conception through birth and until death. Analogously, one could understand species essences as the information determining which compositions of chemical elements lead to living beings. 'Abdu'l-Bahá's concept of species essences may be equivalent to the assumption of the existence of an objective, reproducible fitness function. In mathematical evolution models, the fitness function guides evolution because it "decides" which members survive and which die. Of course, the strict link between biological species as a reproductive community and species essences, assumed in classical biology, is lost in such a generalized concept of species essences.

5.3.4 *Human Identity during Ontogeny and Phylogeny.* In Chapter 47 of *Some Answered Questions,* 'Abdu'l-Bahá elaborates on the comparison between the development of the embryo and the evolution of the human species on earth. 'Abdu'l-Bahá puts forward the major conclusion, that the human species remains original throughout the development of humanity on earth:

And in the same way, man's existence on this earth, from the beginning until it reaches this state, form and condition, necessarily lasts a long time, and goes through many stages until it reaches this condition. But from the beginning of man's existence he has been a distinct species. In the same way, the embryo of man in the womb of the mother was at first in a strange form; then this body passed from shape to shape, from state to state, from form to form, until it appeared in the utmost beauty and perfection. But even when in the womb of the mother and in this strange form, entirely different from its present form and figure, it was the embryo of a distinct species, and not the embryo of an animal. Man's species and essence have undergone no change whatsoever. Now, assuming that the traces of organs which have disappeared actually existed, this is not a proof of the impermanence and the nonoriginality of the species. At the most it proves that the form, appearance, and organs of man have evolved. But man was always a distinct species, a man, not an animal. . . . For the originality of the human species and the independence of the essence of man, is clear and evident.[211]

This quote starts with the major conclusion drawn by 'Abdu'l-Bahá in Chapter 47 of *Some Answered Questions*. Although humanity undergoes an evolution on this planet, changes in all respects as the embryo does in the mother's womb, still ". . . from the beginning of man's existence he is a distinct species." Here 'Abdu'l-Bahá extends the analogy between ontogeny and the evolution of humanity. The embryo is human from the time point of conception, although during ontogeny it changes in all respects. In the same manner, the human "species and essence" exists from the beginning of the universe and does not change during evolution; it remains original. A similar statement is given in another chapter:

To recapitulate: just as man in the womb of the mother passes from form to form, from shape to shape, changes and develops, and is still the human species from the beginning of the embryonic period—in the same way man, from the beginning of his formation in the matrix of the world, is also a distinct species—that is, man—and he has gradually passed from one form to another. Therefore, this change of appearance, this evolution of organs, this development and growth, does not prevent the originality of the species.[212]

The embryo in the womb of the mother starts as a single cell and passes through many states, until it obtains maturity and strength to survive in this world. Throughout all this development, beginning with a single cell, this embryo is human. The biological aspects of the embryonic growth depend necessarily on the DNA as a (more or less) constant, "time-invariant" origin of development. The genome, the DNA, guides the necessary formation of the organs and their mutual interactions. Changes, mutations, or defects in the genome generally tend to ruin the new life. The embryo is human from the time point of conception, its DNA is human, not that of fishes, nor that of higher primates. It maintains its particular genome, its potential to express human characteristics, through all the stages of development from conception to birth.

Just as the embryo remains human, "man, from the beginning of his formation in the matrix of the world, is also a distinct species." According to this view, the human "species and essence" is a time-invariant law of nature, but its physical expressions have a temporal origin, and evolve and change over time.[213] The evolution of humanity, and of every creature on this planet, depends upon the intelligible timeless order, designated "essences" by 'Abdu'l-Bahá.

5.4 Parallel Evolution

How literally are we to understand 'Abdu'l-Bahá's analogy between phylogeny and ontogeny? If, on the one hand, it is understood to present a general philosophical understanding about the fundamental nature of the universe, and about the metaphysical origin of complex order in our world, then this analogy should be accepted as a convincing argument that essentialism and evolution are not mutually exclusive. Because the "European philosophers" (e.g., Büchner, Spencer, and Haeckel), representing an important philosophical school of modern evolution at the turn of the nineteenth century, believed in mechanistic evolution and rejected essentialism in general (which they equated with typological thinking), 'Abdu'l-Bahá's argument is an important counterargument to the mechanistic world view.

If, on the other hand, 'Abdu'l-Bahá's analogy is understood to argue for a particular scientific concept of how biological life evolved on earth, then it can be understood to support parallel evolution. The analogy between human phylogeny and embryonic ontogeny particularly invites this interpretation. In this case, statements such as: "But from the beginning of man's existence he has been a distinct species . . . a man, not an animal"[214] and "Man, from the beginning, had this perfect form and composition, and possessed the potentiality and capacity for acquiring inner and outer perfections,"[215] might be understood to refer to the biological evolution of humanity, where "beginning" indicates the time point of the first appearance of the human species on earth. In this case, 'Abdu'l-Bahá's arguments would present a picture of biological evolution radically different from the theories of modern evolution biology.

In a parallel evolution model, a biologically distinct line of the human species would exist from the beginning of life on earth, i.e., at the stage of very primitive life forms, until modern *Homo sapiens sapiens*. Because the originality of species is a general principle, distinct lines of parallel evolution would have to be assumed for each individual biological species. The following statement of 'Abdu'l-Bahá, if understood in a biological sense, would support this: "All beings, whether universal or particular, were created perfect and complete from the first, but their perfections appear in them by degrees."[216]

As indicated in the introduction, some authors understand 'Abdu'l-Bahá's statements as a proposal for parallel evolution. In such an interpretation, the terms "species," "man," and similar ones are assumed to refer to the biological organisms. But in view of the different species concepts introduced in this article, it should be clear that a mere biological interpretation of these terms is insufficient and may result in misleading interpretations of 'Abdu'l-Bahá's teachings. Consequently, any biological interpretation of this concept requires one to find corresponding biological species definitions in the Bahá'í writings. Philosophically, it is not difficult to argue for a model of parallel evolution, but if one claims that it also describes biological reality, then it must be supported by evidence from applied biology. Otherwise, such a claim would "begin with words and end with words."[217]

5.4.1 *Practical Problems with the Concept of Parallel Evolution.* There exists no necessary correlation between the human embryo being human from the time point of conception and human phylogeny being biologically human all the way down. Such a concept is not implicit in the paradigm of classical biology nor in that of modern biology. Lamark, however, proposed a similar idea. According to Mayr: "Lamark attributed it [i.e., the creation of new species] to a *deus ex machina*, spontaneous generation. Each evolutionary line, according to him, was the product of a separate spontaneous generation of simple forms which subsequently evolved into higher organisms."[218] But this theory, although prominent at the end of the nineteenth century, does not explain the known paleontological and biological data.[219] It requires that new simple starting points of new species be continually created. Such a constant creation is not found.

If one prefers to understand 'Abdu'l-Bahá's writings as teaching parallel evolution, then a series of questions must be answered if this concept is to be taken seriously:

(1) Parallel evolution requires at least a single branching point. Every biological species appeared at a certain time point for the first time on earth. Where did it come from? According to 'Abdu'l-Bahá, "there is no doubt that in the beginning the origin was one: the origin of all numbers is one and not two."[220] All kingdoms originate from the same root. With respect to the chemical elements, there is no distinction between the higher kingdoms; there are no atoms specialized just for vegetables but not for animals or humans. If all kingdoms have the same root, a model of parallel evolution requires points to be defined where the vegetable, animal, and human species branched from their common roots.

(2) A biological definition of the term *species* must be developed that is compatible with the concept of parallel evolution and with the known facts of biology. In particular, the documented cases of speciation[221] would have to be taken into account. Of course, specia-

tion in this context means speciation according to the modern species definition. A redefinition would require some care to avoid getting trapped in unspecific species definitions which would be of little practical value for applied biology.

(3) Because all the species existed from the beginning in the primordial soup, the maximal number of species must have lived at that time and became constantly reduced due to extinctions.[222] What was the distinction between all these species?

(4) Comparing the similarity between the DNA sequences of various organisms, one definitely obtains a tree-like pattern compatible with neo-Darwinism, but not a star pattern as expected in the case of a single branching point, and not a network, which would indicate no phylogenetic relation at all. A theory of parallel evolution would have to explain why DNA sequence similarities among human beings (e.g., the mitochondrial Eve) reflect biological relationships, whereas DNA sequence similarities between various species would not account for such relationships.

(5) Apparently, all multicellular higher taxa stem from a very few eukaryontic cells. In a model of parallel evolution, one either has to assume that all higher taxa branch from those few eukaryontic cells, or one would have to explain how the eukaryontic cell was reinvented millions or even billions of times for each existing species.

Parallel evolution would be plausible if the space of possible forms of living organisms were strongly bounded and the transition within these possible forms along the developmental line of a species very likely. Such a type of evolution is generally designated convergent evolution. An astonishing case of convergent evolution is the extinct marsupalian wolf in Australia which had much in common with the European wolf. To establish parallel evolution, one would have to prove that due to the bounds within which life is possible, the reinvention of the same organs, the same organelles, and often the same or very similar DNA sequences was inevitable. Without such a proof the concept of parallel evolution would remain unsubstantiated. The assumption of parallel evolution produces more problems than it solves. Therefore, it is considered in this essay to be the less likely interpretation of the analogy between phylogeny and ontogeny.

5.4.2 *'Abdu'l-Bahá's Talk Given in San Francisco*. There is a statement in one of the talks 'Abdu'l-Bahá gave during his journey through North America, published in *The Promulgation of Universal Peace*, where a biological interpretation supportive of a parallel evolution model appears to be inevitable. Shoghi Effendi, however, considers the translation of 'Abdu'l-Bahá's talks in this book as "too inaccurate, in some places, to use them as an absolute basis for discussing some points"[223]; consequently, a revised translation of a passage from the talk presented in San Francisco is given here, based on the Persian original.

The reservations of Shoghi Effendi were confirmed when comparing both texts. Certain statements given in the original free English translation are absent in the Persian original. For instance, the passage "in the protoplasm, man is man," which most strongly supports parallel evolution, has no counterpart in the Persian text, as can be seen if one compares the new translations below with the original English translation found in *The Promulgation of Universal Peace*:

> Briefly, the evidences of the intellect of man are manifest and clear. Man is man by reason of this intellectual faculty. Therefore, the animal kingdom is other than the human kingdom. Notwithstanding this, the philosophers of the West have adduced evidences to demonstrate that man had his origin in the animal kingdom. . . . In other words, he was transferred from one state to another until he reached this human shape and form. They say that the manner of man's formation can be compared to the links of a chain, which are connected to one another. However, between man and the ape one link is missing. Great scientists and philosophers have searched for it, some even devoting their whole lives to solving this problem, but until now they have been unable to find that missing link.[224]

First 'Abdu'l-Bahá emphasizes the distinction between the human and the animal kingdoms. After explaining the theory of the European philosophers of the descent of *Homo sapiens* from the animal world, 'Abdu'l-Bahá stresses that no link has been found between *Homo sapiens* and higher primates. Then 'Abdu'l-Bahá describes his position and the position of the "philosophers of the East" concerning Darwinism:

The philosophers of the East say: If the human body was originally not in its present composition, but was gradually transferred from one stage to another until it appeared in its present form [as the philosophers of the West say], then we would postulate that although at one time it was a swimmer and later a crawler, still it was human, and its species has remained unchanged. The proof for this is that the human embryo is at first a mere germ. Gradually the hands and feet appear and the lower limbs become separated from each other, and it is transferred from one form to another, from one shape to another, until it becomes born with this shape and appearance. But from the time it was in the womb in the form of a germ, it was the species of man and not like the embryo of other animals. It was in the form of a germ, but it progressed from that form to this most beautiful form. Therefore, it is clear that the species is preserved.

Provided that we assent [to this theory] that man was at one time a creature swimming in the sea and later became a four-legged creature, assuming this to be true, we still cannot say that man was an animal. Proof of this lies in the fact that in the stage of the embryo man resembles a worm. The embryo progresses from one form to another, until the human form appears. But even in the stage of the embryo he is still man and his species remains unchanged.

The link which they say is lost is itself a proof that man was never an animal. How is it possible to have all the links present and that important link absent? Though one spend this precious life searching for this link, it is certain that it will never be found.[225]

'Abdu'l-Bahá's reference to the missing link cannot be understood to support parallel evolution. Any fossil finding of an ancient human form, which should exist according to the parallel evolution model, could be interpreted as such a missing link. At the time 'Abdu'l-Bahá was in the United States, the question of the missing link was heatedly discussed in scientific circles as well as by the public. It was hotly debated whether or not Darwin's theory of biological evolution also applied to the human species.

The first missing link ever presented, the Piltdown man, was bogus, and it took nearly forty years to discover this forgery.[226] Haeckel[227] presented the Java man, discovered by the Dutch military physician Eugen Dubois in 1891, as the missing link between apes and humanity. The time thought to be required to evolve *Homo sapiens* from ancestral primates varied widely during the nineteenth century. Darwin located this branch point at 30 million years ago.[228]

In contrast, at the beginning of the twentieth century, Haeckel considered time ranges of between 100,000 and 1,000,000 years as necessary for human evolution from ancestral primates. His view corresponded with the general opinion of paleontologists at that time. Most estimates given during the middle of the nineteenth century were much shorter. Those earlier estimates, however, were still dominant in the general public opinion at the time 'Abdu'l-Bahá visited the United States.[229]

A direct link between modern higher primates and *Homo sapiens*, expected by some scientists at the time of 'Abdu'l-Bahá's visit in the States, however, was never found. Today, many fossil findings are known which allow us to trace back human evolution much more accurately. Modern paleontologists generally assume that *Homo sapiens* and the modern higher primates have a common ancestor, but they are not directly linked. Putative predecessors of the human species lived about 5 million years ago in Africa.[230] The branching point between *Homo sapiens* and higher primates is assumed to be at least 10 million years ago.

5.5 The Meaning of the Term "Species"

In several of his talks, 'Abdu'l-Bahá criticized the "theory of some European philosophers" that the human species stems from the animal kingdom. The interpretation of those passages depends critically on the meaning of the term "species" in his writings. Therefore, the various meanings of the term "species" are now carefully analyzed. Any interpretation of 'Abdu'l-Bahá's statements about evolution has to make clear which species definition is being used and why this particular interpretation should be preferred over the others. Here three species concepts are distinguished:

(1) Modern species definitions are characterized by their emphasis on the individual, by *population thinking*. One of the current def-

initions of a species in modern biology sets the boundaries between different kinds by their ability to interbreed: "A species is a reproductive community of populations (reproductively isolated from others) that occupies a specific niche in nature."[231] This is a rather nominalistic concept because the species is not defined by some general rule but, following the Aristotelian tradition, simply by the members of a group of related organisms.

(2) In classical biology species definitions were dominated by Platonic essences, by *typological thinking*. A species was considered to represent an ideal picture of the represented kind (e.g., an ideal cat):

> Every earthly thing is a sort of imperfect copy or reflection of an ideal exemplar or Form that existed timelessly in the Platonic realm of Ideas, reigned over by God. . . . Their individual members came and went, but the species itself remained unchanged. . . . In fact, the word "species" was at one point a standard translation of Plato's Greek word for Form or Idea, *eidos*.[232]

All existing populations were thought to represent, in a fixed way, one particular species essence. And because these species were considered to be created perfectly in their outward forms, any changes within respective populations were thought to be confined to certain narrow limits. Evolution is impossible with this species concept.

(3) Another species concept we may designate as that of the "philosophers of the East." Although the Arabic-speaking philosophers accepted the classical view of fixed essences and a harmonious cosmos, they added to it the idea of "progress toward perfection" (*taraqqí ila'l-kamál*). In other words, the timeless potentiality of creatures was realized through temporal unfoldment. 'Abdu'l-Bahá obviously supports some form of this concept.

This concept applied to evolution implies that the species essences not only contain an "ideal picture of a cat," but also its possible evolutionary pathways (just as Newtonian mechanics not only contains all possible stable constellations of the planets, but also their evolution).

5.5.1 *'Abdu'l-Bahá's Concept of the "Human Species."* In *Some Answered Questions*, 'Abdu'l-Bahá argues in favor of the originality of the human species based on the ideas of a perfect harmonious universe and time-invariant laws of nature. The point of these arguments is that the "species of man" exists eternally without change, so 'Abdu'l-Bahá is clearly not using the terms "human species" or "man" in their modern meaning, where they would refer to a biological population of human beings. 'Abdu'l-Bahá's understanding of the term "species" instead falls under the category of the classical concept of a "species essence." His claim, in Chapter 50 of *Some Answered Questions*, that the human species exists eternally makes sense only within an essentialistic species concept:

> Now we will adduce theological proofs that human existence—that is, the species of man—is a necessary existence, and that without man the divine perfections would not appear. . . . We have many times demonstrated and established that man is the noblest of contingent beings, the sum of all perfections, and that all beings and all existents are centers for the appearance of the divine effulgence—that is to say, the signs of the divinity of God are manifest in the realities of all created things. . . . The world, indeed each existing being, proclaims to us one of the names of God, but the reality of man is the collective reality, the general reality, and the center for the appearance of all the divine perfections—that is to say, for each name, each attribute, each perfection which we affirm of God there exists a sign in man. . . . Consequently, the divinity of God, which is the sum of all perfections, appears resplendent in the reality of man—that is to say, the Essence of Oneness is the possessor of all perfections, and from this unity He casts an effulgence upon the human reality. Man, then, is the perfect mirror facing the Sun of Truth and is its place of appearance: the Sun of Truth shines in this mirror.[233]

'Abdu'l-Bahá describes our world as a mirror reflecting the names and attributes of God. If the "species of man" were missing, this would imply the corresponding non-existence of certain names and attributes of God. As he says in another place, "the names and attributes of God require the existence of objects or creatures upon which they have been bestowed and in which they have become manifest."[234] In this context, the term "species" is certainly not used in a biological sense, but in an essentialistic sense referring to the eternal reality of our universe. In the light of 'Abdu'l-Bahá's statements on evolution as a process of unfolding, "species" here indicates the potential of the laws of nature to form human beings wherever the environment is suitable.

The Guardian of the Bahá'í Faith, Shoghi Effendi, gave a few explanations concerning the originality of the human species: "The Bahá'í Faith teaches man was always potentially man, even when passing through the lower stages of evolution."[235] In a letter Shoghi Effendi wrote:

> We cannot prove man was always man for this is a fundamental doctrine, but it is based on the assertion that nothing can exceed its own potentialities, that everything, a stone, a tree, an animal and a human being, existed in plan, potentially, from the very "beginning" of creation. We don't believe man has always had the form of man, but rather that from the outset he was going to evolve into the human form and species and not be a haphazard branch of the ape family.[236]

Shoghi Effendi states that the *originality of species* is based on the principle that "nothing can exceed its own potentialities." This principle means that the ability of the human species to show forth intelligence was not developed during evolution, but was potentially present from the beginning of the universe.

5.6 Summary

'Abdu'l-Bahá does not accept the idea that creation and evolution are two mutually exclusive concepts, or that the development of our universe is accidental, without a purpose, goal, or destiny. He does not deny the facts that are generally used to support biological evolution, but he criticizes the frequently made conclusion of "some European philosophers" (such as Büchner and Haeckel) that evolution excludes the existence of a Creator, creation, and a higher purpose for our universe. He emphatically argues against the idea that

Darwinism alone can explain the origin of complex order out of "primeval simplicity."[237]

In support of the concept of the originality of the species, 'Abdu'l-Bahá refers to the argument of a perfect harmonious universe (originating from Plato) and to the existence of timeless universal laws of nature, a concept that was firmly accepted in physics and chemistry in the second-half of the nineteenth century. Both arguments imply that if the human species as a potential reality was missing, this would render the universe imperfect and incomplete.

The first of the two arguments was well established in Occidental philosophy and was understood to represent a strong counterargument against evolution. The concept of a perfect harmonious universe implies that all possible forms of life exist from the very beginning of creation. As God is timelessly perfect, His creation, reflecting His names and attributes, is also eternally complete. Consequently, the origin of the universe is presupposed to be essentially complex. But 'Abdu'l-Bahá formulated an understanding of Plato's harmony argument radically different from the philosophic concepts of classical Western biology, because he expanded this old concept to include evolution.

The constancy of matter and energy, and the time invariance of the laws of nature were understood by Büchner and Haeckel to exclude creation. By his argument, 'Abdu'l-Bahá reversed a well-known interpretation of those concepts to support creation. He considers it evident that a certain composition of chemical elements which today results in a human being (or a myoglobin molecule) some time ago would have produced the same human being (or the same kind of myoglobin molecule) and nothing else. If the same composition under the same boundary conditions always produces the same outcome, then the evolution of humanity is not a principally unpredictable, irreproducible outcome of haphazard self-creations, but the unfolding of potential characteristics inherent in laws of nature. In neo-Platonic language, evolution translates the timeless species essences into actuality, and in Bahá'í terminology, evolution realizes mirrors capable of reflecting the names and attributes of God.

By the analogy between human ontogeny and phylogeny, 'Abdu'l-Bahá demonstrated that the assumption of a human species essence does not contradict the evolution of *Homo sapiens* on earth. Although the fertilized human egg passes through many very different phases, it is human from the time point of conception. Its "being human" does not prevent all those changes; the genetic information is even a necessary precondition for the unfolding of all the inherent potentials of this new member of human society. Just as the information stored in DNA chains regulates the development of growing organisms and unfolds their hidden potentials during the life of their "hosts," species essences "guide" evolution on cosmological and geological time scales. Thus the existence of a universal law predefining "humanity" or other species may be understood as a necessary precondition for making the evolution of a complex biosphere possible. Interestingly, the constancy of the genome discovered by modern microbiology, strengthens 'Abdu'l-Bahá's argument.

Because of the conviction of many Western philosophers and biologists that evolution and the existence of species essences are mutually exclusive, this analogy is an important and original element in 'Abdu'l-Bahá's concept of evolution. 'Abdu'l-Bahá's concept, however, although closely related to Plato's essences, should not be mistaken with the typological thinking current in classical biology. The major purpose of 'Abdu'l-Bahá's arguments is to show the compatibility between evolution and creation.

CHRIST PRESIDES OVER CREATION

This title page from Thomas Burnet's *Sacred Theory of the Earth* (1690) shows Jesus Christ straddling the first and last stages of the earth's development. Shown in a sequence of seven spheres, Burnet attempted to explain the present form of the world by natural events, rather than a single act of creation.

Section 6

Spiritual Dimensions of the Human Origin Discussion

After the publication of Darwin's *The Origin of Species*, it became obvious that his concept of evolution undermined the classical, largely biblical worldview of creation prevalent in the Occident. In natural theology, the existence of well-adapted, complex life forms were considered to strongly support the biblical picture of a world originating from a powerful and benevolent Creator. Because Darwin, according to Dennett, reduced the origin of species to a "mindless, algorithmic process of evolution,"[238] the philosophy of modern biology together with other influences destroyed the foundation of natural theology and undermined belief in creation.

The problem of morality under the influence of a materialistic form of Darwinism was seen rather early. Many of the nineteenth-century materialists, however, assumed that reason would be sufficient to formulate generally accepted moral values. For instance, Haeckel says about his monistic, quasi-religious movement: "This monistic religion and ethics differ from all others, for we base it exclusively on pure reason. It is a worldview grounded in science, experience, and reasonable belief."[239] Büchner considers the

Golden Rule to be the basis of any workable ethics and solidarity the quintessence of morality.[240]

Mayr clearly sees the tendency of Darwinism to destroy classical value systems:

> Biology has an awesome responsibility. It can hardly be denied that it has helped to undermine traditional beliefs and value systems. Many of the most optimistic ideas of the Enlightenment, including equality and the possibility of a perfect society, were ultimately (although very subconsciously) part of physico-theology. It was God who had made this near-perfect world. A belief in such a world was bound to collapse when the belief in God as designer was undermined.[241]

Mayr tries to solve this problem by grounding human values on Darwinism:

> If, instead of defining man as the personal ego or merely a biological creature, one defines man as mankind, an entirely different ethics and ideology is possible. It would be an ideology that is quite compatible with the traditional values of wanting to "better mankind" and yet which is compatible with any of the new findings of biology. If this approach is chosen, there will be no conflict between science and the most profound human values.[241]

Ward, however, severely doubts that "metaphysical Darwinism" is sufficient to ground human values:

> Only a theory that is completely certain should be allowed to undermine this moral sense. Metaphysical Darwinism is far from being such a theory. Indeed, its inability to account for the moral consciousness in a satisfactory way is one of the strongest arguments for its incompleteness as a total explanation of human behavior, and therefore of the evolution of life.[242]

Thus, Darwin's new theory revolutionized not only the biological sciences, but it challenged a whole worldview, particularly the concepts of human purpose and destiny. These far-reaching consequences were seen and discussed soon after the publication of

Darwin's *Origin of Species*. Many of the more popularized publications about Darwin's theory directly addressed religious and philosophical issues, and often claimed that the "new worldviews" were the direct consequence of the "new facts" of modern sciences.

6.1 Implications of the Unity of Nature

Why should particular biological results challenge worldviews and, to use Dennett's words, threaten "to leak out, offering answers—welcome or not—to questions in cosmology (going in one direction) and psychology (going in the other direction)"?[243] This challenge is a direct consequence of the idea of the unity of nature. Haeckel based his concept of the unity of nature on the agreement of physical and chemical forces in the inorganic as well as organic world. From this he concluded: "the unity of natural forces or alternatively the monism of energy."[244] Weizsäcker formulates this principle in more traditional physical terms, whereas Dennett applies the concept of natural selection to cosmology as well as to psychology. Thus, if such a unity of nature exists, the fundamental laws which bring forth the complex order of our biosphere should be relevant in all "directions." If we assume that our universe does not divide up into several disconnected parts of reality, then we should assume a unity in the fundamental principles ruling this universe.

In contrast, to escape the consequences of materialism, many Protestant theologians divided the world into two contrary parts: a materialistic and a spiritual one. By this separation of reality into a world of facts and a world of values, religion was thought to be immune against the attacks of materialistic philosophy.[245] A similar separation was recently proposed by Gould.[246]

The Bahá'í Faith upholds the concept of the unity of our reality. 'Abdu'l-Bahá explains that everything in our universe stems from a single root: "for there is no doubt that in the beginning the origin was one."[247] 'Abdu'l-Bahá often repeats that "truth is one" and makes this principle the reason for the harmony that should exist between science and religion.[248] Thus, if the unity of nature is assumed, in the last analysis the fundamental driving forces should be the same in particle physics, the evolution of life, cultural and scientific development, and in human ethics and moral behavior.

6.1.1 *Evolution and Human Values.* Since Laplace, many have considered mechanics to be "atheistic." Haeckel formulated this view: "Once Laplace based the fundamental laws of our world in mathematics, all inorganic natural sciences became mechanistic and consequently purely atheistic."[249] At the time of Laplace, the complex order of the biosphere, however, was still considered to require an explanation which could not be given by mechanics alone. The complex forms of life were still accepted as a good argument in support of the existence of a benevolent Creator. Darwin's natural selection filled this "gap" by providing the means to explain complex biological order on mechanistic grounds.

Thus, many of Darwin's contemporaries understood Darwinism to show that complex biological order doesn't require an external origin. According to Büchner: "Neither does nature know a supernatural beginning, nor a supernatural continuation; as all begetting and all devouring, she is in herself origin and end, birth and death. Of her own resources, she procreated the so-called creation and humanity as its apex."[250] In the same spirit, Haeckel presented atheism as a direct consequence of Darwin's discovery, although he himself preferred the term monism for his new belief. Explaining the concept of atheism, Haeckel states that "this 'god-less worldview' essentially agrees with the monism and pantheism of our modern natural sciences. . . . It is only another expression for the non-existence of an otherworldly, supernatural deity."[251]

From the very beginning, Darwinism was understood to challenge the foundation of the classical worldview. This consequence of the new theory was seen by friend and foe alike. Societies were founded to support and distribute these new "scientific" ideas. In 1881 Ludwig Büchner co-founded the *Deutschen Freidenkerbund.* To spread his monistic religion, Haeckel promoted the *Deutschen Monistenbund* in 1906 in Jena. He himself considered his "new faith" to be a competitor against Christianity: "It is obvious that the Christian worldview must be replaced by this monistic philosophy."[252] According to

Büchner, "science must replace religion, faith in a natural and absolute world order must substitute for belief in spirits and ghosts, and natural morals must overcome artificial dogmas."[253] In Great Britain, similar campaigns were supported by Huxley and Spencer.

The existence of a final cause, goal, or destiny for evolution has been denied by many Darwinists. Not only in the past, but also today, Darwinism is often presented as incompatible with belief in traditional religion. Dawkins formulates this rejection rather drastically. He claims that only "scientifically illiterate" people assume a purpose in nature:

> Nature is not cruel, only pitilessly indifferent. This lesson is one of the hardest for humans to learn. We cannot accept that things might be neither good nor evil, neither cruel nor kind, but simply callous: indifferent to all suffering, lacking all purpose. . . . In a universe of electrons and selfish genes, blind physical forces and genetic replication, some people are going to get lucky, and you won't find any rhyme or reason in it, nor any justice. The universe that we observe has precisely the properties we should expect if there is, at the bottom, no design, no purpose, no evil and no good, nothing but pitiless indifference.[254]

According to modern meta-biology, life and finally humanity is the "product of a blind, algorithmic process." It has to escape the "slings and arrows of outrageous fortune in a tough external world."

If all biological characteristics did develop on the path of evolution, this should also be true for instincts and social behavior. Following Herbert Spencer, Haeckel supposed human social behavior to be the consequence of instincts: "Social duties . . . are only highly developed forms of social instincts which are found with all higher animals living in social groups."[255] Similar positions were also formulated by Büchner. Haeckel applied the rule of the survival of the fittest to human history. From the obvious lack of morality in most historical events, he concludes that no higher moral order exists.

In the case of the oxygen-binding ability of a myoglobin molecule, it is certainly only of academic interest whether this particular characteristic is the result of *ad hoc* self-creation or whether it reveals the timeless properties of the chemical elements. But in the case of social laws, this question has implications for daily life. Whether those laws are arbitrary, mere conventions introduced by powerful groups within our society to serve their particular interests, or whether they reflect some objective, God-given order, makes a great deal of difference. If social laws and concepts are not grounded in a fundamental structure of nature or in some higher order, but are arbitrary *ad hoc* creations, then "anything goes" as formulated by the German philosopher Paul Feyerabend.[256]

On the one hand, social norms would then be partly based on social instincts inherited from our predecessors. In this case, a "natural social order" would be determined by social instincts adapted from an environment that was inhabited by human beings several million years ago. For instance, the ability of humanity to address the problems of racism and war is often evaluated on the basis of our animal heritage: "Uncritical assent is given to the proposition that human beings are incorrigibly selfish and aggressive and thus incapable of erecting a social system at once progressive and peaceful, dynamic and harmonious, a system giving free play to individual creativity and initiative but based on cooperation and reciprocity."[257]

On the other hand, the part of our norms which are not bound by archaic patterns of behavior would be absolutely arbitrary and very likely would serve only the interests of certain influential groups. Then the deconstructionists would be correct in stating that any concept of our world has the same level of validity. Some are not better than others.[258] Alan Sokal caricatured such a view by saying that then even the laws of nature would be the result of social agreements and lack objectivity.[259]

6.1.2 *Values Based on a "Complex Origin."* But what if moral values are not arbitrary? There are certainly moral values which are constructive and others which destabilize a society. If we assume that nature has inherent purpose, then our behavior would have adapted at least partly to this purpose. In a reality that mirrors the names and attributes of God, human behavior would not be confined by the achievements of the past, but could change according to human destiny, and could be realized during evolution. If evolution serves a God-given destiny, evolutionary achievements not only reflect the history of evolution but also its goals. Then our behavior is not only determined by our animal heritage, which undoubtedly exists, but also will adapt to our evolutionary destiny.

Does such an approach help us to formulate social concepts and moral value systems that solve the actual problems of our time? As proposed by the leading body of the Bahá'í Faith,[260] any definitely new insight and solution for the question of the "natural social order" must consider traditional religious value systems. Whereas the interactions between electrons or planets are fixed by the laws of physics, laws of social interaction are (at least to some extent) not fixed. They can be willfully modified and they are known to have changed throughout history. What freedom do we have to choose values compatible with a peaceful, progressive society? Are there objective sources for human values? It is certainly difficult, if not impossible, to answer such questions by scientific means. Our social concepts, however, create facts in this real world by means of our deeds, and in this real world we have to manage our lives. One can at least objectively study the impact of certain values on human behavior. For instance, what practical consequences does faith in purpose in life have on human conduct?

Should we simply trust in our "traditional values"? This solution may work locally, but worldwide there are too many different traditional value systems for each one to be applied to a world society. Thus, lastly, we have to refer to some kind of trial and error, to an evolutionary strategy. If social interactions are dependent on a timeless reality, the success of a community depends on their "fitness" to foster a lively community. In this case, social laws are subject to the "survival of the fittest," where the fitness would be set by an unknown but objective "fitness function." Thus, the multiple value systems which are offered on the market of the world have to be tested to see whether or not they serve their purpose.

According to the Bahá'í Faith, the purpose of religion is to educate humanity: "The purpose underlying the revelation of every heavenly Book, nay, of every divinely-revealed verse, is to endue all men with righteousness and understanding, so that peace and tranquillity may be firmly established amongst them."[261] Thus, religious value systems can be investigated to see whether or not they serve their self-defined purpose.

6.2 At Home in the Universe

Teachings about the purpose and destiny of life are the central subjects of virtually every religion. For instance, Bahá'u'lláh, the prophet-founder of the Bahá'í Faith, states in his Hidden Words:

> O Son of Man! Veiled in My immemorial being and in the ancient eternity of My essence, I knew My love for thee; therefore I created thee, have engraved on thee Mine image and revealed to thee My beauty.

> O Son of Man! I loved thy creation, hence I created thee. Wherefore, do thou love Me, that I may name thy name and fill thy soul with the spirit of life.[262]

In 'Abdu'l-Bahá's talks on the subject of evolution addressed to his Western followers, he attempts to resolve the question of how evolution can be compatible with creation and a purpose of life. 'Abdu'l-Bahá did not address the particular mechanisms of the evolution of different forms of life. As the appointed leader of the young Bahá'í community, he recognized the tendency of Darwinism to "leak out" to give answers to problems in cosmology and social evolution as well.

According to the author of this essay, the purpose of 'Abdu'l-Bahá's arguments is to show that our cosmological, biological, and social order is not arbitrary, accidental, or trivial, but that it is based on a potential complex order existing from the very beginning.

On the one hand, it may be impossible to detect purpose by scientific means. On the other hand, our belief in the existence or absence of a non-arbitrary purpose for our universe has huge implications for our visions of the future! If mankind has a non-trivial destiny, we may be able overcome archaic patterns of aggressive behavior and the destructive aspects of "social instincts" inherited from our predecessors. The conviction of the destiny of a peaceful future invests us with the necessary will, fortitude, and optimism to take the required actions to establish a peaceful and progressive society. Such "positive thinking" may be a necessary precondition to solving the world's problems. We are not "gypsies at the edge of the universe."[263] We really should feel "At Home in the Universe."[264] The future will demonstrate whether the "meme"[265] of the "selfish gene" or the meme of "All men have been created to carry forward an ever-advancing civilization"[266] will enable humanity to create a "progressive and peaceful, dynamic and harmonious" society.

NOTES:

Section 1: Introduction

1. M. Gell-Mann, *The Quark and the Jaguar* (New York: WH Freeman, 1994) and C. F. von Weizsäcker, *Aufbau der Physik*, 2nd edition (München: Carl Hanser Verlag, 1986).
2. D. C. Dennett, *Darwin's Dangerous Idea* (New York: Simon & Schuster, 1995).
3. E. Mayr, *One Long Argument* (Cambridge: Harvard University Press, 1991).
4. R. Dawkins, *The Selfish Gene*, new edition (Oxford: Oxford University Press, 1989), p. 1.
5. C. Darwin, *The Origin of Species* (London: Penguin Books, 1985).
6. R. Dawkins, *The Blind Watchmaker* (London: Longmans, 1986) and E. Mayr (1991).
7. Mayr, *One Long Argument*, p. 68.
8. Dawkins, *Blind Watchmaker*, p. 287.
9. W. Howells, *Getting Here: The Story of Human Evolution* (Washington: Compass Press, 1993) p. 4.
10. E. Mayr, *The Growth of Biological Thought* (Cambridge: Harvard University Press, 1982) p. 626.
11. T. Beardsley, "Darwin Denied: Opponents of Evolution Make Gains in Schools," *Scientific American*, vol. 273, no. 1 (1995) pp. 12-14.
12. For details see Keven Brown's accompanying essay: *'Abdu'l-Bahá's Response to Darwinism: Its Historical and Philosophical Context.*
13. The origin of these talks in Palestine is described in the foreword of the book *Some Answered Questions*: "The talks between 'Abdu'l-Bahá and Laura Clifford Barney took place during the difficult years, 1904-1906, when he was confined to the city of Akká by the Turkish government and permitted to receive only a few visitors. At the time he was under constant threat of removal to a distant desert confinement. As interlocutor, Miss Barney arranged for one of 'Abdu'l-Bahá's sons-in-law, or for one of the three distinguished Persians of his secretariat of that period, to be present during the talks to insure accuracy in recording his replies to the questions asked him. 'Abdu'l-Bahá later read the transcriptions, sometimes changing a word or a line with his reed pen. They were later translated into English by Miss Barney. The original Persian texts are today a part of the Bahá'í archives of Haifa." (From the publisher's foreword to the 1964 edition) Miss Barney published these talks under the title *Some Answered Questions* (hereafter cited as *SAQ*).
14. During his visit to the United States in 1912, 'Abdu'l-Bahá gave public talks on many occasions. Many talks were recorded in Persian and in English. They were published under the title *The Promulgation of Universal Peace* (cited below as *PUP*) in English and as *Khatibát-i Hadrat-i 'Abdu'l-Bahá* in Persian.
15. J. Hatcher and W. Hatcher, *The Law of Love Enshrined* (Oxford: George Ronald, 1996).
16. L. Büchner, *Kraft und Stoff*, 21st edition (Leipzig: Theodor Thomas, 1904).
17. L. Büchner, *Sechs Vorlesungen über die Darwin'sche Theorie von der Verwandlung der Arten und die erste Enstehung der Organismenwelt*, 2nd edition (Leipzig: Theodore Thomas, 1868).

18. E. Haeckel, *Die Welträtsel*, 11th Edition (Stuttgart: Kröner, 1984).
19. Ibid., p. 30.
20. Ibid., p. 29.
21. Ibid., p. 366.
22. Ibid., p. 480.
23. Ibid., p. 507.
24. J. E. Esslemont, *Baha'u'llah and the New Era* (Wilmette: Bahá'í Publishing Trust, 1980).
25. A. Khursheed, *Science and Religion: Towards the Restoration of an Ancient Harmony* (London: Oneworld Publications, 1987).
26. B. H. Conow, *The Bahá'í Teachings: A Resurgent Model of the Universe* (Oxford: George Ronald, 1990).
27. J. Savi, *The Eternal Quest for God* (Oxford: George Ronald, 1989).
28. C. Loehle, "On Human Origins: A Bahá'í Perspective," *The Journal of Bahá'í Studies*, vol. 2, no. 4 (1990), pp. 67-73 and C. Loehle, *On the Shoulders of Giants* (Oxford: George Ronald, 1994).
29. A. Abizadeh, "Commentary to Craig Loehle Article," *The Journal of Bahá'í Studies*, vol. 3, no. 1 (1990) pp. 45-58; I. Ayman, "Response to Commentary on 'On Human Origins'," *The Journal of Bahá'í Studies*, vol. 5, no. 2 (1992) pp. 67-71; K. Brown, "Response to Commentary on 'On Human Origins'," *The Journal of Bahá'í Studies*, vol. 5, no. 4 (1994) pp. 59-62; J. S. Hatcher, "Response to Commentary on 'On Human Origins'," *The Journal of Bahá'í Studies*, vol. 5, no. 2 (1992) pp. 60-66; C. Loehle, "Response to Commentary on 'On Human Origins'," *The Journal of Bahá'í Studies*, vol. 5, no. 2 (1992) pp.72-76.
30. Keven Brown, "Response to Commentary on 'On Human Origins,'" *The Journal of Bahá'í Studies*, vol. 5, no. 4 (1994) pp. 59-62.
31. W. S. Hatcher, "A Scientific Proof of the Existence of God," *The Journal of Bahá'í Studies*, vol. 5, no. 4 (1993) pp. 1-16, and Hatcher (1996).
32. Esslemont, *Baha'u'llah and the New Era*, p. 206.
33. Khursheed, *Science and Religion*, p. 91.
34. Conow, *A Resurgent Model of the Universe*, pp. 59-60.

Section 2: "Species" and "Evolution" in Occidental Biology

35. Mayr, *Growth of Biological Thought*, p. 38.
36. Ibid., pp. 305-306.
37. Qtd. in Mayr, *Growth of Biological Thought*, p. 141.
38. Although Hume in 1779, criticized the design argument, he could provide no mechanism for the generation of the diverse order of life. (See Dennett, *Darwin's Dangerous Idea* or E. Sober, *Philosophy of Biology* (Oxford: Oxford University Press, 1993) But without such a mechanism the design argument remains valid, since the existence of complex order requires an explanation. R. Dawkins states in *The Blind Watchmaker*: "But what Hume did was criticize the logic of using apparent design in nature as *positive* evidence for the existence of

God. He did not offer any *alternative* explanation for apparent design, but left this question open."

39. Many chemists assume that the chemical characteristics of a particular molecule are entirely determined by the laws of quantum mechanics, e.g., the Schrödinger equation. (See for instance P. Dirac, "Quantum Mechanics of Many-Electron Systems," *Proc Roy Soc A*, vol. 123 [1929] pp. 714-733) Whenever this molecule is formed, it shows exactly the same physical and chemical properties. This means that in chemistry one assumes a time-invariant reality in the form of quantum mechanical laws that define "chemistry" independently of actually existing molecules. Consequently, the properties of a molecule potentially exist even before it appears in this universe for the first time.

40. W. Heisenberg, *Das Teil und das Ganze* (München: Piper, 1969), and F. Hund *Geschichte der physikalischen Begriffe: Die Entstehung des mechanischen Naturbildes*, vols. 543, 544 (Mannheim: Bibliographisches Institut, 1978).

41. I. Prigogine, *Vom Sein zum Werden* (München: Piper, 1979). I. Prigogine and I. Stengers, *Dialog mit der Natur* (München: Piper, 1981).

42. P. Holmes, "Poincaré, celestial mechanics, dynamical-systems theory and 'chaos'," *Physics Reports*, vol. 193, no. 3 (1990) pp. 137-163.

43. Quotd in Mayr, *Growth of Biological Thought*, p. 305.

44. Ibid., p. 865.

45. Ibid., p. 257.

46. Ibid., p. 261

47. Ibid., p. 260; the text in square brackets is added by the author.

48. Mayr, *Growth of Biological Thought*, p. 404.

49. Mayr, *One Long Argument*, p. 42.

50. Mayr, *Growth of Biological Thought*, p. 310.

51. These natural laws were considered to be secondary causes. The Creator himself was the Primary Cause, but by means of the secondary causes He was believed to rule the world. The mechanization of the world culminated in the concept of Laplace, that the world started a long time ago and is now following its world trajectory like clockwork as predicted by Newton's laws.

52. Mayr, *Growth of Biological Thought*, p. 104 ff.

53. Ibid., p. 115. Helmholtz studied medicine as well as physics and mathematics. He made important contributions to physics, chemistry, and medicine. In 1847 he wrote his famous treatise about the conservation of energy. Three years later, he measured the velocity of neuronal excitation along nerve fibers. He therefore showed that the neurons work by material means and do not require some special vital substance for their functioning.

54. Büchner, *Kraft und Stoff*.

55. E. Haeckel, *Anthropogenie oder Entwicklungsgeschichte des Menschen*, vol. 2 (Leipzig: Wilhelm Engelmann, 1891) p. 851 ff.

56. Haeckel, *Die Welträtsel*, p. 27.

57. At a naturalist's meeting in Göttingen in 1854, the Swiss physiologist Jacob Moleschott explained that the brain secretes thoughts, as the kidneys secrete urine. This statement provoked a comment from the philosopher Hermann Lotze: "Listening to colleague Moleschott, one gets the impression that he is right" (E. Bloch, *Das Materialismusproblem, seine Geschichte und Substanz*, vol. 7 [Frankfurt a.M.: 1972] p. 289.)

58. Kraft, *Der Wiener Kreis: Der Ursprung des Neopositivismus* (Wien: Springer Verlag, 1968).

59. Mayr, *Growth of Biological Thought*, p. 528.

60. Qtd. in Mayr, *Growth of Biological Thought*, p. 353.

61. Today Lamark is mostly known for his assumption that learned characteristics can be inherited. This idea does not go back to Lamark, but is was generally accepted by the scientists of his time. Darwin and Haeckel also believed in the inheritance of acquired characteristics. See for instance E. Mayr, "Evolution," *Scientific American*, vol. 239, no. 3 (1978) pp. 46-55.

62. Qtd. in Mayr, *Growth of Biological Thought*, p. 529.

63. T. de Chardin, *Le Phénomène humain* (Paris: Édition du Leuil, 1947).

64. Mayr, *One Long Argument*, p. 67.

65. S. J. Gould, "The Evolution of Life on the Earth," *Scientific American*, vol. 271, no. 4 (1994) pp. 85-91.

66. T. Dobzhansky, F. J. Ayala, G. L. Stebbins, and J. W. Valentine, *Evolution* (San Francisco, 1977).

67. L. E. Orgel, "The Origin of Life on the Earth," *Scientific American*, vol. 271, no. 4 (1994) pp. 77-83.

68. M. Eigen, *Steps Towards Life: A Perspective of Evolution* (Oxford: Oxford University Press, 1992), and Orgel (1994).

69. Gould, "The Evolution of Life on the Earth," *Scientific American*, vol. 271, no. 4 (1994).

70. Alberts, et al., *Molecular Biology of the Cell*.

71. The probability for replication errors in RNA viruses is approximately a single error per gene and copy. In the case of DNA viruses and higher organisms, it is in the order of one error in 1000 genes. (See M. Eigen, "The origin of genetic information: viruses as models," *Gene*, vol. 135, no. 1-2 (1993) pp. 37-47; and M. Eigen, "Viral quasispecies," *Scientific American*, vol. 269, no. 1 (1993) pp. 42-49.

72. Alberts, et al., *Molecular Biology of the Cell*.

73. Mayr, *Growth of Biological Thought*, p. 591.

74. Dawkins, *Blind Watchmaker*, p. 43.

75. The huge effect of cumulative selection can be illustrated by throwing dice to get the six 100 times. On the one hand, if I take 100 dice and try to get all 100 dice to show a six on a single throw of all 100 dice, on the average I would have to throw $6^{100} \sim 7 * 10^{77}$ times until all dice show a six. If I threw the hundred dice every second from the time the universe began with the Big Bang, this would not be sufficient to get the requested result even once. On the other hand, if I take each die of the hundred dice individually, throw it until it shows a six and keep it then, I would have to perform about 600 throws. In the first case it was an all or none selection. Only if all hundred dice would show the six in a single throw, would it be selected. In the second case, the sixes were sampled cumulatively, one six was accepted after the other. Although this is not a good example to show the evolution of complex biological order, it clearly shows the huge distinction between "all and none" and cumulative selection.

76. Neo-Darwinistic evolution requires the mutation rate, that is, the number of mutations per generation, to obey certain limits. If it is too large, the genetic

information defining a species will be lost within a few generations. If it is too small, only the locally fittest sequence of a given species will survive, but there will be no further progress. At the optimal mutation rate, not only the locally fittest sequence does survive, but also a large number of closely related ones. This set of sequences forms the so-called quasi species (Eigen, 1993). Another important property is that the sequence path between different but closely related species must not be too long. The probability to progress in the sequence space to increasingly complex biological forms of life must be considerably above zero. The requirements of the fitness landscape to favor the progress of evolution in the sequence space are studied by S. Kauffman, *At Home in the Universe* (New York: Oxford University Press, 1995). It is shown from first principles that evolution would be impossible if the fitness-sequence relation were quasi-random.

77. There exist two types of cellular organization: the primitive prokaryonts and the more complex eukaryonts. Prokaryonts contain no nucleus. In eukaryontic cells the DNA is packed into the cell nucleus. (Alberts, et al. [1989]; C. de Duve, "The birth of complex cells," *Scientific American*, vol. 274, no. 4 [1996] pp. 50-57.) The eukaryonts are assumed to have organized by means of the fusion of prokaryonts. There still exist some relics of these ancient precursors. Some organelles, such as the mitochondria, until today have their own DNA. All higher taxa, plants and animals, are formed by eukaryont cells. The agreement in the complex organization of all eukaryontic cells is understood to indicate that all eukaryontic taxa originate from a small group of eukaryontic cells.

78. C. G. Sibley, J. A. Comstock, and J. E. Ahlquist, "DNA hybridization evidence of hominoid phylogeny: a reanalysis of the data," *Journal of Molecular Evolution*, vol. 30, no. 3 (1990) pp. 202-236.

79. Mitochondria are organelles, the "organs" of the cells, which produce energy rich molecules designated as ATP (adenosine triphosphate). This chemical energy stored in those molecules is degraded in many energy demanding processes inside the cells, such as copying DNA or contracting muscle fibers. Those mitochondria have their own DNA. Because mitochondria lack the sophisticated proofreading machinery of its host cell, the mutation rate of mitochondrial DNA is large compared to the mutation rate of the host's DNA. Recently mitochondrial DNA has been used to estimate the biological relationship between humans around the world (A. C. Wilson, and R. L. Cann, "The recent African genesis of humans," *Scientific American*, vol. 266, no. 4 [1992] pp. 68-73.) According to this study modern *Homo Sapiens* originated about 200,000 years ago in Africa.

80. Dawkins, *The Blind Watchmaker*; Dayhoff, "Computer Analysis of Protein Evolution," *Scientific American*, July (1969) pp. 86-95; and Eigen, *Steps Towards Life*.

81. Dopazo, et al., 1993; Eigen 1993.

82. Mayr, *One Long Argument*.

83. Mayr, *Growth of Biological Thought*, p. 271; text in brackets added by the author.

84. Ibid., p. 69.

85. The phenomena of the aging of materials and the behavior of non-equilibrium

dynamic systems, however, require us to introduce history into physics and chemistry. Only recently have those subjects obtained specific interest in physics and chemistry. (Gell-Mann [1994], Land [1991], Prigogine [1979], Prigogine and Stengers [1981], or R. Ruthen, "Trends in nonlinear dynamics. Adapting to complexity," *Scientific American*, vol. 268, no. 1 [1993] pp. 110-117.

86. Mayr, *Growth of Biological Thought*, pp. 69-70.
87. Ibid. p. 46.
88. Ibid. p. 263.
89. Ibid., p. 363ff.

Section 3: The Origin of Complex Order in Our Universe

90. R. Dawkins, *The Blind Watchmaker*.
91. William Paley was one of the British theologians and naturalists who saw in the wonders of nature, and particularly biology, the best proofs of the existence of God. In 1805 Paley published his famous book *Natural Theology*. It contains several proofs for the existence of God using the *argument by design*. Those proofs were based on the complexity and adaptedness of life. For instance, he elaborated the *watchmaker argument*: Just as the existence of a well-designed watch proves the existence of a watchmaker, the existence of the well-adapted biosphere proves the existence of an intelligent designer. See E. Sober, *Philosophy of Biology* (Oxford: Oxford University Press, 1993) for a discussion.
92. K. Ward, *God, Chance and Necessity* (Oxford: Oneworld, 1996).
93. Dawkins, *The Blind Watchmaker*, p. xii.
94. For instance, the Grand Unification Theory in high energy physics described by M. Gell-Mann, *The Quark and the Jaguar*.
95. Bahá'u'lláh, *Tablets of Bahá'u'lláh Revealed after the Kitáb-i-Aqdas* (Haifa: Bahá'í World Centre, 1982) p. 142.
96. 'Abdu'l-Bahá, *Promulgation of Universal Peace*, p. 307.
97. In modern physics, the second law of thermodynamics states that locally entropy (that is, disorder) is always generated but never destroyed. A decrease of entropy in a small volume element can be obtained by a free energy influx, which corresponds to an influx of "negative entropy," equivalent to an outflow of entropy. Systems which exchange energy with their environment are called *open systems*. The planet earth is such an open system. Light from the sun enters the geosphere, and the surplus of energy is reemitted into the universe in form of thermal radiation. The resulting free energy difference drives non-equilibrium processes, such as weather, and provides our planet with the necessary means to develop life. Thus, the second law of thermodynamics does not contradict evolution; it defines necessary conditions for the development of complex biological order.
98. Dawkins, *The Blind Watchmaker*, pp. 7 and 9.
99. 'Abdu'l-Bahá, "Tablet to Forel," in John Vader, *For the Good of Mankind: August Forel and the Bahá'í Faith* (Oxford: George Ronald, 1984) p. 78.

100. E. Haeckel, *Die Welträtsel*, 11th edition, p. 308.

101. Ibid., p. 301.

102. L. Büchner, *Kraft und Stoff*, 21st edition, p. 11.

103. E. Haeckel, *Die Welträtsel*, p. 281.

104. P. W. Atkins, *The Creation* (Oxford: Freeman & Company Limited, 1981).

105. J. A. Wheeler, "Information, Physics, Quantum: the Search for Links," in *Proceeding of the 3rd International Symposium on the Foundation of Quantum Mechanics*, (Tokyo: 1989) pp. 354-368

106. Here Wheeler's (1989) idea is simplified. But the argument also holds for the more complex form of the idea proposed by Wheeler.

107. If the understanding of the left-hand side zero takes several years of dedicated studies of theoretical physics, such a zero is also certainly not trivial, and not self evident.

108. Dennett, *Darwin's Dangerous Idea*, p. 63, emphasis by Dennett.

109. Ibid, p. 184, emphasis by Dennett.

110. The chemistry of different galaxies can be studied by means of the optical spectra of atoms and molecules. If the chemical laws were different in distant galaxies, which also means earlier galaxies due to the limited speed of light, one would expect to find absorption and excitation spectra different from those we find today. But according to scientific studies, the chemistry is the same within the known universe.

111. Dawkins, *The Blind Watchmaker*, p. 317.

112. E. Mayr, *One Long Argument*, pp. 86-87.

113. If oil is continually heated from below, a hexagonal pattern of convection cells appears (I. Prigogine, *Vom Sein zum Werden* [München: Piper, 1979]). In this particular case, the order is maintained by energy dissipation.

114. E. Mayr, *Growth of Biological Thought*, p. 63.

115. Monod, *Le Hasard et la Nécessité*, pp. 129-130.

116. As shown by modern mathematics (D. Hofstadter, *Gödel Escher Bach* (New York: Basic Books, 1979), the randomness of a sequence of numbers or characters cannot be proven. Good counter examples are pseudo random number generators. Although the numbers of good generators fulfill nearly every test for randomness, they are completely deterministic, reproducible, and therefore not random. This means that Monod's argument is not well founded because the apparent randomness of DNA sequences does not prove their actual randomness.

117. Monod, *Le Hasard et la nécessité*, pp. 111-112.

118. Ibid., pp. 160-161.

119. Dawkins, *The Blind Watchmaker*, p. 317.

120. A small protein may consist in 130 of its building blocks, the amino acids. There are twenty different naturally occurring amino acids. The number of all possible sequences ($20^{130} \sim 10^{170}$) of this small protein with 130 amino acids exceeds by orders of magnitude the estimated number of neutrons in our universe or its estimated age given in seconds (C. F. von Weizsäcker, *Aufbau der Physik* 2nd edition (München: Carl Hanser Verlag, 1986). Because changes in the sequence often result in the complete loss of the function of the protein, it is not likely that even a single small protein endowed with a highly specific and efficient function was generated by pure chance during the existence of the uni-

verse. The probability of creating a complete organism by accident is again many, many orders of magnitude lower than the probability of forming a simple protein. Using such probabilistic arguments the accidental existence of life can be practically excluded.

121. In principle, self-creative evolution would make the current interpretation of fossil findings doubtful. These interpretations ground on the assumption that the physical, chemical, and biological laws and principles we know today apply in exactly the same way to those ancient forms of life. Self-creative evolution, however, assumes the *ad hoc* creation of essentially new characteristics.

122. K. R. Popper, *Objective Knowledge* (Oxford: The Clarendon Press, 1972).

123. Ward (1996) argues similarly: "To say that such a very complex and well-ordered universe comes into being without any cause or reason is equivalent to throwing one's hands up in the air and just saying that anything at all might happen, that it is hardly worth bothering to look for reasons at all. And that is the death of science."

124. Dawkins, *The Blind Watchmaker*, pp. 41 and 49.

125. Ibid, p. xvi.

126. Ibid, p. 62.

127. Ward, *God, Chance and Necessity,* p. 18.

128. S. Kauffman, *At Home in the Universe.*

129. Dennett, *Darwin's Dangerous Idea,* p. 47.

130. Ibid, p. 59.

131. The "algorithmic complexity" (AC) of a given sequence of symbols is the length (number of bits) of the shortest possible algorithm, the shortest possible text of computer code to produce this sequence. In the worst case, the AC of a particular sequence is determined by the length of this sequence as it is, plus the necessary commands to print it. But often the AC is much smaller than the length of a given sequence. For instance, a sequence consisting in the character 'a' repeated one million times can be produced by a loop that repeats 1,000,000 times the command to print 'a.' Thus, the AC measures the internal complexity of a sequence of symbols. It is "simple" if it can be compressed to a short text of code.

132. Of course, one can reject Kolmogorov's algorithmic complexity as a reasonable measure for biological complexity. But one would have to present a "more reasonable" definition for it. Without such a definition, Dennett's claim that his evolution algorithm explains biological complexity by a simple algorithm becomes meaningless.

133. It is obvious that mankind has produced sequences of symbols, for instance books, of large algorithmic complexity. Consequently, such books can be produced only by algorithms with a large AC, but not by those with a small AC. If the evolution of the biosphere is the product of an algorithm, the AC of this algorithm cannot be smaller than the AC of its product, that is, natural DNA sequences and the artifacts of human culture. This conclusion follows directly from the definition of AC. Consequently, the AC of the evolution algorithm must exceed the AC of any natural or human product. Some human products are considered to have a high AC; therefore, the evolution algorithm cannot be simple. According to Dawkins (1986), assuming a complex origin is not an expla-

nation for the evolution of life: "To explain the origin of the DNA/protein machine by invoking a supernatural Designer is to explain precisely nothing, for it leaves unexplained the origin of the Designer." Taking Dawkins by his own word implies that the assumption of an evolution algorithm does not explain the existence of a complex biosphere, because it was shown above that this algorithm cannot be of "primeval simplicity." The problem of the origin of complex life was merely shifted to the question of the origin of the algorithmically complex evolution algorithm.

134. A well-known example is the Bénard instability of oil when heated from below (Prigogine (1979); I. Prigogine, and I. Stengers, *Dialog mit der Natur* (München: Piper, 1981). Beyond a certain temperature gradient, the oil forms hexagonally ordered convection cells. Probably no one would claim that the Bénard instability was created during its discovery and did not potentially exist before in the laws of fluid dynamics.

135. Dawkins, *The Blind Watchmaker,* p. 73.

136. S. Spiegelman, "An *in vitro* analysis of a replicating molecule," *American Scientist*, vol. 55 (1967) 63-68.

137. A herd of monkeys hammering on typewriters, or computers producing random sequences of characters, would (given enough time) produce sonnets of Shakespeare, Einstein's general relativity, etc. They would, however, be unable to select such excellent pieces of work out of the remaining garbage. Thus the difficult step is not to produce a wide range of variability but to find the needles in the haystack.

138. Selection can be compared with learning. Nobody can understand mathematics by eliminating non-mathematical thoughts, but only by learning mathematics. A removal of non-mathematical ways of thinking is, of course, necessary, but certainly by no means sufficient for the education of a good mathematician.

139. J. Hatcher, and W. Hatcher, *The Law of Love Enshrined* (Oxford: George Ronald, 1996).

Section 4: Top-Down Evolution: Assuming a Voluntary Origin

140. 'Abdu'l-Bahá, "Letter to Forel," in *For the Good of Mankind, August Forel & the Bahá'í Faith*, ed. by J.P. Vader, (Oxford: George Ronald, 1984) p. 75.

141. S. J. Gould, "The evolution of life on the earth," *Scientific American*, vol. 271, no. 4 (1994) pp. 85-91.

142. S. Kauffman, *At Home in the Universe* (New York: Oxford University Press, 1995) and "Climbing Mount Improbable: Richard Dawkins," *Nature*, vol. 382, no. 6589 (1996) pp. 309-310.

143. W. S. Hatcher gives a careful formal analysis of Aristotle's proof of the existence of God in *Logic and Logos* (Oxford: George Ronald, 1990) and J. Hatcher and W. Hatcher, *The Law of Love Enshrined* (Oxford: George Ronald, 1996).

144. 'Abdu'l-Bahá, "Letter to Forel," p. 76.

145. See, for instance, D. Hofstadter, *Gödel Escher Bach* (New York: Basic Books, 1979).

146. For a discussion of this argument, see R. Dawkins, *The Blind Watchmaker*, and E. Sober, *Philosophy of Biology*.

147. In *The Blind Watchmaker* Dawkins states: "But of course any God capable of intelligently designing something as complex as the DNA/protein replicating machine must have been at least as complex and organized as that machine itself. Far more so if we suppose him *additionally* capable of such advanced functions as listening to prayers and forgiving sins. To explain the origin of the DNA/protein machine by invoking a supernatural Designer is to explain precisely nothing, for it leaves unexplained the origin of the Designer."

148. Bahá'u'lláh, *Gleanings from the Writings of Bahá'u'lláh* (Wilmette: Bahá'í Publishing Trust, 1971) pp. 61,63.

149. Ibid., p. 184.

150. Ibid., p. 65.

151. 'Abdu'l-Bahá, *Promulgation of Universal Peace*, pp. 462-463.

152. See also B. H. Conow, *The Bahá'í Teachings: A Resurgent Model of the Universe* (Oxford: George Ronald, 1990).

153. 'Abdu'l-Bahá, "Letter to Forel," pp. 71-72. A similar and more detailed description of the hierarchical structure of the kingdoms of nature can be found in 'Abdu'l-Bahá, *Promulgation of Universal Peace,* p. 258.

154. Ibid., p. 73.

155. In an e-mail group Juan Cole posted: " 'Abdu'l-Bahá accepts an essentially Aristotelian notion of a hierarchy of types of soul, where soul really means a set of abilities or faculties. Thus, plants have a vegetative soul, which is equivalent to the faculty of growth/reproduction. Animals have an animal soul which is equivalent to the faculty of deliberate movement. Humans have a rational soul, which is equivalent to the faculty of rational thinking. These 'souls' or capacities are seen to exist apart from matter, perhaps in the World of Forms, but are 'attracted' by matter when it is arranged in a certain way." (cited with permission of the author)

156. 'Abdu'l-Bahá, *Promulgation of Universal Peace,* p. 285; see also p. 350. Conow, in *A Resurgent Model of the Universe*, describes the journey of the atoms through the kingdoms.

157. In nonrelativistic mechanics formulated by Newton, mass points were the central objects of consideration, and kinetic and potential energy were certain characteristics of these mass points. Einstein reversed this relation. Energy became the central entity, and matter one possible form of energy. Today, information is considered to be a form of matter. But according to the expectations of J. A. Wheeler ("Information, Physics, Quantum: the Search for Links," in *Proceeding of the 3rd International Symposium on the Foundation of Quantum Mechanics*, (Tokyo: 1989) 354-368 and C. F. von Weizsäcker (*Aufbau der Physik* 2nd edition (München: Carl Hanser Verlag, 1986) one can consider an analogous reformulation of physics similar to the transformation from nonrelativistic to relativistic physics: information may become the fundamental entity of our universe, its substance; and energy and matter only particular aspects of it, its forms.

158. It is well known that physical theories generally have a limited range of applicability. For instance, Newton's mechanics apply if the velocities of the mass

points are small compared to the speed of light, if the considered length scale is small compared to cosmological dimensions but large compared to the de Boglie wavelength of ordinary electrons, etc. Analogously, in a hierarchical order of nature, certain types of characteristics may only be detectable in sufficiently complex systems, but not necessarily at the atomic or molecular level.

159. E. Mayr, *Growth of Biological Thought*, p. 131.

160. 'Abdu'l-Bahá, *Some Answered Questions*, p. 201.

161. W. S. Hatcher, "A Scientific Proof of the Existence of God," *The Journal of Bahá'í Studies*, vol. 5, no. 4 (1993) pp. 1-16; and Hatcher, *Law of Love Enshrined*.

162. Hatcher, *Law of Love Enshrined*, p. 54.

163. Hatcher, "A Scientific Proof of the Existence of God," *The Journal of Bahá'í Studies*, vol. 5, no. 4 (1993) p. 12.

164. Ibid, p. 13.

165. Ibid.

166. G. Dicks, "Comment on 'A Scientific Proof of the Existence of God'," *The Journal of Bahá'í Studies*, vol. 6, no. 3 (1994) pp. 75-80.

167. W. S. Hatcher, "Reply to Gordon Dicks' comment on 'A Scientific Proof of the Existence of God'," *The Journal of Bahá'í Studies*, vol. 6, no. 3 (1994) pp. 81-85.

168. 'Abdu'l-Bahá, "Letter to Forel," p. 75.

169. Hatcher, *Law of Love Enshrined*, p. 13.

170. During the nineteenth century chance was not considered to be important for evolution. Ludwig Büchner explicitly denies the existence of chance in the process of the development of life: ". . . but chance . . . does not exist in nature, where at last everything occurs in a natural, necessary way" (*Kraft und Stoff*, 21st edition [Leipzig: Theodor Thomas, 1904] p. 112) Consequently, Büchner as well as Haeckel based evolution entirely on necessary causes.

171. Büchner, *Kraft und Stoff*, p. 84.

172. In principle, Hatcher assumes in his argument rejecting neo-Darwinism that there exists only a weak correlation between DNA sequences, the genotypes, and the fitness of their respective phenotypes by assuming only "sparse" improving mutations. He assumes that the fitness values are more or less randomly scattered through the sequence space. And, indeed, for such a sequence-fitness relation, evolution would be by far too slow, if not impossible. Of course, the possibility of progressive evolution in a fitness landscape is not trivial and is subject to intensive mathematical studies. (M. Eigen, Steps towards Life—A perspective of evolution (Oxford: Oxford University Press, 1992); Kauffman (1995); I. Prigogine, Vom Sein zum Werden (München: Piper, 1979); I. Prigogine and I. Stengers, Dialog mit der Natur (München: Piper, 1981); R. Ruthen, "Trends in nonlinear dynamics. Adapting to complexity," Scientific American, vol. 268, no. 1 (1993) pp. 110-117). Evolution models can account only for the known fossil records if there exists a sufficiently strong sequence-fitness relation (Kauffman [1996])

Estimates of the possible speed of evolution have an analogy in the protein folding problem. The a priori probability of obtaining a correctly folded protein by searching through all possible states is much too low for even fairly small proteins to fold within reasonable times (C. B. Anfinsen, "Principles that Govern the

Folding of Protein Chains," Science, vol. 181, no. 49096 [1973] 223-230). A small water soluble protein has typically 130 amino acids. If for simplicity we assume four different conformations for each monomer, that total protein has about 4130 ~ 1080 different possible conformations. If during the folding process the protein would have to find its native conformation by purely random search, on the average, it would need 1060 years if it tries one conformation per pico second. Because it is known that those proteins fold within seconds or hours, in practice, the protein appears to search roughly 1017 conformations instead of 1080 ones. The folding pathway of the protein is determined by the free energy of each of the possible states. Only if this free energy landscape satisfies certain requirements and prevents the protein from searching the complete conformational space during folding is protein folding possible. (R. L. Baldwin, "Pieces of the folding puzzle," Nature, vol. 346 [1990] 409-410) Thus, the folding of the protein is not purely random, but is guided by a "fitness function," by the conformational free energy landscape. This conformational free energy is encoded in the particular amino acids sequence; it enforces adoption of those conformations which lead to rapid folding. In a similar way, a high sequence-fitness correlation would help for fast evolution. Consequently, the possibility of neo-Darwinism as a horizontal evolution model cannot be excluded a priori by mean as a simple probability argument.

173. Hatcher, *Law of Love Enshrined*, p. 14.
174. Loehle, *On the Shoulders of Giants*, p. 110.
175. K. Ward, *God, Chance and Necessity* (Oxford: Oneworld, 1996) pp. 132-133.
176. Ibid., p. 183.
177. Bahá'u'lláh, *Gleanings from the Writings of Bahá'u'lláh*, p. 68.
178. Monod, *Le Hasard et la nécessité*, pp. 111-112.
179. Ibid., pp. 187-188.
180. Dawkins, *The Blind Watchmaker*, p. 50.
181. Gödel proved that the randomness of a sequence of numbers cannot be ascertained. Perfect pseudo random number generators, for instance, are purely deterministic, even if they meet nearly every test for randomness.
182. If one puts crystalline sugar in a glass of tea, the sugar dissolves and after some time it becomes distributed all over the volume of the tea in the glass. On average, the sugar performs a directed motion, from the bottom to the middle of the glass. If one would follow the path of a single sugar molecule, however, one would detect a random Brownian motion. The molecule would go up and down without preference to any direction. Only when looking at the average motion of many molecules can a directionality of the sugar motion be seen.
183. Bahá'u'lláh, *Gleanings*, p. 4.

Section 5: Evolution and the Originality of Species

184. See Keven Brown's essay.
185. Bahá'u'lláh, *Gleanings*, pp. 79-80.
186. Mírzá Abu'l-Fadl Gulpáygání, *Miracles and Metaphors* (Los Angeles: Kalimát Press, 1981) p. 9.
187. 'Abdu'l-Bahá, *Some Answered Questions*, p. 177, cited below as *SAQ*.

188. *SAQ,*, p. 191; provisional revised translation by Keven Brown.

189. Ibid.

190. Ibid., pp. 191-192.

191. E. Mayr, *Growth of Biological Thought*, p. 363.

192. *SAQ*, pp. 177-178; provisional revised translation by Keven Brown.

193. Ibid., p. 196; see also 'Abdu'l-Bahá, "Letter to Forel," pp. 74, 77.

194. *SAQ*, p. 179; provisional revised translation by Keven Brown.

195. Ibid.

196. Ibid.

197. *SAQ*, p. 181; provisional revised translation by Keven Brown.

198. Some pre-Darwinian approaches to evolution, which Mayr does not consider to represent "real" evolution, because they are still based on an essentialistic species concept, assumed saltations or "mutations" in the species essence, thus the appearance of a new species is accompanied by the creation of a new species essence. Maupertius in 1756 proposed the following concept of speciation: "Could we not explain in this way how from only two individuals the multiplication of the most various species could have resulted? Their first origin would have been due simply to some chance production, in which the elementary particles would not have kept the order which they had in the paternal and maternal animals: each degree of error would have made a new species; and by repeated deviations the infinite diversity of animals which we know today would have been produced." (Mayr, *Growth of Biological Thought*, 403.)

199. According to Mayr (*The Growth of Biological Thought*, p. 305), during the nineteenth century, the harmonious universe argument was considered one of several strong arguments against Darwinism that for a long time hindered the invention of evolution theories: "The second was the concept of an animate cosmos, a living, harmonious whole, which made it so difficult in later periods to explain how evolution could have taken place, because any change would disturb the harmony."

200. *SAQ*, p. 233; provisional revised translation by Keven Brown.

201. 'Abdu'l-Bahá, *Selections from the Writings*, p. 157.

202. Bahá'u'lláh, *Tablets*, p. 140.

203. 'Abdu'l-Bahá, *Má'idiy-i Ásmání*, vol. 2, p. 68; provisional translation by Keven Brown.

204. *SAQ*, p. 181; provisional revised translation by Keven Brown.

205. Ibid., pp. 182-183.

206. Ibid., p. 199.

207. E. Mayr, *One Long Argument*.

208. *SAQ*, pp. 182-183; provisional revised translation by Keven Brown.

209. In classical biology until the beginning of the eighteenth century, the animal world was thought to consist in a single scale of animal organization, the *scala naturae*, starting from the most primitive animals and ending in humanity as the apex of creation. In classical biology parallel ontogeny was understood to mean that the higher animals in their embryonic growth start on a primitive level of the *scala naturae*, and continue through the intermediate levels until they reach their own place. This concept should not be mistaken for evolution; it is designed to apply to a static biosphere. For instance, the French anatomist Étienne Serrès considered "the whole animal kingdom . . . ideally as a single ani-

mal, [which] . . . here and there arrests its own development and thus determines at each point of interruption, by the very state it has reached, the distinctive characters of the phyla, the classes, families, genera, and species." (Mayr, *Growth of Biological Thought*, p. 472) Serrès thought of the *scala naturae* as a continuous scale of increasingly complex organisms. A particular species simply got stuck at a certain point of this scale. This concept became known as the Meckel-Serrès law. Later Agassiz extended this law to the fossil records so that the embryo not only should go through the more primitive stages of life, but it also should reflect the extinct predecessors of its own class: "It may therefore be considered as a general fact . . . that the phases of development of all living animals correspond to the order of succession of their extinct representatives in past geological times. As far as this goes, the oldest representatives of every class may then be considered as embryonic types of their respective orders or families among the living." (Mayr, quoted in *Growth of Biological Thought*, p. 474)

210. In his *Origin*, Darwin used the parallelism between ontogeny and phylogeny as an argument in favor of evolution. Here this parallelism is no longer thought to result from the general law of increasing complexification in the *scala naturae*, as proposed by Meckel and Serrès, but each embryo was considered to repeat individually the evolution of its own species. Ernst Haeckel (*Die Welträtsel*, 11th edition, p. 111) reformulated the Meckel-Serrès law into the law of recapitulation: "Ontogeny is a concise and compressed recapitulation of phylogeny, conditioned by laws of heredity and adaption." This law became popular and strongly influential in biology, especially in embryology. Around the beginning of this century this law became more and more questionable and was shown to be wrong at least in its extreme variants.

211. *SAQ*, p. 184; provisional revised translation by Keven Brown.

212. Ibid., p. 194.

213. It is interesting to note that Monod used the same example to explain that human evolution should not be compared with ontogeny, because the embryo develops according to its inherent genetic potentials, and evolution, according to Monod, consists in new creations.

214. *SAQ*, p. 184; provisional revised translation by Keven Brown.

215. Ibid., p. 194.

216. Ibid., p. 199.

217. Bahá'u'lláh, *Tablets*, p. 52.

218. Mayr, *Growth of Biological Thought*, p. 403.

219. 'Abdu'l-Bahá certainly is not a Lamarkian. 'Abdu'l-Bahá (*SAQ*, Chapter 51) proposes that the less complex species appeared first: "first the mineral, then the plant, afterward the animal, and finally man." For Lamark the sequence is reversed. He assumed an evolution towards increasing complexity and perfection. Each species started simple and slowly accumulated perfections. For him, speciation, i.e., the appearance of new species, is a continuous process which should occur even today. Humanity is the result of the evolution of "ancient worms," whereas "modern worms," which appeared only recently, did not have much time to acquire perfections, and are still at the beginning of their evolution to develop elaborate morphologies.

220. *SAQ*, p. 181.

221. The *World Wide Web*, Talk.

Origins Archive <http://www.talkorigins.org/faqs/faq-speciation.html> has a long list of articles reporting discovered speciations.
222. R. A. Kerr, "Who Profits from Ecological Disaster?," *Science*, vol. 266 (1994), pp. 28-30.
223. Shoghi Effendi, letter 19 March 1946 to an individual, cited from a Memorandum of the Research Department of the Universal House of Justice, dated 19 March 1995.
224. 'Abdu'l-Bahá, *Promulgation of Universal Peace*, pp. 358-359; the retranslation was done from 'Abdu'l-Bahá, *Khitábát*, Vol. 2, pp. 301-304.
225. Ibid.
226. W. Howells, *Getting Here: The Story of Human Evolution* (Washington: Compass Press, 1993).
227. Haeckel, *Die Welträtsel*, p. 116.
228. R. Leakey, *The Origin of Humankind* (London: Weidenfeld & Nicolson, 1994).
229. Haeckel (*Über den Ursprung des Menschen - Vortrag, gehalten auf dem 4. Internationalen Zoologen-Congress in Cambrigde, am 26. August* 1898, 12th edition [Leipzig: Kröner Verlag, 1916] p. 62) writes in the printed version of his talk given at the 4th International Congress on Zoology, August 20, 1898 in Cambridge: "Whereas recently some anthropologists assumed the existence of humanity on earth to be about one million years, most guess her duration to be half a million years or less; in any case, it is generally agreed upon that it took at least a hundred thousand years. However, this age is much larger than generally considered in the middle of the nineteenth century and still erroneously taught at schools today." The fact that the time spans required for considerable evolution estimated in the middle of the nineteenth century were generally rather short compared to modern time tables can be inferred from one of Cuvier's statements against evolution. He argued that the mummified humans and animals found in ancient Egypt do not show any signs of change compared to their modern relatives. He concluded from this fact that the modification of species predicted by evolution theory did not take place. Interestingly, Büchner (*Sechs Vorlesungen*, 2nd edition, p. 57) in his early rebuttal of Cuvier's argument did not argue that the time since the burial was too short for the evolution of obvious differences in the morphologies, as would be a modern response, but instead he claimed that the environment in Egypt must have been particularly stable, which prevented those expected changes.
230. J. D. Clark, et al, "African Homo erectus: old radiometric ages and young Oldowan assemblages in the Middle Awash Valley, Ethiopia," *Science*, vol. 264, no. 5167 (1994) pp. 1907-1910; Howells, *Getting Here*; M. G. Leakey, et al, "New four-million-year-old hominid species from Kanapoi and Allia Bay, Kenya," *Nature*, vol. 376, no. 6541 (1995) pp. 565-571; I. Tattersall, "Out Of Africa Again . . . and Again," *Scientific American*, vol. 276, no. 4 (1997) pp. 46-53; T. D. White, G. Suwa, and B. Asfaw, "Australopithecus ramidus, a new species of early hominid from Aramis, Ethiopia," *Nature*, vol. 371, no. 6495 (1994) pp. 306-312; G. Wolde Gabriel, et al, "Ecological and temporal placement of early Pliocene hominids at Aramis, Ethiopia," *Nature*, vol. 371, no. 6495 (1994) pp. 330-333.
231. Mayr, *Growth of Biological Thought*, p. 263.
232. D. C. Dennett, *Darwin's Dangerous Idea*, p. 36.

233. *SAQ*, pp. 195-196; provisional revised translation by Keven Brown.
234. *PUP*, p. 219.
235. Shoghi Effendi, *Unfolding Destiny*, p. 458.
236. *Arohanui—Letters from Shoghi Effendi to New Zealand* (Suva, Fiji Islands: Bahá'í Publishing Trust, 1982) p. 85.
237. R. Dawkins, *The Blind Watchmaker*, p. xvi.

Section 6: Spiritual Dimensions of the Human Origins Discussion

238. Dennett, *Darwin's Dangerous Idea*, p. 63.
239. Haeckel, *Die Welträtsel*, p. 507.
240. Büchner, *Kraft und Stoff*, p. 411.
241. Mayr, *Growth of Biological Thought*, pp. 80-81.
242. Ward, *God, Chance and Necessity*, p. 178.
243. Dennett, *Darwin's Dangerous Idea*, p. 63.
244. Haeckel, *Die Welträtsel*, p. 325.
245. H. Albert, *Traktat über kritische Vernunft*, 5th edition (Tübingen: Paul Siebeck, 1991); E. von Kitzing, "Ist eine Einheit von Religion und Wissenschaft denkbar?," *Tagungsband zur 10 Jahrestagung der Gesellschaft für Bahá'í Studien im deutschsprachigen Europa*, vol. 4 (1997) pp. 77-102.
246. S. J. Gould, *Rocks of Ages* (New York: Ballantine, 1999).
247. *SAQ*, p. 181.
248. See 'Abdu'l-Bahá, *Paris Talks*, pp. 136-137, 146.
249. Haeckel, *Die Welträtsel*, p. 331.
250. Büchner, *Kraft und Stoff*, p. 178.
251. Haeckel, *Die Welträtsel*, p. 369.
252. Ibid, p. 429.
253. Büchner, *Kraft und Stoff*, p. 411.
254. R. Dawkins, *River Out of Eden* (London: Weidenfeld & Nicolson, 1995).
255. Haeckel, *Die Welträtsel*, pp. 446-447, and Büchner, *Kraft und Stoff*, p. 407.
256. P. Feyerabend, *Erkenntnis für freie Menschen*, vol. 1011 (Frankfurt a.M.: Suhrkamp, 1980).
257. The Universal House of Justice, *The Promise of World Peace* (1985).
258. J. Derrida, "Structure, sign, and play in the discourse of the human sciences," in *The languages of criticism and the sciences of man: The structuralist controversy*, ed. by Richard Macksey and Eugenio Donato (Baltimore: John Hopkins University Press, 1970).
259. A. Sokal, "Transgressing the Boundaries: Toward a transformative hermeneutics of quantum gravity," *Social Text*, vol. 14, no. 1-2 (1996) pp. 46-47.
260. In the *The Promise of World Peace*, published during the UN year of peace, the Universal House of Justice stressed the importance of considering religious value systems as the solution to the burning problems of our world: "No serious attempt to set human affairs aright, to achieve world peace, can ignore religion."
261. Bahá'u'lláh, *Gleanings*, p. 206.
262. Bahá'u'lláh, *Hidden Words*, numbers 3-4.

263. Monod, *Le Hazard et la necessité*, pp. 187-188.

264. S. Kauffman, *At Home in the Universe* (New York: Oxford University Press, 1995).

265. Dawkins, in *The Selfish Gene*, proposes "memes" as entities which correspond to genes. Memes are the ideas which form our culture and which, similarly to genes, struggle selfishly for their own replication and survival.

266. Bahá'u'lláh, *Gleanings*, p. 215.

BIBLIOGRAPHY

'Abdu'l-Bahá. *Má'idiy-i Ásmání* (The Heavenly Bread). Part 2. Comp. `Abdu'l-Hamíd-i Ishráq Khávarí. New Delhi: Bahá'í Publishing Trust, 1984 (Reprint of vols.2, 5, and 9 formerly published in Tehran).

_____. *The Promulgation of Universal Peace*. Talks Delivered by 'Abdu'l-Bahá during His Visit to the United States and Canada in 1912. Comp. Howard MacNutt. Wilmette: Bahá'í Publishing Trust, 1982.

_____. *Some Answered Questions*. [=SAQ] Trans. Laura Clifford Barney. Wilmette: Bahá'í Publishing Trust, 1981.

_____. "Tablet from 'Abdu'l-Bahá to August Forel," John Paul Vader. *For the Good of Mankind, August Forel and the Bahá'í Faith*. Oxford: George Ronald, 1984.

_____. *Paris Talks*. London: Bahá'í Publishing trust, 1972

Abizadeh, A. "Commentary to Craig Loehle's Article." *The Journal of Bahá'í Studies* Vol. 3, No. 1 (1990) pp. 45-58.

Albert, Hans. *Traktat über kritische Vernunft*. 5th ed. Tübingen: Paul Siebeck, 1991.

Alberts, Bruce, et al. *Molecular Biology of the Cell*. 2nd ed. London: Garland Publishing, 1989.

Anfinsen, C. B. "Principles that Govern the Folding of Protein Chains." *Science*. 181.49096 (1973) pp. 223-230.

Atkins, P. W. *The Creation*. Oxford: Freeman & Company, 1981.

Ayman, I. "Response to Commentary on 'On Human Origins'," *The Journal of Bahá'í Studies*. Vol. 5, No. 2 (1992) pp. 67-71.

Bahá'u'lláh. *The Hidden Words*. London: Bahá'í Publishing Trust, 1932.

_____. *Gleanings from the Writings of Bahá'u'lláh*. Wilmette: Bahá'í Publishing Trust, 1971.

_____. *Tablets of Bahá'u'lláh Revealed after the Kitab-i-Aqdas*. Haifa: Bahá'í World Centre, 1982.

Baldwin, R. L. "Pieces of the folding puzzle." *Nature*. Vol. 346 (1990) pp. 409-410.

Beardsley, T. "Darwin Denied: Opponents of Evolution Make Gains in Schools." *Scientific American.* Vol. 273, No. 1 (1995) pp. 12-14.

Bloch, Ernst. *Das Materialismusproblem, seine Geschichte und Substanz.* Vol. 7. Frankfurt a.M., 1972.

Brown, Keven. "Response to Commentary on 'On Human Origins'," *The Journal of Bahá'í Studies.* Vol. 5. No. 4 (1994) pp. 59-62.

Büchner, Ludwig. *Sechs Vorlesungen über die Darwin'sche Theorie von der Verwandlung der Arten und die erste Enstehung der Organismenwelt.* 2nd ed. Leipzig: Theodor Thomas, 1868.

————. *Kraft und Stoff.* 21st ed. Leipzig: Theodor Thomas, 1904.

de Chardin, T. *Le Phénomène humain.* Paris: Édition du Leuil, 1947.

Clark, J. D. et al. "African Homo erectus: Old Radiometric Ages and Young Oldowan Assemblages in the Middle Awash Valley, Ethiopia." *Science.* 264.5167 (1994) pp. 1907-1910.

Conow, B. H. *The Bahá'í Teachings: A Resurgent Model of the Universe* Oxford: George Ronald, 1990.

Darwin, Charles. *The Origin of Species.* London: Penguin Books, 1985.

Dawkins, Richard. *The Blind Watchmaker.* London: Longmans, 1986.

————. *The Selfish Gene.* Oxford: Oxford University Press, 1989.

————. *River Out of Eden.* London: Weidenfeld & Nicolson, 1995.

Dayhoff, "Computer Analysis of Protein Evolution." *Scientific American* (July 1969) pp. 86-95.

Dennett, Daniel C. *Darwin's Dangerous Idea.* New York: Simon & Schuster, 1995.

Derrida, J. "Structure, Sign, and Play in the Discourse of the Human Sciences." *The Languages of Criticism and the Sciences of Man: The Structuralist Controversy.* Ed. Richard Macksey and Eugenio Donato. Baltimore: John Hopkins University Press, 1970.

Dicks, G. "Comment on 'A Scientific Proof of the Existence of God'." *The Journal of Bahá'í Studies.* Vol. 6, No. 3 (1994) pp. 75-80.

Dirac, Paul. "Quantum Mechanics of Many-Electron Systems." *Proc Roy Soc* A 123 (1929) pp. 714-733.

Dobzhansky, T., F. J. Ayala, G. L. Stebbins, and J. W. Valentine. *Evolution*. San Francisco: 1977.

Dopazo, J., A. Dress, and A. von Haeseler. "Split decomposition: a technique to analyze viral evolution." *Proceedings of the National Academy of Sciences of the USA*. Vol. 90, No. 21 (1993) pp. 10320-10324.

de Duve, C. "The birth of complex cells." *Scientific American*. Vol. 274, No. 4 (1996) pp. 50-57.

Eigen, Manfred. *Steps towards Life: A perspective of evolution*. Oxford: Oxford University Press, 1992.

_____. "The origin of genetic information: viruses as models." *Gene*. Vol. 135, No. 1-2 (1993) pp. 37-47.

_____. "Viral quasispecies." *Scientific American*. Vol. 269, No. 1 (1993) pp. 42-49.

Esslemont, J. E. *Bahá'u'lláh and the New Era*. Wilmette: Bahá'í Publishing Trust, 1980.

Feyerabend, Paul. *Erkenntnis für freie Menschen*. Vol. 1011. Frankfurt a.M.: Suhrkamp, 1980.

Gell-Mann, Murray. *The Quark and the Jaguar*. New York: WH Freeman, 1994.

Gould, S. J. "The Evolution of Life on the Earth." *Scientific American*. Vol. 271, No. 4 (1994) pp. 85-91.

_____. *Rocks of Ages*. New York: Ballantine, 1999.

Gulpáygání, Mírzá Abu'l-Fadl. *Miracles and Metaphors*. Los Angeles: Kalimát Press, 1981.

Haeckel, Ernst. *Anthropogenie oder Entwicklungsgeschichte des Menschen*. Vol. 2. Leipzig: Wilhelm Engelmann, 1891.

_____. *Über den Ursprung des Menschen - Vortrag, gehalten auf dem 4. Internationalen Zoologen-Congress in Cambrigde, am 26. August 1898*. 12th ed. Leipzig: Kröner Verlag, 1916.

_____. *Die Welträtsel*. 11th ed. Stuttgart: Kröner, 1984.

Hatcher, John S. "Response to Commentary on 'On Human Origins'." *The Journal of Bahá'í Studies*. Vol. 5, No. 2 (1992) pp. 60-66.

Hatcher, John and William. *The Law of Love Enshrined.* Oxford: George Ronald, 1996.

Hatcher, William S. *Logic and Logos.* Oxford: George Ronald, 1990.

_____. "A Scientific Proof of the Existence of God." *The Journal of Bahá'í Studies.* Vol. 5, No. 4 (1993) pp. 1-16.

_____. "Reply to Gordon Dicks' comment on 'A Scientific Proof of the Existence of God'." *The Journal of Bahá'í Studies.* Vol. 6, No. 3 (1994) pp. 81-85.

Heisenberg, Werner. *Das Teil und das Ganze München.* Piper, 1969.

Hofstadter, D. *Gödel Escher Bach.* New York: Basic Books, 1979.

Holmes, P. "Poincaré. "Celestial Mechanics, Dynamical-systems Theory and 'Chaos'." *Physics Reports.* Vol. 193, No. 3 (1990) pp. 137-163.

Howells, W. *Getting Here: The Story of Human Evolution.* Washington: Compass Press, 1993.

Hund, Friedrich. *Geschichte der physikalischen Begriffe: Die Entstehung des mechanischen Naturbildes.* Vols. 543, 544. Mannheim: Bibliographisches Institut, 1978.

Kauffman, S. *At Home in the Universe.* New York: Oxford University Press, 1995.

_____. "Climbing Mount Improbable: Richard Dawkins." *Nature.* Vol. 382, No. 6589 (1996) pp. 309-310.

Kerr, R. A. "Who Profits from Ecological Disaster?" *Science.* Vol. 266 (1994) pp. 28-30.

Khursheed, Anjam. *Science and Religion: Towards the Restoration of an Ancient Harmony.* London: Oneworld Publications, 1987.

von Kitzing, Eberhard. "Ist eine Einheit von Religion und Wissenschaft denkbar?" *Tagungsband zur 10 Jahrestagung der Gesellschaft für Bahá'í Studien im deutschsprachigen Europa.* Vol. 4 (1997) pp. 77-102.

Kraft, Viktor. *Der Wiener Kreis: Der Ursprung des Neopositivismus.* Wien: Springer Verlag, 1968.

Land, G. "The Evolution of Reality." *Journal of Bahá'í Studies.* Vol. 3, No. 1 (1991) pp. 19-30.

Leakey, Richard. *The Origin of Humankind.* London: Weidenfeld & Nicolson, 1994.

Leakey, Richard et al. "New Four-million-year-old Hominid Species from Kanapoi and Allia Bay, Kenya." *Nature.* Vol. 376, No. 6541 (1995) pp. 565-571.

Loehle, C. "On Human Origins: A Bahá'í Perspective." *The Journal of Bahá'í Studies.* Vol. 2, No. 4 (1990) pp. 67-73.

_____. "Response to Commentary on 'On Human Origins'." *The Journal of Bahá'í Studies.* Vol. 5, No. 2 (1992) 72-76.

_____. *On the Shoulders of Giants Oxford.* Oxford: George Ronald, 1994.

Mayr, Ernst. "Evolution." *Scientific American.* Vol. 239, No. 3 (1978) pp. 46-55.

_____. *The Growth of Biological Thought.* Cambridge: Harvard University Press, 1982.

_____. *One Long Argument.* Cambridge: Harvard University Press, 1991.

Monod, Jaques. *Le Hasard et la Nécessité.* Paris: Édition du Leuil, 1970.

Orgel, L. E. "The origin of life on the earth." *Scientific American.* Vol. 271, No. 4 (1994) pp. 77-83.

Rabbani, Shoghi. Letter 19 March 1946 to an individual, cited from a Memorandum of the Research Department of the Universal House of Justice, dated 19 March 1995.

_____. *Unfolding Destiny: The Messages from the Guardian of the Bahá'í Faith to the Bahá'í Community of the British Isles.* London: Bahá'í Publishing Trust, 1981.

_____. *Arohanui - Letters from Shoghi Effendi to New Zealand.* Suva, Fiji Islands: Bahá'í Publishing Trust, 1982.

Popper, K. R. *Objective Knowledge.* Oxford: The Clarendon Press, 1972.

Prigogine, I. *Vom Sein zum Werden.* München: Piper, 1979.

Prigogine, I. and I. Stengers. *Dialog mit der Natur.* München: Piper, 1981.

Ruthen, R. "Trends in nonlinear dynamics. Adapting to complexity." *Scientific American.* Vol. 268, No. 1 (1993) pp. 110-117.

Savi, J. *The Eternal Quest for God.* Oxford: George Ronald, 1989.

Sibley, C. G., J. A. Comstock, and J. E. Ahlquist. "DNA Hybridization Evidence of Hominoid Phylogeny: A Reanalysis of the Data." *Journal of Molecular Evolution.* Vol. 30, No. 3 (1990) pp. 202-236.

Spiegelman, S. "An in vitro analysis of a replicating molecule." *American Scientist.* Vol. 55 (1967) pp. 63-68.

Sober, E. Philosophy of Biology. Oxford: Oxford University Press, 1993.

Sokal, Allan. "Transgressing the Boundaries: Toward a transformative hermeneutics of quantum gravity." *Social Text.* Vol. 14, No.1-2 (1996) pp. 46-47.

Tattersall, I. "Out Of Africa Again ... and Again." *Scientific American.* Vol. 276, No. 4 (1997) pp. 46-53.

Universal House of Justice. *The Promise of World Peace* (1985).

Ward, K. God, *Chance and Necessity.* Oxford: Oneworld, 1996.

Wheeler, J. A. "Information, Physics, Quantum: the Search for Links." *Proceeding of the 3rd International Symposium on the Foundation of Quantum Mechanics.* Tokyo (1989) pp. 354-368.

von Weizsäcker, C. F. Aufbau der Physik. 2nd ed. München: Carl Hanser Verlag, 1986.

White, T. D., G. Suwa, and B. Asfaw. "Australopithecus ramidus, a new species of early hominid from Aramis, Ethiopia." Nature 371.6495 (1994) 306-312.

Wilson, A. C. and R. L. Cann. "The recent African genesis of humans." *Scientific American.* Vol. 266, No. 4 (1992) pp. 68-73.

WoldeGabriel, G. et al. "Ecological and temporal placement of early Pliocene hominids at Aramis, Ethiopia." *Nature.* Vol. 371, No. 6495 (1994) pp. 330-333.